Britain's 15-inch-gauge Railways
Duffield Bank to Perrygrove

Britain's 15-inch-gauge Railways

Key:
- ● Railway location
- ▲ Private line, with limited opening

Inverness

Aberdeen

Craigtoun Park
St Andrews

EDINBURGH

GLASGOW

Berwick-on-Tweed

Heatherslaw

NEWCASTLE

Carlisle

Ditflin Lake
Raphoe   Londonderry

BELFAST

Thorpe

Saltburn

Scarborough

Sligo

Newry

Ravenglass
& Eskdale

Lightwater
Valley

Ripon

Barrow-in-Furness

YORK

Westport House
Westport

Blackpool   Zoo Park
PRESTON   LEEDS   Hull

Athlone

Lakeside
Southport   Windmill Farm   Grimsby

DUBLIN

Haigh Hall Country Park   Kirklees   Cleethorpes Coast

**Irish
Republic**

Knowsley Safari Park   MANCHESTER
LIVERPOOL   Warrington   SHEFFIELD

Rhyl   Gulliver's World   Sherwood Forest

Conwy
Valley
Museum   Eaton Hall
Stoke-on-Trent

Markeaton Park   NOTTINGHAM

Aylsham   Bure Valley
Wroxham

DERBY

Shrewsbury   Wolverhampton   Twinlakes Park
Melton Mowbray   NORWICH

Fairbourne   LEICESTER   Diss

Rhiw Valley   Bressingham
Museum

Tramore   Waterford
Leisure Park   Rosslare

Aberystwyth   BIRMINGHAM

CORK

West Midlands
Safari Park   Northampton   Billing Aquadrome

Fishguard   Hereford   Evesham Vale   Gulliver's Land   Ipswich
Milton Keynes

Oakwood   Perrygrove   Blenheim Park

SWANSEA   Oxford   Hertford

CARDIFF   LONDON

BRISTOL   Swindon

Combe Martin
Wildlife Park   Clevedon   READING   Croydon

Longleat   Marwell
Zoological
Park   Dover

Barnstaple   Taunton   Salisbury   Romney, Hythe
& Dymchurch

Paultons Park   SOUTHAMPTON

EXETER   Portsmouth   BRIGHTON

Bournemouth

Newquay   Lappa
Valley   Torquay

PLYMOUTH

Penzance   Hayle
Paradise Park

Map courtesy of David Henshaw *Miniature Railway Magazine*

Britain's 15-inch-gauge Railways

Duffield Bank to Perrygrove

David R. Jones

Silver Link Publishing Ltd

This book is dedicated to the memory of

Sir Arthur Percival Heywood (3rd Bart)
(1849-1916)
of Dove Leys and Duffield Bank, Derbyshire
Inventor – Promoter – Visionary – Perfectionist
and
Henry Greenly
(1876-1947)
Locomotive Designer – Railway-builder – Genius

'If you seek their memorials…'

First published in 2013

British Library Cataloguing in Publication Data

A catalogue record for this book is available from the British Library.

Softcover   ISBN 978 1 85794 416 7
Hardback Limited Edition
                   ISBN 978 1 85794 417 4

Silver Link Publishing Ltd The Trundle
Ringstead Road
Great Addington
Kettering
Northants NN14 4BW

Tel/Fax: 01536 330588
email: sales@nostalgiacollection.com
Website: www.nostalgiacollection.com

Printed and bound in the Czech Republic

Frontispiece: 'Let's be 'aving you!' *Sutton Belle* and LNER No 6284 attract 'police' interest during a Second World War-themed weekend at Humberstone North Sea Lane station on 13 August 2011.
D. Holroyde

Markeaton Lady and train built by Exmoor Steam Railway in 1996, seen at Markeaton Park, Derby. *J. Stirland/ Exmoor Steam Railway*

Contents

Acknowledgements

First and foremost, I must thank those who have preceded me in telling the story of the 15-inch-gauge with all its romance, colour and incident; they are recorded in the 'Further reading' section of this book. In recent years much research has been made available in print or on the Internet and I have tried, where possible, to incorporate fresh insights and new discoveries into the classic version of events. Others will judge how far I have succeeded!

I am deeply grateful to Peter Townsend of Silver Link Publishing Ltd and his colleagues for taking this project on board, and for their expertise in its design and presentation, not least for the inclusion of such a large number of coloured illustrations. Many experts in the field have generously assisted me with their time and knowledge, including Simon Townsend (who gave great encouragement at all stages

and suggested the contact with Silver Link Publishing), David Henshaw (who read the text in draft), and Peter Bryant (who reviewed the Gazetteer entries for operating railways and museums, and generously allowed me to draw information from the 'Miniature Railway World' website).

I am honoured that Sir Peter Heywood Bt has written the Foreword for this book.

Peter Scott, compiler of *Minor Railways*, has generously supplied track plans for the three 'main lines' – Bure Valley, Ravenglass & Eskdale, and Romney, Hythe & Dymchurch – for inclusion in this book.

Among many others who have helped with the provision of information I would like especially to thank Phil Ashworth and David Vere of the Heywood Society; Chris Walker, Librarian of the Narrow Gauge

Railway Society; Richard Sheppard of Trent & Peak Archaeology; Anthony Coulls of the National Railway Museum; June Stirland of Exmoor Steam Railway; and Jenny Pengelly on behalf of Burton Lazars PCC. The staffs of Derbyshire Record Office, the North-East Midlands Photographic Record, Cumbria Archives Centre (Kendal) and Hampshire Record Office have all responded patiently to my enquiries, as have Phil Soanes at the Strumpshaw Steam Centre, Jean Maskell at Ardkinglas Estate Office, Alexandra Beavis at King's College, London, and Katie Holdsworth at Warner Leisure Hotels.

I am most grateful to the staff of all the railways I have visited for their universal helpfulness and welcome, in particular Austin Moss at the Windmill Farm Railway, Christine Maisey at Bressingham Steam Museum, David Nelson at the Perrygrove Railway, Don Clark at the Lakeside Miniature Railway, Stuart Ross at the Kirklees Light Railway, Mike Woodroffe at the Rhiw Valley Light Railway, and Andrew Grass at the Grosvenor Garden Centre – who has the rare privilege of an office in the former Eaton Railway locomotive shed! Peter van Zeller at the Ravenglass & Eskdale Railway, despite a heavy workload, kindly gave me information by telephone. Numerous individuals have helped with queries, as well as offering photographs from their personal collections, in particular Peter Green, Jason Murgatroyd, Bill Parkes, Peter Scott, Donald Sills, Derek Smith, Geoff Sutton and David Verity.

No one interested in the 15-inch-gauge could fail to be inspired by the achievement of James Waterfield of Boston, the creator of the magnificent Heywood Collection at the Perrygrove Railway. It was a memorable experience to hear him speak on Sir Arthur Heywood's life and work, introduced by the sound of bells – Sir Arthur's change-ringing composition, 'Duffield'.

My children and grandchildren have listened to me 'talking railways' for as long as they can remember, and I thank them for their patience! I owe a huge debt to my wife, Ros, not only for reading the manuscript more than once and preparing captions, but for her tolerance while books, notes and photographs overflowed into numerous parts of our house, and holiday travel inevitably involved 'dropping in' at sundry railways en route! Fortunately we share the same favourite line, but how often has she heard the phrase 'You can sit and have a coffee, while I just…' For enduring cold, windy days at Cleethorpes and Rhyl, and waiting in pitch darkness to see the night Dining Special arrive at Dungeness, I thank her.

Photograph credits

I am most grateful to the following friends and enthusiasts for kindly allowing their work to be used to illustrate this book: Eliot Andersen, David Armstrong, Phil Ashworth, Simon Bowditch, Jim Cleaver, Peter Green, David Holroyde, Jason Murgatroyd, Bill Parkes, John Robinson, Ben Rolfe, Peter Scott, Derek Smith, Geoff and Mark Sutton, and David Verity. The view of Higham Park is from the collection of Paul Moore (www.flickr.com/rhedae).

Several photographs have kindly been contributed by organisations: the locomotive *Pearl* is by courtesy of King's College, London; the Zborowski family tomb is by courtesy of Burton Lazars Parochial Church Council; the Long Tunnel at Duffield Bank is reproduced by permission of Trent & Peak Archaeology from its survey report on 'Loner's Lair'; and the Cricket St Thomas viaduct is from the archive of Warner Leisure Hotels. The classic 1896 view of the Duffield Bank train (cover) and the c1962 view of the Duffield Bank incline are from versions in the North-East Midland Photographic Record, copyright of Derbyshire County Council (the Bromby Collection and www.picturethepast.org.uk). Two photographs have been taken from the wonderful Ray Ruffell Collection held by the publisher, and images have also been kindly supplied by the Exmoor Steam Railway (J. Stirland), Kirklees Light Railway, Lappa Valley Railway, Ravenglass & Eskdale Railway and Sherwood Forest Railway managements.

Where not specifically credited, photographs were taken by myself.

David R. Jones

Foreword by Sir Peter Heywood Bt

The history of 15-inch-gauge is fascinating. It is a story that is full of enthusiastic people with great ideas and with the determination to carry them through, when that is often a lifetime's work. The result is a great series of inventions, discoveries and experiments leading to the design and building of engines and rolling stock, and the creation of 15-inch lines in many locations, both public and private, that provide so much pleasure to so many people every year.

This excellent book traces the history of this journey over the last 150 years in a comprehensive and well-structured way. It contains a large amount of information, which must have been very difficult to bring together, and David Jones has done a superb job in creating a joined-up story of the people, the events and the equipment over all these years.

When my father Oliver was a small boy, he and his sister Joan often went to Doveleys, the big Heywood family home in Staffordshire. The house was owned by his uncle Sir Percival Heywood, and many other aunts and uncles lived there too. In the grounds of the house were some old railway tracks, with a small flat-bed that they could sit on and punt themselves along the line.

Their grandfather Sir Arthur Heywood had died four years before my father Oliver was born. But Oliver's father and his uncles and aunts used to tell him about their interesting adventures as children, when their father Sir Arthur had built his pioneering railway in the grounds of their home at Duffield Bank in Derbyshire. The line wound upwards from the house into the woods, arriving at the top at the Tennis Ground where there was a station. We have a number of fascinating photographs in our family album. The children used to act as guards and signal operators, and they used to make journeys in the dining carriage and the saloon car and the sleeping car. It was a wonderful world of extravagant fun. Their father built a total of six engines in his lifetime, and named three of them after his daughters – Effie, Ella and Muriel.

Sir Arthur Heywood is widely acknowledged as the founder of 15-inch-gauge, so the story of this book more or less starts with him. I have enjoyed retracing his steps with our good friends James Waterfield and Frances and Michael Crofts. We climbed up the steep gradients at Duffield Bank until we found the old Tennis Ground, immediately recognisable from the old photographs, but now very much grown over. Then we clambered through the tunnels, which were still in good shape, marvelling at all the work that Sir Arthur and his team did to create this extravaganza in his garden. Then we came to some small valleys and saw where the bases of the bridges were. Nothing lasts for ever, and it is now all long gone.

But actually, it has not gone. Quite a lot of Arthur Heywood replicas have been built by some Heywood enthusiasts, a number of them by James Waterfield. I have so enjoyed driving his Ursula, and being on the footplates of Effie and Muriel (now called River Irt) at Ravenglass, and visiting the estate of the Duke of Westminster at Eaton Hall with Robin Butterfield, riding round the grounds on the reinstated tracks. We have searched the grounds at Doveleys, prodding the earth and finding evidence of the old tracks as they crossed the fields, and locating the concrete bases of the old bridges. Part of the original line is still there, right next to the house, and there is an old train shed in a thicket in the garden.

But for me, the best is to go to Perrygrove in the Forest of Dean. This is the end of the story in this excellent book. Michael and Frances Crofts have created a wonderful railway that is as close as possible to the long-gone line at Duffield Bank. What a pleasure it is to dress up on a summer's evening, and to squeeze eight grown adults into James Waterfield's beautiful reconstruction of Sir Arthur's dining carriage, and to steam gently up the track, being pulled by Ursula driven by James, stopping at every station so that superb finger food and delicious wine can be served through the windows, with Richard playing some classic records on an old gramophone. It is the essence of Victorian extravagance, still living on.

Just before the end of her long life, we took my Aunt Joan to Perrygrove, and she rode again on the same flat-bed that she had ridden on as a little girl 80 years before. It is moments like this that join it all up. It's so good to enjoy our history, and that's what this book is all about. I commend it to you.

Let's honour and thank all those pioneers who have made this journey possible, and who continue to do so today.

And now, to conclude, some words from the diary of my Great Aunt Effie Heywood, who I met when she was an old lady and I was a small boy, written about her father, Sir Arthur Heywood.

'Arthur Percival Heywood, eldest son of Sir Thomas Percival Heywood, was born in 1849. He was educated at Eton and Trinity College, Cambridge.

At an early age he showed signs of great engineering ability, but his wish to enter the Royal Engineers was not approved of by his father, much to his sorrow. It was in the days when opposition to paternal commands was not to be thought of and Arthur had to content himself with experiments at home.

This was a great pity, for he was a real genius in this line. It was a peculiar fancy of Sir Thomas Percival to bring up his sons in no profession.

He was the kindest man on earth, there was nothing he would not do for his family or for other people. Countless were the individuals and charities he helped. A stern man in some ways, demanding the best from his dependants, he was a most genial man. He was a trifle diffident at times, a great talker and a good speaker. Being thwarted in his wish to enter the engineering profession, he found an outlet for his talents in an experimental railway and in designing and building additions to the two houses he occupied.

On his marriage, his father bought Duffield in Derbyshire for him. It stood on the slope of the hillside above the then small country village of Duffield. Arthur made small additions to it, but it was not until 1896 that he made very large alterations and additions. The result was a long rambling house of whitish stone with various levels to suit the slope on which it stood.

Here, at Duffield, Arthur constructed a model railway and workshops of every description.

In these shops, which comprised a machine shop, carpenters, erecting, saw shops, a foundry, smithy and many other buildings, he built his model engines and rolling stock.

The railway was a demonstration of what could be practically made on a narrow gauge, and many experts took hints therefrom.

He also laid for the Duke of Westminster a similar line from the big station up to Eaton Hall for the conveyance of visitors, coal, etc.

All the locomotives (save the boilers) and rolling stock were constructed for both lines in the workshops at Duffield.

If motor traction had not come into use the War Office would have adopted his system of light railway building.

Petrol-propelled engines held no interest for him – it was steam that was his love. His inventive powers were enormous, and when not expended on engineering he was planning and building additions to Duffield (as his family increased) and later, when he inherited it, to Doveleys.

He loved his house to be well run; he liked his stables, his gardens and park, his home farm to be complete, and he had an almost old-fashioned idea of 'living in state'.

At the death of his father he succeeded to the Baronetcy, and to Doveleys, but although he made the latter place his headquarters he always went to Duffield for part of the year and had all his county interests in Derbyshire.

Headlamp

Fifteen inches. 380 millimetres (381mm, some purists would say). A curious gauge for a railway, yet one that has been used for more than 140 years, and for decades was regarded as the minimum gauge for the practical conveyance of passengers or goods. For many people it has meant just a chance encounter with a pleasure line at the seaside, or in a country park, for others the experience of riding a main-line train in miniature at Ravenglass or New Romney. Some might stop to wonder why the same gauge has been adopted so widely, from the Lappa Valley in Cornwall to Great Yarmouth and from Banff in Scotland to Dungeness on the South Coast.

This book attempts to set out the story of 15-inch-gauge lines, their uses, and some of the colourful characters who have created and operated them: gentlemen amateurs, visionary enthusiasts, skilled engineers, and hard-headed businessmen in the developing leisure industry. Pleasure has always been a key element, beginning with the self-indulgent private tracks of wealthy landowners and enthusiasts – for as long as there have been railways, there have been railway enthusiasts! But the serious purposes of these lines should not be forgotten – whether or not they succeeded. They did provide the first mechanised transport for some of the great English landed estates, though never so many as was hoped; they might have been found as the first mechanised warfare transport; and they did move millions of tons of granite in Eskdale and assist the construction of the D-Day oil pipeline in the Second World War.

The story of locomotive development follows, covering the classic designs of Arthur Heywood, Henry Greenly and his contemporaries, and the innovative builders of both steam and internal-combustion power since the 1930s. With so many 15-inch-gauge railways in operation – about 38 in Great Britain and Ireland – at the present day, there is a huge variety to be seen and enjoyed, and live steam

building continues to flourish in the 21st century. The same is true of rolling stock, with classic vehicles still in use alongside modern designs, some having passed through many hands to reach the venues where they run today. The infrastructure of 15-inch-gauge railways does have common ground with larger narrow-gauge lines on the one hand, and the smaller 'miniature' gauges on the other, but both permanent way and architecture have features of technical and historic interest.

Mark Timothy at Wroxham in 2009.
G. Sutton

A summary description is given of each of the lines that can be enjoyed today, i.e. those that are expected to operate during 2013. An important distinction has to be kept in mind between lines that operate as attractions in their own right, and those that are an integral part of a theme or safari park. In the latter cases, the visitor is required to pay for entry to the wider attraction – or at least some part of it – before travelling on the railway. In recent years, as the historic importance of these railways has been more widely appreciated, some superb collections of museum exhibits have been formed, and a summary of these is also provided.

It is a remarkable fact that almost the whole

story of the 15-inch-gauge can be illustrated from equipment that has been preserved or re-created in replica, and this indeed has inspired the author to attempt the present book. It is very far from being the first on 15-inch-gauge railways, and it will not be the last. Some books have been general histories or surveys of miniature railways, while others have dealt in great depth with particular aspects or certain types of locomotive. Unfortunately, many books are now out of print and scarce, and these works have been listed for 'Further reading' in the hope that the reader will be inspired to delve further into the story. Equally impressive are the publications on individual lines, ranging from full-length studies to guide books and collections of artistic photographs, which have been noted where possible in the accounts of each line.

For much of its history, 15 inches was regarded as the 'minimum gauge' for the efficient operation of a public railway. That, of course, is no longer the case, as lines with gauges of 12½ and 10¼ inches have become well-established in recent decades, and modelling enthusiasts have successfully built and operated lines on gauges as small as 7¼ inches, leading to something of a revival for the private 'garden' railway. With the exception of the **Fairbourne Railway** – which operated on the 15-inch-gauge for much of its life – these are excluded from the present book, but are well covered in the general gazetteers and websites covering miniature railways. Equally, there are other small-gauge railways – 18, 20 and 21 inches – of a similar character, which have also been largely excluded apart from a brief account of the (defunct) **Sand Hutton** line, which underwent a hasty and opportunist conversion to the 18-inch gauge as it neared completion.

The distinction between a 'miniature' railway and a 'narrow-gauge' one has produced much debate. It is the fascination of the 15-inch-gauge lines that the two traditions are combined equally, some displaying perfect scale-model engineering while others use locomotives and rolling stock of the largest possible size consistent with stability in motion. George Ottley, in his *Bibliography of British Railway History*, explains that:

'The essential difference centres upon the design of the locomotives. Narrow Gauge locomotives allow the driver to sit, if not to stand, in his cab, and traditionally to have space enough for a fireman. On Miniature railways this practical, indeed humane, requirement has to take second place to the over-riding principle that the locomotives must be standard gauge prototypes in miniature. This means the driver must squat in his cab and look ahead over the roof.'

More than one writer has recounted being frightened when first introduced, as a small child, to the 'hissing, snorting monster' of a small steam engine. The author, on the contrary, recalls feeling rather inclined to pet *King George* and *Princess Elizabeth* on the **Lakeside Miniature Railway** at Southport in the 1950s and being totally fascinated by the rituals of firing up, taking water, oiling round and polishing, which occupied the driver at the end of each run! These simple pleasures can be recaptured, and shared with children and grandchildren, on so many different lines, all over Britain, today. The fascination of such railways was summed up in the account of 'The White City Express' in the 1909 Souvenir Handbook of the White City Exhibition at Trafford Park in Manchester:

'One of the earliest things the baby of the house talks about is the "Choo-Choo", and a train of carriages with engine, etc, is among the most popular of Christmas and Birthday gifts to the young. The liking for the Railway does not, like that for dolls and tin soldiers, die out with years but only grows and takes on more importance.'

Thanks to the patience and indulgence of his long-suffering parents, the author's own early memories of narrow-gauge railways include discovering the remains of the miniature railway (10¼-inch gauge?) that ran until about 1950 on the summit of the Great Orme at Llandudno, and following the track to where some abandoned carriages could be pushed out of their doorless shed – wonderful playthings! – and exploring the moribund wagons and signals of the Ffestiniog Railway at what must have been Blaenau Ffestiniog Central station around the same year.

If this book encourages readers to look

out for and explore different lines, it will have achieved all the author's hopes. Very likely one may become attached to a favourite line, to be visited whenever opportunity allows – many have a preservation society or Friends organisation, which can be joined to keep in touch or to offer voluntary support. The author will try to keep his own preference a secret, unless perhaps the merest hint escapes at the very end of the book. And every enthusiast must be allowed to have a favourite engine too, whether on the same or on a different line, be it old or new. Strange and irrational it may be, but the author tended on his earlier visits to the **Waveney Valley Railway** at Bressingham to let *Rosenkavalier* run past and wait to ride behind the 'identical twin', *Männertreu*. Love at first sight perhaps?

1. History of the 15-inch-gauge to 1945

In the beginning...

The ultimate origin of the 'minimum gauge' is probably untraceable. Railways themselves, in the modern world, began in the mining districts of Germany and Central Europe in the 15th and 16th centuries when it was found that tubs or trucks with crude rollers could be guided relatively smoothly along tunnels by wooden baulks laid next to the walls. Some adits would have been little wider than the space needed for a medieval miner and his pick, so gauges of not much more than 15 inches might have existed at a very early date. Later, in 19th-century England, the Good Luck lead mine at Middleton Wood in Derbyshire used track just 11 inches wide, while other nearby mines had gauges around 15 inches – sometimes retaining the ancient form of wooden rails with iron 'plates' nailed on top, illustrating the origins of the term 'platelayer'.

In Britain several narrow-gauge railways existed in the early 19th century, when improved transport links (especially by river and canal) enabled larger-scale production and distribution of minerals such as slate. The greatest single innovation came in 1836, when the Spooner family promoted the construction of the **Ffestiniog Railway** linking the quarries of the Blaenau Ffestiniog district with the new harbour developed by the Madocks family at Porthmadog, on their Tremadog estate. Crucially, the Ffestiniog retained the track gauge of just under two feet (1ft 11⅝in

or, by coincidence, 60cm) used in the local quarries, and maximised its carrying capacity by maintaining an even downhill gradient. Loaded trains ran the 13 miles to Porthmadog by gravity and horses were needed only to return the empty trucks. In 1863 the railway converted to steam traction and began to carry passengers. It was, and remains to this day, an engineering wonder, and the '2-foot gauge' was adopted in many parts of the world for routes involving sharp curves, steep gradients, and intensive traffic. The **Darjeeling Himalayan Railway**, now awarded World Heritage Status, was subsequently built to follow the line of a twisting mountain road for the best part of 50 miles.

Yet some engineers wondered whether the '2-foot gauge' could not be further reduced, saving land and materials costs, and still perform useful work. Smaller lines could also be laid in relatively confined spaces, and provide a highly pleasurable hobby for amateurs! The earliest known small-gauge garden railway was built by one Captain Robert Rodney (later 6th Baron Rodney) of Alresford in Hampshire in 1843. A simple circle of 400 yards diameter, it was apparently in a cutting and included – like so many later pleasure lines – a tunnel for fun, and was worked by steam. Similar ventures were recorded at Far Sawrey in the Lake District in the 1860s (a 300-yard line owned by a steamboat engineer, Charles Fildes), and at Ardkinglas on the shore of Loch Fyne in Argyll in the 1870s. The latter was owned by George

'Homes of the Pioneers': Doveleys lies within Doveleys Riverside Garden Centre, and 78 Derngate is open within museum hours, with an entrance charge. Staughton Manor and Higham Park are in private ownership, and not open to the public.

Left: Doveleys, childhood and final home of Sir Arthur Percival Heywood.

Right: 78 Derngate, Northampton, modernised for Wenman Bassett-Lowke by Charles Rennie Mackintosh. *B. Rolfe*

Below: Staughton Manor, site of Jack Howey's personal railways.

Frederick William Callender, who had been a contemporary, at Eton College, of Arthur Percival Heywood – of whom we shall hear much more presently. The Ardkinglas line extended to about 500 yards on piles along the loch shore and might well have been seen, if not actually travelled on, by Queen Victoria when she visited the estate in 1875; the gauge, on the evidence of a single surviving

Higham Park, inherited by the youthful Count Louis Zborowski. *P. A. Moore*

pair of wheels, was 12 inches. The Heywoods, interestingly, maintained a connection with the area in later years by renting the shooting on the Loch Fyne estate. It is probable that a gauge of at least 18 inches was used at Far Sawrey, the mechanical equipment for both boats and locomotives possibly being supplied by Isaac Watt Boulton of Ashton-under-Lyne.

On the industrial scene, the Crewe Locomotive Works of the London & North Western Railway had introduced a system of 18-inch-gauge railways as early as 1862. This was remarkable not only for using tiny steam locomotives to move 15-ton loads of materials and supplies, but also for being fitted into an existing layout of workshops, doorways and roadways. Similar lines later appeared at the Horwich railway workshops and at the Government Arsenals, Woolwich perhaps being the best known. Overseas, evidence has been found of a 14-inch-gauge forestry railway at Changa Manga south of Lahore (now in Pakistan), established in the late 19th century, which ran until 1921 powered by bullocks!

What was needed was for a visionary promoter, with wealth, extensive private land and engineering skill, to bring together all the elements of the 'minimum gauge' on such a scale as to impress his contemporaries.

Heywood and the Duffield Bank 'Experimental' Railway

Arthur Percival Heywood was born on Christmas Day 1849, the eldest son of Sir Thomas and Margaret Heywood. Arthur's grandfather, a Manchester banker and MP, had been granted a baronetcy for political services in 1838, and in 1831 he had bought a country estate at Dove Leys (nowadays usually written as Doveleys) in Denstone on the Staffordshire and Derbyshire border. Significantly, Arthur's aunt Mary Elizabeth Heywood had married the Rev George Henry Sumner, Rector of Alresford in Hampshire, and family visits before the death of Lord Rodney in 1864 may well have made the young Arthur aware of the circular, steam-operated pleasure railway.

Sir Thomas was, in some ways, an enlightened man of his generation. He was happy for his seven surviving children to receive an education, and take an amateur interest, in any field of their choice. On the other hand, they were never allowed to compromise their status as landed gentry by practising professionally or commercially during his lifetime. Sir Thomas himself had purchased a second-hand lathe and tools as a hobby; Arthur revealed an amazing gift for everything mechanical, though it is said that the only practical instruction he ever had came from an old fishing-rod maker. During

The initials of Arthur Heywood's parents, rebuilding date and family motto, at Doveleys House.

Arthur's teens it appears that an offer from Colonel du Kane of enrolment in the Royal Engineers had come and gone; a commission in a regular regiment might have been acceptable to Sir Thomas, but military engineering was clearly not. Already, Arthur was making a 4-inch-gauge model railway in a workshop at Dove Leys, completed just before he went up to Trinity College, Cambridge. There was also a hand-pushed or pedal-operated 9-inch-gauge railway with three little stations to amuse his younger siblings. He remarked that the latter was stable enough 'provided persons did not attempt to ride on the ends and edges of the carriages and wagons' – we can imagine all sorts of juvenile thrills and spills. He devoted much time thereafter to calculating the perfect gauge for the carriage of two people seated side-by-side, or a useful payload of goods, which he fixed at 15 inches, the 'minimum gauge' from which he never wavered thereafter. His locomotives would be 3ft 10in wide (slightly over three times the track gauge), and his carriages just 2 inches narrower.

At Cambridge Arthur studied what then passed for the new subject of Applied Science, in which he alone obtained a First, but his leisure hours spent at Cambridge railway station and the local locomotive depot were undoubtedly far more beneficial for his future life. In 1872 he married his first cousin, Margaret Effie Sumner, the daughter of the

Rev George and (his aunt) Mary Elizabeth previously mentioned. Sir Thomas bought a house and estate at Duffield Bank, 6 miles north of Derby, for the newly married couple and it proved to be the happiest of family homes and the ideal base for Arthur's mission to promote 15-inch-gauge railways. He needed no encouragement, but had any been wanted Duffield was also a favoured residential area for the senior engineers of the Midland Railway Works at Derby, to which he apparently had free access.

As it grew between 1874 and 1897, the **Duffield Bank Railway** served a multitude of purposes. First and last, of course, it was a rich man's indulgence, creating probably the finest garden railway ever built, a delight to his father and to his own children, with ornamental stations, signal boxes, viaducts and the obligatory tunnels. Built on a steep hillside, it presented engineering difficulties that compelled Heywood to address basic questions such as 'What is actually the steepest gradient that a steam locomotive can climb?' and 'What is the sharpest curve that a locomotive can be made to traverse?' Necessarily, these led to 'What is the ideal type of locomotive for such a railway?' and 'What kinds of rolling stock would be the most efficient?'

The Duffield Bank Railway was, essentially, in two parts. To the north of the house were the extensive workshops including a design office and erecting shops for locomotives and carriages, and from the nearby locomotive shed a single track ran south, then rounded a 25-foot-radius hairpin bend to climb northwards up the escarpment of the hill at a gradient of 1 in 12. When first built, such a gradient would have been considered virtually impossible for a locomotive using the simple adhesion of steel wheel on steel rail; Heywood's designs, with their weight carried equally on all the driving axles, were able to haul a payload equal to their own weight. At the top of the incline, a double-looped layout rather like a pair of spectacles ran north and south along the hill (formerly millstone grit quarries) taking in two main stations, two viaducts and three tunnels, around which the locomotives could be run continuously for evaluation – or the owner, his family and friends could simply play trains from station to station. In later years the 'bottom level' included a spur from the workshops to the nearby road with a crane for the hoped-for dispatch of equipment to clients!

Like other engineering geniuses – there is a slight similarity to Isambard Kingdom Brunel – Heywood tended to believe that everything had to be invented, or re-invented, from scratch. He had visited the **Ffestiniog Railway** and observed, perceptively, that it had made the best of an existing slate quarry wagon gauge rather than considering the ideal for its heavy traffic. He had possibly seen Robert Fairlie's experimental double-bogie locomotive, *Little Wonder*, being tested there in 1870, although if

so it gave him an absolute conviction against the use of flexible-bogie machines. Heywood's Duffield Bank and Eaton Hall locomotives are described more fully later; highly successful for their specific tasks, they were nevertheless so individualistic that no engine building company was willing to produce them on a commercial basis, and this possibly became a negative factor in the minds of potential customers for private railways. Of wider application was Heywood's system for applying sand to the rails for adhesion, using a current of dry air induced by a steam ejector; he publicised the device after a fatal steam tram disaster in Huddersfield in July 1883, and it was adopted by, amongst others, Francis Holt at the Midland Railway Works in Derby.

Arthur Heywood might well, by his own inclination, have become a military engineer. He never lost his interest in fortifications and armaments and a large part of his mission at Duffield Bank was to convince the Royal Engineers that very small-gauge railways were the ideal battlefield transport for artillery, munitions and troops in the large-scale conflict which so many Victorians saw looming over the horizon. Even the dining and sleeping carriages that ornamented Duffield Bank might have found some military use for staff officers, though one can all too easily imagine what the troops would have thought of such luxuries! The timber trestle viaduct was intended specifically to impress the War Office as a structure that could be built in a week by just a

The infamous 1-in-12 gradient at Duffield Bank was still clearly visible in 1962, but has since become totally overgrown; the 25-foot-radius curve was at the extreme right of the picture. *Derbyshire CC (The Bromby Collection and www.picturethepast. org.uk*

few men. Despite several research visits, one as late as 1903, the Engineers were never wholly convinced by Heywood's enthusiasm. As time went on, and artillery vastly increased in size, the Royal Arsenals came to adopt 18 inches as the minimum industrial railway gauge; in the Great War, when it came, the armies on both sides were to build vast networks of 1ft 11⅝in (60cm) lines in support of the trenches.

Another potential application for small railways, in Heywood's mind, was the landed estate itself. Steam was already applied to the work of threshing and, to a lesser extent, ploughing, and crude early versions of 'self-moving' (traction) engines were churning up the roads preceded by men with red flags. Large public institutions, and businesses such as quarries and brickyards, also needed to move several thousand tons of goods per year between fixed points. At that time carting by horses cost between 10 and 15 times as much per ton-mile as a conventional railway; it was labour intensive and often cruel to the draught animals. It was easy to see how 15-inch-gauge railways would be an elegant solution to the movement of visitors and supplies from the local railway station to the Great House, milk churns from the 'model' dairy to the station, timber from plantations to the sawmill, and coal or fertiliser to the farms – all in small, neat railway wagons slipping easily through gates and barn doorways, pulled by locomotives that did not wear ruts in the driveways. No opportunity was lost in demonstrating Heywood's vision to Duffield Bank visitors, but one has to wonder whether the lavish expense of the system – signal boxes, telephones, hand-laid ballasted track, ornamental station buildings and the like – did not detract somewhat from its utilitarian value. By the early 20th century a small steam road tractor – readily available from firms such as Garrett or Wallis & Stevens – could be bought for just half the cost of one of Heywood's railway locomotives.

The Duffield Bank Railway and workshop facilities did not long survive their creator's death in 1916, the locomotives and rolling stock mostly going to the re-equipment of the defunct **Ravenglass & Eskdale Railway** in Cumbria. Some of the trackbed was turned into woodland walks by the new owners after 1916, and the site has been further altered by new building, though parts of the trackbed were clearly visible in the 1960s and 1970s. An archaeological survey of the area around the 'Long Tunnel' in 2009-10 found it to be remarkably intact, despite being partially incorporated into a new house! Interestingly, the tunnel dimensions at Duffield Bank (7 feet high, 5 feet maximum width) were a self-imposed restriction on the size of passenger carriages; far larger vehicles have since operated on the 15-inch (and even smaller) gauges, and indeed Heywood's later vehicles for the Eaton Railway could not have run through the Duffield Bank tunnels.

Significantly, although a number of estate railways were built, only one was commissioned directly from Heywood, and that was for one of the wealthiest landowners in England, the Duke of Westminster. Designed after a visit by the Estate Agent to a Duffield Bank open day in 1894, it was completed just before the death of Sir Thomas Heywood – one of his last

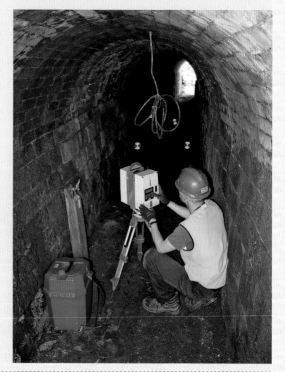

Dr Strange-Walker of Trent & Peak Archaeology surveys the Long Tunnel at Duffield Bank in 2010. *Trent & Peak Archaeology Unit*

The original carriage shed at Eaton Hall now serves as the locomotive depot for *Katie*

visits was to see it working – and naturally the strictures against Arthur working commercially had been relaxed for such a noble client. The inspiration for the line almost certainly came from the first Duke's son, Victor Alexander (Grosvenor), who had been an avid railway enthusiast before his early death in 1884. The Hon Cecil Parker (the Duke's nephew) acted as his Agent, and presumably caught the same enthusiasm in a less virulent form. The agent of the Duke of Rutland had also attended the 1894 event, but remained immune.

The Eaton Railway

The extent of the Eaton Hall estate was such that the main line of 3 miles, from the Hall to Balderton station (on the GWR Chester to Shrewsbury and Paddington line) and a branch of three-quarters of a mile from Belgrave Lodge to the estate works at Cuckoo's Nest, were built entirely over the Duke's land and opened in 1896. Heywood supervised the tracklaying personally and supplied the railway materials, locomotives, carriages and wagons from his own workshops at Duffield Bank. The steel sleepers and the elaborate coal storage shed were supplied by Handyside of Derby. The cost was £5,890 including rolling stock. Harry Wilde, Heywood's assistant engineer at Duffield Bank, worked on the project and stayed on as

driver – later compiling a unique and evocative photographic album of the line at work. The elegant open and closed carriages transported the Duke's guests to shooting parties on the estate, King Edward VII, Queen Alexandra and Winston Churchill being carried in the same month – Churchill apparently preferring the train ride to the shooting! Heavy overhaul of the steam locomotives proved difficult after Heywood's death in 1916, and for its last 20 years the Eaton Hall line was operated mainly by internal combustion locomotives of the 'Simplex' type, continuing to move coal, timber and building materials throughout the working week.

The Second World War led to Heywood's handsome locomotives being broken up for scrap metal at Balderton station – some of the saddest railway photographs the author has ever seen. Had the line survived just a few years after its 1947 closure, who knows what might have happened by way of preservation? The 'silver lining' was that the remaining Eaton Hall equipment went to the **Romney, Hythe & Dymchurch Railway** to contribute towards its post-war revival, and much has survived to the present day. Even more happily, a relatively short oval line starting from the original goods depot near the Hall was created in 1996 by the present Duke, complete with a replica Heywood locomotive and two carriages, which are usually operated on the three Sundays each year when the gardens are opened to the public for charity.

The Dove Bank, Blakesley Hall and Sand Hutton railways

Although Sir Arthur Heywood had a direct involvement with only the first of these, all three exemplified the gentleman's private estate railway 'as it might have been'. It was hardly to be expected that Arthur would not seek to build a line at Dove Leys, his father's family seat. The little railway powered by hand or pedals seems to have survived until about 1887. On inheriting the property in 1897, Heywood planned to extend the line to the nearest railway station – Norbury to the north or Rocester to the south, both on the Uttoxeter to Ashbourne branch line – and introduce his latest types of locomotive, as being built for Eaton Hall. Unfortunately (unlike the Duke of Westminster) he did not own all the intervening land and, as the owners were unwilling to give Heywood a railway 'wayleave', the plans for the **'Dove Bank Railway'** were never fulfilled. The line seems to have got as far as Dove Cliff Farm (the trackbed with cinder ballast has been found about half a mile away from Dove Leys), and several wagons and a rail-bending machine were certainly in use.

Sir Arthur seems to have been a very private man, and left no record of his feelings at the very limited spread of the ideas to which he had devoted his life and fortune. Perhaps the management of his property, the life of his family, and his interests in Church of England affairs and campanology sufficiently occupied his time in the latter years of his life. His youngest daughter Effie recorded in a memoir that he was the kindest of men, though expecting the best from his dependants – genial, if occasionally stern. 'He loved his house to be well run; he liked his stables, his gardens and park, his home farm to be complete, and he had an almost old-fashioned idea of "Living in State".' All were true characteristics of both her father and her grandfather Sir Thomas, and could never have been sustained after Sir Arthur's death in 1916 in the economic conditions of a World War.

In 1903 a civil engineer and railway shareholder named Charles William Bartholomew (who had been a contemporary of Heywood at Trinity College, Cambridge) built a 15-inch-gauge line linking Blakesley Hall to Blakesley station (near Towcester, Northamptonshire), where he had the use of a private platform. It is thanks to the meticulous researches of Dr Bob Tebb that the family has been rescued from almost total obscurity. Like Heywood, Bartholomew acquired his home as a gift from his family (who had played an important role in coal-mining and river and canal transport in South Yorkshire) on his marriage in 1876,

A Heywood-style building in the grounds of Doveleys – a silent witness to the ambitions of the Dove Bank Railway.

and he embraced his new role of country squire with open arms; his ecclesiastical tastes were towards stained glass rather than campanology. His marriage was unfortunately not an enduring one and, following the departure of Lucy Bartholomew from the scene in the 1880s, her role was taken over by a young cook and housekeeper named

Charles Bartholomew was a shareholder of this railway, which served Blakesley station. The notice was photographed at Bressingham Steam Museum.

Sarah Floyd. In later years the playwright George Bernard Shaw became a friend of Bartholomew through shared motoring interests, and Sarah's hurried 'gentrification' may even have provided the real-life model for the play *Pygmalion* and the subsequent musical *My Fair Lady*! Interestingly, Shaw also came to know Wenman Bassett-Lowke, through the Fabian Society.

Charles Bartholomew inherited a large fortune on the death of his father in 1895, and became an avid railway enthusiast as well as a keen pioneer motorist. The **Blakesley Miniature Railway** served the purposes of an estate and pleasure railway, bringing visitors, fuel and supplies to the house, the home farm, and his private electrical generating station. Crucially its equipment marked a turning point towards scale model engineering. Beginning with a 4-4-0 steam locomotive and a set of ten carriages to the design of the American Cagney brothers – giving himself a brand-new train set 'straight out of the box' – Bartholomew then experimented with two of the earliest internal-combustion locomotives on any railway. His friends included Wenman Joseph Bassett-Lowke of the Northampton firm of model engineers, who possibly helped to maintain the Cagney locomotive; visits to Blakesley certainly helped to convince Bassett-Lowke of the practicality of 15-inch-gauge lines for carrying the paying public. Bartholomew loaned his Cagney in 1909 to help out on Bassett-Lowke's **Sutton Coldfield Railway**, shortly after Henry Greenly had been commissioned to design the pioneering 'steam outline' petrol locomotive *Blacolvesley* for Blakesley Hall – one of the most handsome of his early designs.

Bartholomew derived much of his wealth from ownership of the Wombwell Main Colliery and other mineral rights, and although he died in 1919 Sarah kept the line operational until 1939. Henry Greenly brought a visitor to see – and possibly to purchase – *Blacolvesley* just three years earlier. Although the track was lifted in 1940, and the equipment dispersed by auction in 1943, *Blacolvesley* has happily survived in treasured private preservation after a chequered middle age. Blakesley Hall itself was demolished in 1958.

The most interesting landed estate railway, in many ways, was that built by Sir Robert James Milo Walker in the grounds of his family home at **Sand Hutton** to the east of York. A Major in the Coldstream Guards, and said to be the richest man in the British Army (owning 7,000 acres of land), he had succeeded his father and come into his inheritance at the age of ten. After leaving Cambridge University in 1911 (again, a Trinity College student!) he was free to build his own railway, three-quarters of a mile in length with a bridge across a pond and a short tunnel. Bassett-Lowke supplied one locomotive, *Synolda* – named after Sir Robert's fiancée, Emily Synolda Thursby-Pelham – and four coaches; there were also some home-made additions. It was probably through the influence of Sir Arthur Heywood that Harry Wilde from the Eaton Railway arrived on the scene to give practical advice. On return from war service, Sir Robert determined to develop the estate to its fullest potential, equipping it with a fire brigade and extending the railway to Claxton brickworks and the local Warthill railway station. To cover these, and further extensions serving farms and settlements northwards to

Barnby, he obtained a Light Railway Order in 1919 allowing the line to cross public roads and carry passengers.

All these plans might have been carried out to the 15-inch-gauge; Sir Robert approached the firm of Judd of York for additional rolling stock, and Henry Greenly sent a design for a 2-8-4 tank locomotive, almost certainly intended for Sand Hutton, to the North Eastern Railway engineers who were Sir Robert's technical advisors. However, opportunism intervened; a large quantity of 18-inch-gauge equipment from the Government's closed Deptford Meat Factory came onto the market at the end of 1920, and proved too good a bargain for Sir Robert to resist. *Synolda*'s last duties were to operate gauge conversion trains over the existing line. Coincidentally, Sir Robert and Synolda divorced in 1921, and in an episode worthy of 'Thomas the Tank Engine' *Synolda* (the engine, not Lady Walker) was locked up in the disused ornamental tunnel for some time, stripped of her name and builder's plates!

Although strictly outside the scope of this book, the 18-inch-gauge line finally extended to nearly 7½ miles (a branch across the River Derwent to Scrayingham was never built), and Sir Robert's enthusiasm for the economic possibilities of the landed estate railway was given the fullest airing in *The Railway Magazine* in

Little and large at Eaton Hall: Bassett-Lowke's *Synolda* with the Eaton four-wheel brake van, 24 August 2008

May 1924. The fresh equipment included no fewer than four Hunslet-built industrial tank locomotives, No 1 being named *Esme* after Sir Robert's new fiancée, Esmé Ethel Alice de Beaumont, doubtless on the 'better-luck-this-time' principle. Passenger services were operated on Saturdays using a capacious Hudson bogie carriage, complete with a refreshment service.

Sir Robert died in July 1930, and his trustees closed the railway to passengers immediately and to goods in 1932; the local farmers had already formed a co-operative to use road transport – avoiding trans-shipment costs at Warthill station – and the Claxton brickworks had run out of the local clay. What remained of the Hall was demolished around 1960 and it is now the site of Sand Hutton School; recent work in the grounds has revealed a few traces of the 15-inch-gauge line. But visitors to the Armley Mills industrial museum near Leeds can still enjoy the prototype of the 18-inch-gauge locomotive design, *Jack* (built by the Hunslet Engine Co in 1898) having been preserved by Leeds Museums & Galleries after 60 years at work hauling fireclay at the Woodville Clay Pits in Derbyshire.

Toys for wealthy gentlemen: the Staughton Manor, Higham Park and Hardwick Manor railways

Of course, all the 'landed estate' railways included a substantial element of fun for the owning families, and it is perhaps a fine

distinction between these and the purely pleasure lines of the extremely rich. But it is at this point that the influence of Wenman Joseph Bassett-Lowke comes to the fore. His background and miniature railway interests are described in more detail in the next section, but by 1910 his model shop in High Holborn, London, had become a 'Mecca' for miniature and model railway enthusiasts – especially those for whom money was of little or no object.

One of the first among such happy people was John Edwards Presgrave Howey (universally known as 'Jack'), son of John Howey, born at Melton Grange near Woodbridge, Suffolk, in 1886. His father, already a millionaire, had inherited a large property in Melbourne, Australia, from a bachelor uncle in 1871. J. E. P. Howey had a brother, Richard, ten years younger; both were motor-racing enthusiasts, and Richard would be tragically killed at a hill-climb in France in 1926.

Howey's first locomotive was a 9½-inch-gauge 4-4-2 supplied by Bassett-Lowke in 1911 and tried out at Melton Grange. He married in the same year, moving to a leased house, Staughton Manor near Huntingdon, in 1912. Not being the actual landowner seems not to have troubled Howey in the slightest, and he commissioned Henry Greenly to build a three-quarter-mile line, complete with wooden scale models of the Forth Bridge and a country station. Howey was present at the opening of **Rhyl Miniature Railway** on 1 May 1911, where he talked his way onto the footplate, and thoroughly 'caught the 15-inch-gauge bug' driving the engine. By 1913 Greenly was back at Staughton Manor widening the line to the 15-inch-gauge. Characteristically, Howey ordered an entirely new design of enlarged locomotive – the 4-6-2 'Gigantic' type named after his infant son, *John Anthony*.

At this point war intervened. Captain Howey, serving as an observer with the Royal Flying Corps, was shot down in 1915 and survived only by taking control from his (dead) pilot and crash-landing the plane. He was taken prisoner but repatriated to Switzerland in 1917. Staughton Manor was already too small for his ambitions, so he moved to London after the war while looking round for a bigger challenge. Power-boat racing and motor-racing

were his current enthusiasms; as one of the 'Brooklands Set', he formed a close friendship with Count Louis Zborowski. Howey owned a Leyland racing car, bought from the legendary John Godfrey Parry-Thomas, but self-evidently his driving was less suicidal than his contemporaries. On the railway front, he sold *John Anthony* to Narrow Gauge Railways Ltd to advance his burning desire to take over the **Ravenglass & Eskdale Railway**, but that was to prove an ambition too far.

Count Louis Vorrow Zborowski, born in 1895, was perhaps the most flamboyant of all the miniature railway pioneers. The son of Count Eliott Zborowski, a Russian-Polish aristocrat – who had been killed while motor-racing as early as 1903! – his maternal grandmother was no less than an Astor, endowed with fabulous wealth from their property in Manhattan, including several blocks on Fifth Avenue. Louis's mother, Countess Margaret, purchased the estate of Higham Park at Bridge, just east of Canterbury, in 1910, but died three months later.

Thus at the age of 16 Count Louis became one of the richest young men in the world by inheriting £11 million and Higham Park, where he built up a fleet of 30 racing cars, including two versions of the famous 'Chitty-Bang-Bang' machines powered by aircraft engines. A 27-litre 'Higham Special', unfinished at his death, was later to become 'Babs', Parry-Thomas's fatal speed record contender at Pendine Sands. Discovering that his motor-racing friend Jack Howey had the same passion for railways, they began to look around for a suitable site to fulfil their vision of a fast main line in miniature. Typically impatient, in 1923 Zborowski commissioned a local firm to construct a line in the grounds of Higham Park (it might eventually have encircled the estate for fast running) and ordered Bassett-Lowke to rush the completion of a final Class 30 locomotive, the parts for which had been lying around the firm's Northampton works since 1914.

Count Louis's wife, Vi, had been a Gaiety actress and they were both (again, like the Howeys) well-known in the world of London theatre. Life at Higham Park in the summer of 1924 must have epitomised the 'roaring twenties': young actresses mingling with the 'Brooklands Set' racing their fast cars around the lanes of Kent. And if not already terrified by the improvised explosive devices that Zborowski liked to detonate for fun in his statuary and swimming pool, the actresses were likely to be carried off and tied to the track of the **Higham Railway** – to be rescued in the nick of time from the advancing locomotive by the Count himself, in the role of hero!

By this time, a site for the **Romney, Hythe & Dymchurch Railway** had already been found, and Zborowski had ordered the first two of Greenly's magnificent 4-6-2 locomotives (*Green Goddess* and *Northern Chief*) from Davey, Paxman of Colchester. He intended to devote himself fully to the new venture after 'just one more' motor race, the Italian Grand

Prix at Monza. There, on 19 October 1924, his Mercedes skidded on a patch of oil and hit a tree. Zborowski died instantly. He was buried next to his father, mother and infant brother in the churchyard of Burton Lazars near Melton Mowbray. His widow immediately decided to sell Higham Park, and the little railway was dismantled in 1924-25 as quickly as it had been built. His Bassett-Lowke locomotive, named *Count Louis* by its new owners, became the mainstay of the **Fairbourne Railway** in Wales before being happily preserved and, very recently, restored to full working order.

Many other private 15-inch-gauge railways have been built, and several still exist – such as the delightful little **Rhiw Valley Railway** around farmland at Manafon near Berriew in mid-Wales. However, special mention must be made of the **Hardwick Manor Railway**, which, despite its short life, made a significant contribution to other passenger-carrying lines. The builders were R. Barnard Clayton and Douglas Clayton, the owners of Cannon Ironfounders of Bilston, who acquired two incomplete sets of castings for Bassett-Lowke Class 30 locomotives. The first was assembled by 1933 and named *Douglas Clayton* to run on a short line in the grounds of his house at Bredons Hardwick near Tewkesbury. The rolling stock included a magnificently furnished three-compartment covered coach. The line closed in

Above: Count Louis Zborowski was buried in the family tomb at Burton Lazars near Melton Mowbray. On his tombstone his second name is spelled 'Vorow' with only one 'r'. *Burton Lazars PCC*

Right: Attention to detail: the restored boiler backhead of *Count Louis* includes a J. T. Lowke manufacturer's plate.

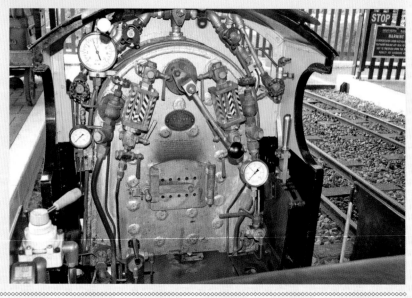

1948, after Douglas's death, and the working and unfinished locomotives went to the **Sutton Miniature Railway** where both were rebuilt and put to work (as *Sutton Belle* and *Sutton Flyer*); both have survived to this day in the Sutton Collection at the **Cleethorpes Coast Light Railway**. The rolling stock and a signal box had a less fortunate fate after sale to the **Fairbourne Railway**; the splendid GWR-style coach was allowed to rot in the Welsh sea air until its body was beyond repair, while the signal box was demoted to an ice-cream kiosk!

Seaside railways and international exhibitions: Bassett-Lowke, Greenly and Miniature Railways of Great Britain Ltd

It is, of course, with the seaside or pleasure park railway that many people rightly associate the 15-inch-gauge. They began in the democratic United States while such lines were still the preserve of the wealthy few in Great Britain. The four brothers Cagney (Timothy, David, Charles and Thomas) established in 1898 the **Miniature Railroad Company** with the prestigious business address of 'Broadway, New York', and offered equipment in a variety of track gauges. A simple, robust, type of 4-4-0

steam locomotive was offered as motive power pulling up to ten diminutive open coaches, sometimes provided with canopies.

The first such venture in Britain was operated by one Captain Paul Boyton at the Earls Court Exhibition of 1901, using the narrowest Cagney gauge of 12⅝ inches, and in the same year he opened a 15-inch-gauge line at the Glasgow International Exhibition (in what is now Kelvingrove Park) with twice the carrying capacity. Other short, and short-lived, lines quickly followed at Wolverhampton in 1902 (both gauges being laid down), at the Alexandra Palace, London, in 1903-04, at White City, Manchester, in 1909, and at Edge Lane, Liverpool, in 1913. The moving spirit in these large-scale exhibitions was a Hungarian showman by the name of Imre Kiralfy. As we have seen, Charles W. Bartholomew used a Cagney engine at his Blakesley Miniature Railway, and one of the 'exhibition' locomotives seems to have paid the occasional visit there. A Cagney opened the Kürsaal line at Southend about 1920, and it may well have been the authentic 'Blakesley Hall' Cagney that was seen on George Horsefield's private line at Dean's Mill in Sussex in the late 1930s.

The early years of King Edward VII's reign

Sutton Flyer, one of the Clayton 4-4-2s, is dwarfed by a former Liverpool Garden Festival coach at Cleethorpes.

were fruitful ground for the miniature railway. Holidays with pay, though not yet universal, were commonplace for industrial workers, who now had access to recreational facilities ranging from public parks, endowed by philanthropists in their home towns, to seaside resorts that might even be near enough for a cheap day excursion. Seaside entertainment was already a flourishing, if occasionally tawdry, business, with music halls, fairgrounds, piers and donkey rides. Mechanisation was already appearing with the 'tunnel railway' in which customers were drawn, seated in carriages, through a series of scenes or tableaux arranged in a circle. Purpose-built steam engines for these came from the fairground manufacturers, Savage's of King's Lynn in Norfolk.

A British entrepreneur to take up the miniature railway idea was needed, and was immediately found in **Wenman Joseph Bassett-Lowke** (1877-1953) of Northampton. The son of Joseph Thomas Lowke, an agricultural engineer and boiler-maker, Wenman had left school at 13 to serve an apprenticeship with his father at the Central Engine & Boiler Works before spending short periods in an architect's office and with Crompton Parkinson, the electrical engineers. His real passion was model-making and, encouraged by a travelling engineering salesman and by his future business partner Harry Foldar Robert Franklin (a book-keeper at J. T. Lowke & Sons), he made good use of the facilities of his father's works. By 1902 he had already started to visit continental model and toy fairs; in that year he commissioned the first model to his own standards and, even more significantly, met Henry Greenly, who would become his chief designer.

Bassett-Lowke was a complex man – summed up by his biographer Roland Fuller as an 'author, broadcaster, a keen businessman, an excellent organiser, an inveterate traveller, a skilled photographer and a superb showman'. Although a gregarious character, hating to do things alone, Bassett-Lowke tended to be highly opinionated and his works staff (including, in later times, his niece Janet) sometimes found him a hard master; throughout his life he was guided by the twin ideals of Fitness for Purpose and Perfection in Miniature. He was keenly interested in modern design (his first house was remodelled by no less an architect than Charles Rennie Mackintosh, and his second, 'New Ways', was the only English house designed by Professor George Behrens of the Bauhaus). Despite his pacifist beliefs, he accepted the substantial income that his business made from the manufacture of screw gauges and naval models for the Government during the First World War. In later life he was, unfortunately, to lead two of his close friends into financial difficulties; Robert Proctor Mitchell lost everything that he invested in the Narrow Gauge Railways Ltd venture, and Henry Greenly would be forced into insolvency in a bizarre libel action grounded in breach of copyright in his engineering drawings. For some obscure reason, Bassett-Lowke often went by the nickname of 'Whynne', which was later carried by one of his 15-inch-gauge locomotives. He was careful to keep his personal interest in miniature railway operation entirely separate from the main Bassett-Lowke business of high-quality model railway equipment, architectural models, and ship models.

A carriage tread-plate of Bassett-Lowke Ltd on the preserved four-wheel carriage in Ravenglass Museum, photographed in March 2012.

Henry Greenly (1876-1947) was the eldest son of Edward Greenly, a senior guard on the Great Western Railway. The family had enjoyed a long association with railways and, even earlier, with stage coaches. Henry inherited his father's happy disposition and his mother's energy and perfectionism. The family moved from Tranmere, Birkenhead, to Queen's Park, West London, in 1887, and at the age of 13 Henry was apprenticed to a Bayswater jeweller where his skill at fine, miniature work became apparent. His love of engineering and railways took him to a local science school, then in 1896 to Regent Street Polytechnic, where he marked out the expansion links and helped machine the cylinders of an 18-inch-gauge model of a Stirling 4-2-2 locomotive from castings made by Bagnalls of Stafford; he also studied building construction. From 1897 he worked in the drawing office and the architectural department of the Metropolitan Railway at Neasden, and quickly developed a love of making locomotive drawings for publication, a taste for journalism (sometimes contentious), and an enthusiasm for photography.

He was a founder member, in 1898, of the Society of Model and Experimental Engineers, and in May 1901 (just months before marrying) he abandoned – to the distress of his father – his promising career with the Metropolitan Railway to take up the editorship of *The Model Engineer* for his friend Percival Marshall. At about the same time he met Wenman Joseph Bassett-Lowke and, with their common interests in railways, models, photography and buildings, the two men became immediate and close friends, travelling together on fact-finding visits to German toy and model manufacturers in 1902 and 1903. In 1904 Greenly visited Sir Arthur Heywood's line at Duffield Bank. Bassett-Lowke famously described Greenly as having 'a mind like quicksilver'.

It was largely due to Greenly that standard scales for British model railways came to be recognised; his first book, *The Model Locomotive*, appeared in 1904 and was to become a standard textbook on the subject. His interest in large models seems to have started with a visit to the 15-inch-gauge Glasgow Exhibition line in 1901, and in 1904 he built his first locomotive for passenger-carrying, the 10¼-inch-gauge

0-4-4 tank engine *Nipper*, which ran at Bricket's Wood near St Albans in 1904, and at Northampton in 1905. It is a noteworthy aspect of his character that, throughout his life, Greenly wrote, drew, corresponded and published endlessly for the benefit of model-makers, yet he retained a close control – bordering on the jealous – over the use of his personal drawings, which led him into legal proceedings on at least three occasions, and finally resulted in his insolvency. The last years of his life were overshadowed by ill health, and he died in 1947 at the age of 70.

Bassett-Lowke and Greenly were inspired by the exploits of Captain Boyton and Charles Bartholomew to set up **Miniature Railways of Great Britain Ltd** – the similarity to the American title was surely deliberate – in 1904, being essentially a group of friends with the same single-minded enthusiasm. The first MRGB operation was, appropriately, at Blackpool, the quintessential Edwardian seaside resort. Forty acres of beach had been purchased by J. W. Outhwaite and W. G. Bean to establish a permanent outdoor pleasure ground, and the **South Shore Miniature Railway** was a circular track of just over 400 yards laid directly onto the sands near the funfair. It combined the appeal of a fairground ride with that of a donkey ride on the sands, but more seriously Bassett-Lowke recognised that the intelligent working man – and his son – among the visitors would be fascinated by the spectacle of the miniature locomotive at work. As he expressed it, 'If the fascination engendered by locomotion at the present day is so intense, the attractive powers of locomotion in miniature must of necessity be greater still.' Being long before the era of political correctness, the boarding point was a wooden station called Gipsyville, adjoining the 'encampment' of the fortune-teller 'Gipsy Lee' (Urania Boswell). The extensive use of wooden buildings at MRGB sites was due partly to their portability, and partly to one of the Directors, Ernest Trenery, being a Northampton timber importer.

The first locomotive, Greenly's pioneer 4-4-2 *Little Giant*, was tested at Eaton Hall by courtesy of the railway-minded Alexander, (second) Duke of Westminster, and during its first week at Blackpool in the Whitsun holiday it pulled 9,000 passengers in three bogie coaches. The line was an immediate success. Better coaches by the tramcar builder, Milnes of Birkenhead, arrived in 1908, but by the next year the wear and tear caused by wind-blown sand in the bearings and working parts was becoming critical, and the Blackpool line closed in the autumn of 1909 when the lease of the site expired.

Wenman Joseph Bassett-Lowke was on his own behalf already interested in the early 10¼-inch-gauge line, first laid near St Albans, which moved to a site next to **Abington Park, Northampton**, in 1905 (the stuffy civic authorities refusing to allow it within the park), then to Sutton Park in **Sutton Coldfield** in 1907. The next year it was widened to 15-inch-gauge and re-equipped by Miniature Railways of Great Britain Ltd, using the second Greenly locomotive, *Mighty Atom*, and (very probably) the original coaches from Blackpool. The 'run' again was about 400 yards, with return loops operated by spring points, a feature to be found on many subsequent miniature railways. The Sutton Park venture would have a succession of closings and re-openings, before being reborn as the Sutton Collection at the **Cleethorpes Coast Light Railway** in 2002. *Mighty Atom* herself has even more recently been preserved – though not as yet restored – at the adjacent Miniature Railway Museum. With the first locomotive from St Albans had come a certain Fred Smithies, who would be seen as senior driver on most of the MRGB lines, while his wife obligingly looked after the family dairy business in Watford – a doyen of the miniature railway world.

The next venture was an inland site at the **Halifax Zoo** and pleasure gardens, opened at Exley Bank near Chevin Edge in May 1910. Here a circular 'run' of 1,700 feet was possible, with a rock cutting and a tunnel. The (second set of) Blackpool coaches were re-used and *Little Giant* was renamed *Little Elephant* to suit its new environment, with a bogie tender to carry more coal and water. The movements, transformations, namings and renamings of the Bassett-Lowke locomotives are a research topic in their own right, as evidenced by the magnificent book by the late Robin Butterell

and John Milner, *The Little Giant Story*. Soon after the outbreak of war in 1914, the Halifax venture closed and the equipment came back to Northampton.

The most ambitious scheme yet for MRGB Ltd was built in April 1911 and opened on 1 May. The **Rhyl Miniature Railway** had a circular track of more than a mile around the Marine Park and Lake near the seafront, on land leased from the Council. Here the buildings, too, were to the design of the multi-talented Henry Greenly, who was truly to become 'all things' to his miniature railway projects. Equipped with another 'Little Giant' type locomotive (the former *Red Dragon* being renamed *Prince Edward of Wales* in anticipation of the Prince's forthcoming investiture at Caernarfon Castle) and six coaches, the line was managed by Albert Barnes and became highly successful. On the August Bank Holiday in 1911 *Prince Edward of Wales* made 93 circuits of the track carrying 5,003 passengers, an incredible performance for such a small machine. After a period of abandonment, much uncertainty and tentative rebuilding, the Rhyl line is now fully restored, securely preserved by a charitable trust, and has just celebrated its centenary in fine style. Long may it flourish!

Immediately after the opening of the Rhyl operation, Greenly was at Southport to oversee the building of a line alongside another Marine Lake for Griffith Vaughan Llewelyn, a local postman, shopkeeper and horticulturalist, and a dentist and mechanical enthusiast called Dr Ladmore. The line began as a single track between the rustic Lakeside and Pierhead (later Princes Parade) stations, along which the train shuttled back and forth. In deference to the Southport floral tradition the lineside included a rock garden. MRGB took no part in the operation of the line, but Llewelyn and his associate vigorously developed **Llewelyn's Miniature Railway** (today the **Lakeside Miniature Railway**). The first Bassett-Lowke locomotive, *George the Fifth*, was sold to Rhyl after only two seasons, and Southport began an active period of buying and selling engines, followed by a bewildering frequency of renamings. The future of seaside pleasure lines was now to lie with a number of local owners, like Llewelyn, rather than with a single promotional company. The reasons for this lie partly in the alternative business interests of Miniature Railways of Great Britain Ltd, and partly in the strategy that its successor, **Narrow Gauge Railways Ltd**, adopted after 1912. Bassett-Lowke never followed the business model of the Cagney brothers, the mass-production of equipment for operation by others world-wide.

The years just before the First World War – the high point of the Edwardian age in Britain, and the belle époque on the continent – were marked by a succession of international trade exhibitions that, alas, did not lead to universal peace and prosperity. These large-scale events, on sites in or near large cities, attracted huge crowds of visitors. Captain Boyton had already demonstrated what 15-inch-gauge railways could do to move the public about, and to provide attractive joy-rides; MRGB Ltd set out to do it on a larger scale. The first venture was a line of a mile in length at the 'Exposition Internationale de l'Est de la France' at Nancy, with stations at the two entrance gates and several halts. Trenery, the timber-importer, was the director responsible for construction, and the line was awarded a 'Diploma de l'Honneur'. Bassett-Lowke gained a gold medal for the feat of having built the working locomotive, *Entente Cordiale*, in only 36 days. To meet the demand for rides, *Mighty Atom* was hastily brought from Sutton Coldfield in the guise of *Ville de Nancy*.

At the same time, Bassett-Lowke was contracted by a firm called Sideshow Railways Ltd to build a half-mile line of peculiar shape on a restricted site at the Industrial Exhibition at the White City, London. Two locomotives were built, though in the event only one (*Red Dragon*) with a set of 'toastrack-seat' coaches was actually needed; ever the publicist, Bassett-Lowke took the unused *Green Dragon* to the Model Engineer Exhibition, where it duly won a gold medal.

The next major international exhibition was held in Brussels from April 1910. The railway was again installed by Ernest Trenery, who had become Managing Director of MRGB earlier in the year, and was a double-track line connecting the two main stations; the trains worked the points and signals automatically by means of treadles. Three locomotives were specially

renamed and sent, of which only *Red Dragon* (aka *King Albert*) seems to have definitely returned to Britain. The exhibition closed in August after a disastrous fire at its 'Grande Palais' building. In the following year another short-lived line appeared at the 'Exposition Internationale du Nord de la France' at Roubaix near Lille, possibly powered by *Entente Cordiale* as used at Nancy. These ventures were proving less profitable than hoped and, to prevent any possible financial embarrassment, the decision to wind up Miniature Railways of Great Britain Ltd was taken in December 1911. Among the assets offered for sale in 1912 were the Sutton Coldfield and Halifax Zoo installations.

A change of direction: Narrow Gauge Railways Ltd

At first sight little seemed to have changed when a successor company was formed. Essentially a partnership between Bassett-Lowke and Robert Proctor Mitchell, the heir to the Polytechnic Tours business and an old friend of Henry Greenly, the new company persevered with continental exhibition lines while looking for larger-scale ventures at home. An early decision was to sell the **Rhyl Miniature Railway** to Rhyl Amusements Ltd, which owned the nearby fairground; from then on it would be inseparable from the highly talented manager and mechanical engineer, Albert Barnes.

Experience to date had suggested that 15-inch-gauge trains could operate successfully over much longer distances, with correspondingly greater earning potential and public appeal. Accordingly, an advertisement was placed in the specialist publication *Models, Railways and Locomotives* for suitable sites. There is a wise adage that one should be cautious what one wishes for, in case the wish comes true; the replies received led Narrow Gauge Railways Ltd towards the derelict 3-foot-gauge **Ravenglass & Eskdale Railway** on the Cumbrian coast and the near-derelict 2-foot-gauge horse tramway at **Fairbourne** on the southern shore of the Mawddach estuary.

At this juncture it is appropriate to meet John Wills, who had come to work for Bassett-Lowke in 1909. Born in 1872, he had trained to be a solicitor like his father, but gave up the law for his twin loves of railways and photography. With Bassett-Lowke and Greenly, he was a co-founder of the Society of Model and Experimental Engineers in 1898 and acted as Company Secretary for both MRGB Ltd and NGR Ltd. A brief spell as Manager of the Bassett-Lowke shop in High Holborn, London, was not his ideal position, but his talents blossomed as a practical railway operator; he is to be seen in very many photographs of the NGR Ltd lines, usually on the footplate of the engine with an instantly recognisable cloth cap set at a curious angle on his head! Almost single-handedly he was to nurse the impoverished **Fairbourne Railway** through to 1940, while running the village shop and Post Office to make ends meet; he died a well-respected 'pillar' of the Fairbourne community.

NGR Ltd needed to earn money from its assets, and June 1912 saw the opening of the most elaborate continental venture yet at the 'Parc des Eaux-Vives' on the shore of Lake Geneva. The **Luna Park Railway** boasted long and short loops, a five-span bridge across an ornamental lake, and a tunnel with decorated concrete portals – Henry Greenly designed it all, including the buildings. A new locomotive, *Bert Whynne* (combining the nicknames of Proctor Mitchell and Bassett-Lowke), and a set of new coaches were sent out with the quick-witted John Wills; detecting the imminent

bankruptcy of the park owners, he removed the engine, coaches, and everything else portable – including the station clock – in the dead of night before the bailiffs descended, and spirited them across the French border! Fortunately, there was an immediate opportunity to redeploy *Bert Whynne* – now renamed *Hungaria* – to an English-style funfair being opened at Angol Park (later called Vidam Park) in Budapest. The line seems to have had a long operating life, certainly as late as 1975, and *Hungaria* is still preserved as a historic exhibit by the Hungarian Transport Museum.

Another Bassett-Lowke locomotive was supplied to a little-documented 'Miniatur-Bahn' or 'Liliput-Bahn' at Breslau in Germany in 1913, and the following year saw the unhappily timed Jubilee Exhibition at Christiana (now Oslo) in Norway to celebrate a century of peace in Europe. This closed on the outbreak of the First World War, but more than a year elapsed before the locomotive (a new and enlarged – Class 30 – type named *Prins Olaf*) and other equipment was brought back to England.

In June 1915 Narrow Gauge Railways decided to take a lease on the 3-foot-gauge **Ravenglass & Eskdale Railway**, originally promoted in 1873 by the Whitehaven Iron Company to serve the Nab Gill and Gill Force mines near Boot in the Eskdale Valley. Bankrupt for most of its existence, it closed in 1913, though not before it had begun to attract tourists to the area; it is very likely that

Seen at Windmill Farm, a Lister 'auto-truck' of this kind maintained the Fairbourne operation until 1940. *Whippet Quick* later gained bodywork, but *Gwril* has no such embellishment.

Robert Proctor Mitchell knew of it through his Polytechnic Tours business. It was unfortunate, with hindsight, that John Wills's early legal training did not detect that the shareholder of the 'old' company who was so keen to offer a lease of the trackbed did not actually have the full power to do so. But work began at once on altering the gauge (mostly by the simple expedient of moving one rail along the existing sleepers), and by the end of 1915 trains were running on the 15-inch-gauge as far as Irton Road. Fully opened in 1916, the railway's new equipment included not only scale model locomotives but also the narrow-gauge locomotives and coaches from Duffield Bank after the death of Sir Arthur Heywood. A heady mixture of amateur enthusiasts and professionals gave the line a character all of its own, in many ways anticipating the era of the railway preservation societies in the 1950s and 1960s; and Bassett-Lowke (as a pacifist) was probably glad to spend his spare time away from Northampton while his firm was fully engaged on Government work. Some of his German friends were interned not far away on the Isle of Man, and he visited and assisted them as much as he could – while also getting his Charles Rennie Mackintosh-designed furniture made by the internees! There is of course extensive literature on subsequent developments at Ravenglass, and as one of the doyens of 15-inch-gauge operation it is extremely well known.

No sooner had the Ravenglass venture become operational than NGR Ltd's attention switched to **Fairbourne** on the Welsh coast. More cautious businessmen, recognising the highly unfinished state of both the holiday development near the hamlet of Friog by Arthur McDougall (of self-raising flour fame) and the efforts of his rival Solomon Andrews at nearby Arthog, might have hesitated, but the Fairbourne Estate Company's ten-year lease of the 2-foot-gauge tramway leading to Barmouth Ferry was immediately accepted, and the gauge reduced as simply as at Ravenglass. A mixed set of coaches, rescued from the Geneva and Oslo exhibition railways, arrived in 1916, together with just one locomotive – an 'improved' (Class 20) type appropriately named *Prince Edward of Wales*. John Wills was tactfully relocated from Ravenglass to Fairbourne following a 'falling-out' with Robert Proctor Mitchell.

The return of peace in 1918 brought renewed prosperity to many parts of the British leisure industry, though not so to Narrow Gauge Railways Ltd. Bassett-Lowke himself was quite ready to withdraw from the operation of 15-inch-gauge railways (his firm began no more locomotives of that gauge itself) and concentrate on rebuilding his model and toy business, which would go on to earn world renown. **Fairbourne** was not making the anticipated profits and, more seriously, the lease of the **Ravenglass & Eskdale** line had been found to be unsound; the trackbed had to be

The Irton Road station building has survived almost unaltered since 1879.

purchased to satisfy its remaining creditors and, in effect, a new owner stepped in, none other than the great Liverpool shipping magnate Sir Aubrey Brocklebank (1873-1929).

Sir Aubrey was already a Director of the Great Western Railway and had a Bassett-Lowke model locomotive, a 7¼-inch-gauge Great Central Railway 'Immingham' Class, at his family seat, Nunsmere at Sandiway, Cheshire. He would certainly have been aware of the Duke of Westminster's railway at Eaton Hall, and his own country house, Irton Hall, could hardly have been nearer to the Ravenglass & Eskdale. In 1916 he purchased Howey's locomotive *John Anthony* (renamed *Colossus*) for use at Ravenglass – the somewhat devious Proctor Mitchell is said to have charged him £800 (twice the price actually handed over to Howey) – and shortly afterwards he ordered a very similar 4-6-2 locomotive, which he named after himself, *Sir Aubrey Brocklebank*.

The opportunity to buy up Narrow Gauge Railways Ltd was timely, not only for revenging himself on Proctor Mitchell, who lost all his original investment, but for developing the Eskdale line in quite a different direction. Having seen the potential of the granite quarry at Beckfoot to supply crushed stone for railway ballast and, in the motor age, road stone, Sir Aubrey determined to redevelop the railway as a fully fledged mineral line. The key installation was a granite crushing plant at Murthwaite, for which Greenly designed the concrete buildings while the heavy machinery was successfully moved to the site on 15-inch wagons. Sir Aubrey was to die in 1929 and his successors then held back from further major investment in the 15-inch-gauge railway.

Ballast for the LMS had proved to be the major output from Murthwaite, so to avoid trans-shipment costs a standard-gauge track was put in from Ravenglass, 'gauntleted' outside the 15-inch-gauge rails, along which full-size wagons were pulled by an early diesel locomotive. An ingenious set of points allowed vehicles of the two gauges, with their different tyre and flange dimensions, to go their separate ways just west of Murthwaite. A well-documented visit by K. E. Hartley in 1929 found some Bassett-Lowke four-wheeled coaches still in use together with the Duffield

Bank and (15-inch-gauge) Sand Hutton vehicles; platform seats had been crammed into the sleeping carriage to carry more passengers. The remains of *Sans Pareil* and boilers from *Colossus* and *Sir Aubrey Brocklebank* still lay around Ravenglass, while their tenders and the chassis of *Ella* were 'out to grass' at Murthwaite.

Effectively, Narrow Gauge Railways Ltd had become simply the legal entity owning the Ravenglass & Eskdale line, in which capacity it survived until 1953. The little operation at **Fairbourne** had not fitted into the grand plans for Eskdale, so in 1921 it had been quietly sub-let to the local Barmouth Motor Boat & Ferry Company, with an option to purchase. Unfortunately, the ferrymen were unable to 'keep their heads above water' in the financial sense as railway operators, and by 1924 the line was back in the hands of the Fairbourne Estate in lieu of unpaid rent. Meanwhile, the locomotive *Prince Edward of Wales* had been sold by Narrow Gauge Railways Ltd to Griffith Llewelyn at Southport, forcing the boatmen to take the worn-out Heywood 0-4-0 *Katie* off Llewelyn's hands in exchange. But for the indomitable John Wills, Fairbourne would probably have 'gone under' completely by 1924.

A main line in miniature: the Romney, Hythe & Dymchurch Railway

The much-overused word 'unique' can safely be applied to the Romney line, the longest and best-known of all the 15-inch-gauge railways, with its large fleet of locomotives and rolling stock. Built and equipped almost without regard for cost, on a completely fresh site, it remains a monument to its creators and their engineer – Henry Greenly, of course!

For the first 40 years of its operation the line was epitomised in the title of John Snell's enthralling book *One Man's Railway*, as the life's work of Captain Jack Howey. But the germ of the idea seems possibly to have begun, not with Howey, but with his friend Count Louis Zborowski. Some time in 1919 Zborowski visited Bassett-Lowke's model shop in High Holborn, London, in company with another émigré, Count Dmitri Pavlovich, a cousin of the last Czar and one of Rasputin's assassins, who had narrowly escaped execution by the Bolsheviks and fled to London. The two noblemen discussed the possibility of a fast, double-tracked main-line railway in miniature, complete with full signalling and stations, along which locomotives could be driven for miles on end 'flat out'. So prolonged and animated was their conversation that the shop manager recalled it years later.

Pavlovich's future life took him in other directions, with a heavy emphasis on womanising – his pursuit of the legendary Coco Chanel preceding that of his rival the Duke of Westminster – though ownership of the Eaton Railway was unlikely to have played any part in the latter's success! The fast railway scheme gained practical form through the motor-racing friendship of Zborowski and Howey. Henry Greenly was engaged as engineer; Zborowski ordered the first two locomotives from Davey, Paxman & Co of Colchester, while the more patient and practical Howey commissioned the search for a suitable site. The outcome was largely due to Greenly's contact with Sir Herbert Walker, Chairman of the Southern Railway, whom he had met in wartime at the Royal Aircraft Factory while Walker was a member of the Armaments Committee, and who had revealed a personal interest in models. A line across Romney Marsh had been planned back in 1884 as a standard-gauge railway, but if built on the small gauge the connection from the Southern's New Romney branch terminus to the western side of Folkestone at Hythe would do the Southern no harm and might even bring extra traffic.

Howey had never lost an interest in the Ravenglass & Eskdale line, and many writers suspect that, but for the emergence on the scene of Sir Aubrey Brocklebank, Howey would have steered Zborowski towards a Cumbrian takeover. If money was no object, the line might have been extended right across the Lake District to Ambleside with tunnels under the Hardknott and Wrynose Passes, a project that would have outclassed even the 2-foot-gauge Welsh Highland! Curiously, the idea of extending the Ravenglass line by means of a 'mountain railway' *over* rather than *under* the Hardknott Pass had been mooted in *The Field* magazine as early as August 1915. But Sir Aubrey had little time for such idle

visions; his newly invested cash was to develop Beckfoot Quarry and the Murthwaite stone-crushing business, and moreover he resented his treatment over the purchase of Howey's *John Anthony* (*Colossus*), even though the profit had been pocketed by Proctor Mitchell. Was Romney always, in the Captain's mind, ever so slightly second best to what might have been done at Eskdale? We shall never know; but on his later holiday visits to the Lake District his tall figure was sometimes to be seen leaning on the wall by the turntable at Ravenglass or Dalegarth, peering at the engine being turned and pondering on missed opportunities…

Being on a new site, and crossing numerous public roads and watercourses, the Romney, Hythe & Dymchurch Railway required all the legal procedures of a Light Railway Order to authorise the purchase of land, the construction of works, and the carriage of passengers. Construction started in May 1926. The first of the locomotives ordered by Zborowski, *Green Goddess*, was tested at Ravenglass in July 1925, taking the place of *Colossus*, which had just suffered a head-on collision with a stone train powered by *Muriel*. Howey purchased the second engine, *Northern Chief*, from the Count's executors and immediately ordered a third, *Southern Maid*. Meanwhile, Henry Greenly obtained an 0-4-0 shunting engine from Krauss of Munich – a cut-down standard industrial design, courtesy of his friend Roland Martens – which was delivered in August 1926. With a dislike of things German rooted in his wartime experience, Howey promptly named it *The Bug*! The next four engines were two three-cylinder 'Pacifics' (later converted to two-cylinder drive) and two 4-8-2s, the latter for the ballast traffic expected for Kent County Council.

The early coaches were somewhat makeshift – standard Bassett-Lowke-type four-wheelers with two compartments – of which no fewer than 105 had been built by 1928. They bore no resemblance whatsoever to main-line trains and gave an appalling ride at 25mph. Eight three-compartment enclosed coaches built by the Clayton Wagon Co in 1928 were much better, and pointed the way for the future. A large number of Heywood-type goods wagons with lift-off tops were provided for freight, as well as two bogie wagons; six hoppers for shingle ballast arrived later from Eskdale, when displaced by the standard-gauge link to Murthwaite.

The route was originally almost all through open land, Dymchurch being the most prominent intermediate station, with a roof, footbridge, bay platforms and turntable. Hythe terminus had four platforms. The line was double-track throughout to New Romney, using second-hand rail from the First World War 60cm-gauge supply lines laid down by both sides. The buildings were all to Greenly's design, drawing heavily on his experience with concrete structures on the continental exhibition lines and at Ravenglass; the footbridge structures at Dymchurch cleverly doubled as gentlemen's toilets! Two large wooden bungalows were erected at New Romney station, 'Red Tiles' for the Howey family and one on the opposite side of the tracks for the Greenlys. We cannot know what Mrs Howey and their two children

The Count's engine: a classic view of *Green Goddess* at New Romney on 19 August 2009. *J. Cleaver*

'He flies through the air, with the greatest of ease': *Northern Chief* prepares to leave New Romney for Aylsham on 20 September 2011.

thought of removing from London to the wilds of Romney Marsh, but they doubtless consoled themselves with the thought that driving steam engines was, for father, at least marginally safer than motor-racing.

An early opportunity to gain publicity came with a Royal visit by the Duke of York (later to be King George VI) to a boys' camp at St Mary's Bay on 26 August 1926; the Duke rode on the locomotive from Jesson Lane to New Romney and back, while Greenly was relegated to sitting in the train, and was never presented to the Royal visitor. Such small incidents can sometimes have a wider significance; Greenly realised that in Captain Howey's eyes he would never be more than a consultant. His daughter, Eleanor Steel, remarked that this was 'the one disheartening incident in his career in which his sense of humour deserted him … his Achilles heel was an almost childlike desire to be noticed.'

The official opening took place on 16 July 1927 and Howey lost no time in planning the extension to Greatstone-on-Sea and Dungeness across the great expanses of shingle. The official enquiry into the proposed extension, in April 1928, received widespread public support; the main constructional problems were the bridge under the main road at New Romney and the station alterations there. The Dungeness end was laid out as a large balloon loop to avoid reversing. It is hard nowadays to imagine the wild and unspoiled nature of the extension as first built, the route from Greatstone being now very heavily built-up with eight level crossings over residential roads and no sea views from the train. Greenly achieved a small revenge, by driving Green Goddess down the new track before the Captain had an opportunity to do so.

For the Dungeness extension, Greenly was commissioned to design two further locomotives based on the Canadian Pacific Railway's 4-6-2, No 2300. The prototype was a typically idiosyncratic Howey choice; on his annual visits to his Australian property he preferred the 'scenic route' crossing the Atlantic and Pacific by liner, and Canada by rail – and Canadian Pacific was generous with footplate passes for such a regular and wealthy traveller. The two machines were to be built at New

Romney by a subsidiary company, Jackson Rigby Engineering, which made parts for small engines and supplied copies of Greenly's drawings. It was almost inevitable that friction would arise over Greenly's multiple roles as a private designer, as consultant to the Romney, Hythe & Dymchurch Railway, and as an associate of Jackson Rigby Engineering. Problems over the boilers brought to a head issues about the ownership of the working drawings. Greenly finally lost patience: one Sunday afternoon in March 1929, when Howey was absent, he took away and burned 'his own' boiler drawings, and was then himself removed from New Romney by four policemen in a taxi! The case brought by the Romney, Hythe & Dymchurch Railway for theft was immediately thrown out by the magistrates, and Greenly's counter-claims were settled out of court, on this occasion much to his advantage; but clearly there was no option but for him to resign his consultancy, leave New Romney before Howey's return, and sell his bungalow home there.

As a result the Captain finally had to swallow his dislike of things German, and accept two boilers supplied by Roland Martens as used on his Krauss-built 4-6-2 designs. The accumulated parts were eventually assembled by the Yorkshire Engine Company of Sheffield and delivered in 1931, complete with five-tone chime whistles by Crosbie of Boston, USA – Nigel Gresley heard them, loved them, and later used the same type on his 'A4' LNER 'Pacifics'. The Krauss locomotives were equipped with distinctive Vanderbilt tenders, one of which suffered a spectacular drawbar failure on the approach to Dungeness; the driver was left sitting helplessly on the tender as Dr Syn – for it was he – accelerated away into the distance! Disaster was fortunately averted as the runaway derailed on the curve before the station, and buried itself shamefacedly in the shingle.

In 1926 Robert (Bob) Hardie came to New Romney from the Ravenglass & Eskdale as Traffic Manager; he had been an associate of Robert Proctor Mitchell in the travel business before 1914 and was thus a link with the erstwhile Narrow Gauge Railways Ltd. In 1934 Howey decided to sell or scrap all the four-wheel coaches and order new 16-foot-long bogie coach frames from Hudsons of Leeds

and bodies from the Hythe Cabinet Works; ultimately there were 54 coaches and two vans. Famous among early experiments with internal combustion was Howey's conversion of his 1914 Rolls-Royce shooting brake to rail traction; fitted with a 45hp engine, it once hauled

Above: The old lighthouse at Dungeness provides a spectacular viewpoint as *Typhoon* departs around the 'balloon loop' towards New Romney in 19 April 2009. *D. Verity*

Right: A strange landscape: *Dr Syn* accelerates across the shingle expanse of Dungeness.

Captain Howey survived the Count for 38 years; his ashes lie in the New Romney rockery next to his beloved railway.

four coaches from New Romney to Hythe at 60.2mph and proved of serious value on winter trains. *The Bug* was sold in 1933, with six four-wheel coaches, initially to Blackpool and subsequently passed on to Belle Vue, Belfast. Howey's circle of friends made the railway a lively social centre, reaching its zenith when he staged a locomotive race from New Romney to Hythe against the world-record speed driver Sir Henry Segrave – despite Howey's superior knowledge of the line it was apparently neck-and-neck to the finish! Segrave is well remembered at Southport for his motor speed attempts on the sands, but presumably he never tried his hand at high-speed locomotive driving on Llewelyn's (extremely short) Miniature Railway.

Between the wars:
seaside lines and pleasure parks

The success of the large-scale operations at Ravenglass and New Romney has perhaps tended to divert attention away from the numerous miniature lines built and operated elsewhere in the 1920s and 1930s. It seemed that no respectable seaside resort (and some less than respectable ones) could afford to be without such an attraction. Different gauges (from 10¼ up to 21 inches) were widely used, but several interesting 15-inch-gauge ones were created by private operators, and through

them vintage locomotives and equipment have survived to the post-Second World War period and the present-day era of enthusiast preservation.

The flagship, in many ways, was the **Rhyl Miniature Railway** with its enviable and highly visible location circling the Marine Lake and its reliable fleet of 'Albion' Class locomotives, locally built by the fairground engineer, Albert Barnes. Links between miniature railways and fairground attractions – physical location, ownership and sometimes both – were now to become a recurrent theme. 1920 saw a small beginning at **Southend**, where a line of about 200 yards was built within the Kürsaal site, operated by an American Herschell-Spillman locomotive and four Bassett-Lowke coaches. Around the same time a second short line may have existed on the seafront near the Pier using a 'Little Giant'-type locomotive, but no details of this seem to have survived. Two years later, **Skegness** added a 15-inch-gauge railway to the attraction of its 'bracing' climate, running from the Pier to Pleasureland along the seaward side of North Parade; trains turned on a balloon loop for the return journey. Only one locomotive is recorded, the well-travelled 'Little Giant' Class *George the Fifth*, which had already seen service at Southport and Rhyl; the Skegness operation closed in 1928 due to site redevelopment and the engine moved on again to the improved Southend line. Down on the banks of the River Medway, the short (and short-lived) **Woodland Miniature Railway** operated at Cuckold's Wood on the Isle of Grain near Rochester from 1923 to 1926, with a new Barnes 'Albion' Class 4-4-2 *Michael*, which was later destined for greater things and is fortunately still in existence today.

In spite of his involvement at Ravenglass, Henry Greenly found time in 1919 to create one of the classic seaside lines at **Margate**. The site already had an interesting history back to 1863, when a restaurant and dance hall were opened in an unused railway terminus at the Mere. Pleasure gardens were laid out on the former salt-marsh by the circus entrepreneur George Sanger in 1880, soon to be accompanied by sideshows, roundabouts and amusement rides. In 1919 it was acquired by John Henry Iles, already a proprietor of parks in three continents, and renamed 'Dreamland' in deliberate homage to Coney Island in New York. Iles immediately commissioned Greenly to design a miniature railway, on the familiar pattern used by Miniature Railways of Great

Britain, producing an irregular circuit of 600 yards with a five-span viaduct and concrete buildings. It was finished in four months and opened in 1920, the same year as the famous Scenic Railway, and the initial motive power was the 'Little Giant' Class *Prince Edward of Wales* (originally *Red Dragon*), displaced from the Rhyl Miniature Railway by the first of the new Barnes 'Albion' Class *Joan*. Six four-wheel coaches also came from Rhyl and, rebuilt as articulated units, provided the rolling stock of the line throughout its life to 1980 – a wonderful tribute to the durable Bassett-Lowke construction. A further link with Rhyl was the purchase of a new 'Albion' Class engine, *Billie*, in 1927. The line was cut back in length in 1924, making room for other attractions, and thereafter operated as an out-and-back run from the Park station, which was rebuilt in the 1930s to an ultra-modern appearance that would not have looked out of place on London Transport's new tube lines.

Returning to the East Coast, the **Yarmouth Miniature Railway** was opened at South

A classic lakeside scene at the Rhyl Miniature Railway in its centenary year.

No longer to be seen, but perhaps to be revived? The 1930s-style station at Dreamland, Margate. *D. Smith*

Denes, Great Yarmouth, by Harold Parkinson and his son, Commander Nigel Parkinson RN, in 1930. The line was only around 600 yards in length, but boasted a terminal station at Pleasure Beach, two island platforms with a footbridge at South Denes, full signalling and a genuine tunnel (underground for 95 feet!). Trains on the return 'leg' had to face a gradient of 1 in 72, but nevertheless carried up to 60 passengers at a time. G. V. Llewelyn sold on the second of the 'Little Giants' to be built (*Mighty Atom*), which we first met at Sutton Coldfield; it ran as *Prince of Wales* while at Southport and Great Yarmouth. The mechanical talents of the Parkinsons produced a petrol-electric locomotive and also a petrol-electric twin-coach railcar set, far ahead of its time, and the three fully enclosed steel-bodied coaches that graced the 'Yarmouth Belle' were among the finest then built. When, in 1937, the Parkinsons took the decision to close the operation due to falling receipts the entire equipment was sold back to **Sutton Coldfield**, so today, by almost miraculous good fortune, *Mighty Atom* and its coaches can be seen in the Sutton Collection at the **Cleethorpes Coast Light Railway**.

Emboldened by their success at Great

Yarmouth, the Parkinsons took on the line at the Kürsaal at **Southend** in 1932 and redeveloped it as a balloon loop of 700 yards with two stations, Lakeside and Central, two halts and the inevitable tunnel feature. A set of five articulated coaches similar to the Yarmouth examples was built, and *George the Fifth* from Skegness was joined by the Class 30 'Little Giant' *Synolda*, which we last met in 1922 being banished into the ornamental tunnel at Sand Hutton. Her fate in the ensuing years is one of the unsolved mysteries of 15-inch-gauge railways; it is just conceivable that *Synolda* may have featured in a short-lived re-opening at Sutton Park by the showman Pat Collins in 1922-23.* Presumably Sir Robert Walker would have gladly sold the 15-inch-gauge engine, for which he had no further use, but after 1924 *Synolda* must then have passed into other hands. The Parkinsons discovered her without any identity in a garage in Cricklewood; although in later decades the firm of M. E. Engineering dealt in small-gauge railway equipment at Edgware Road in Cricklewood, it is doubtful whether they were in business so early as 1930. The Southend rolling stock was supplemented by a 'steam outline' petrol locomotive of 2-4-0

---

* It is also just possible that the Cagney engine from Blakesley Hall was borrowed, as in 1909, Charles Bartholomew having died in 1919, but perhaps more likely that the mysterious 'Exhibition' example seen at Blakesley in 1904-05 emerged again from obscurity. This conjecture is based on the evidence that the Cagney that appeared at Ettrick Bay in 1936 had somehow acquired ornamental 'showman' fittings.

tender type, in which the exhaust was cleverly compressed into 'beats' released by the driving wheels, and later by the petrol-electric railcar set from Yarmouth. Regrettably, the operation closed in 1938 and the equipment was dispersed through the agency of Mr Dunn of Bishop Auckland.

Much further afield, a short circular seaside line was built at **Ettrick Bay** on the Isle of Bute in 1936 as a leisure initiative by the former Rothesay Tramways Company, utilising tram rails about to be superseded by motor bus operation. It had the obligatory tunnel (only 10 yards long!) and was operated by just two staff. The line is of interest in being operated by one of the Cagney 4-4-0 locomotives which had formerly operated at Blakesley Hall, renamed *Samson*, but, like so many others, it did not survive the outbreak of war in September 1939. Mention should also be made of a short (440-yard) line opened between Salt Lake and Coney Beach near the seafront at **Porthcawl** in South Wales in 1932, which had the perhaps dubious distinction of never operating with

steam engines. Two petrol-electric locomotives were locally built, of which the older (*Coney Queen*) is said to have included control gear from a dismantled submarine; it was later given equipment similar to *Silver Jubilee* of 1935, derived from Tilling-Stevens buses of the period – historic enough in itself! The 12 four-wheeled coaches were released from the Romney, Hythe & Dymchurch Railway by the arrival of new bogie stock there, and some may even have originated at one of early Miniature Railways of Great Britain exhibition lines. The Porthcawl operation had a long existence, surviving until the end of the 1986 summer season.

Away from the coast, the Halifax Zoo and Sutton Park lines had already demonstrated that inland sites could support a railway as an ancillary attraction. The Halifax equipment had been sold to the Bunce family, who began, just before 1914, to develop the Sunny Vale Pleasure Gardens at Hipperholme. The venerable locomotive, *Little Giant* (already once renamed *Little Elephant*) had run 100,000

A classic 1980s view of the 1936 petrol-electric locomotive *Coney Queen* hauling early Bassett-Lowke coaches on the Porthcawl Miniature Railway. *Ray Ruffell, Silver Link Publishing collection*

miles – an incredible achievement in itself – and was fully rebuilt by Bassett-Lowke with a new boiler. Bought by Mr Bunce in 1923 and unfortunately given the new name of *Baby Bunce*, it provided the sole motive power shuttling up and down an L-shaped run of little more than 200 yards with three bogie coaches. The **Sunny Vale Miniature Railway** survived for 16 seasons, until the outbreak of war.

On the other side of the Pennines, the enterprising landlord of the Saracen's Head public house near **Warburton** in Cheshire – which already boasted a small racecourse – took the opportunity in 1926 to purchase the Barnes locomotive *Michael* from the erstwhile **Woodland Miniature Railway** near Rochester, probably with its coaches. As the landlord, one George V. Tonner, enjoyed a similar name to the reigning monarch, *Michael* quickly became *George V. Junior*! The short pleasure line crossed the racetrack at one point, and two years later the inevitable happened when a horse tripped over a rail and broke a fetlock; forced into a choice between horse and steam power, the landlord opted for the former and the locomotive moved to its third home.

Miniature railways have operated at two civic parks named Belle Vue, which could easily prove confusing. The first, and the more durable, was set up at **Belle Vue, Manchester**, in 1928 using the Warburton equipment and was quickly extended from 200 to 500 yards, circling a boating pool and, of course, including

a mock tunnel for rolling stock storage. The park's attractions for many years included zoological gardens, brass band performances, and an annual carnival of the railway trades unions from all parts of Britain. Young ladies competed for the title of 'Railway Queen', the victor (or victress?) opening the carnival with a circuit of the line on the footplate; one hopes it was well cleaned to preserve her beautiful costume! It was entirely fitting that *Michael/George V. Junior* should be finally renamed *Railway Queen*, an honourable title that (s)he bears to this day in retirement at his (or her) birthplace at Rhyl. On closure of the Southend Miniature Railway in 1938, Belle Vue acquired valuable equipment in the shape of five bogie coaches and two 'Little Giant' locomotives, the Class 10 *George the Fifth* and the then anonymous Class 30 (which we now know to be *Synolda*), in due course to be named *Prince Charles* while running at Manchester.

Across the Irish Sea, a **Belle Vue Park** was established by Belfast Corporation and endowed in 1934 with a quarter-mile railway from Belle Vue to Belle Hazel, having balloon loops at each end. Motive power was none other than the ex-Romney Krauss-built 0-4-0 that Howey had christened *The Bug*, disliked, and sold in 1933 with six original coaches to a Mr Kamiya at Blackpool, who quickly transferred his interest to Belfast. With the locomotive renamed firstly *Sir Crawford* after a sometime Mayor of Belfast, then *Jean*, the Belfast line

Railway Queen from Belle Vue (Manchester) has rejoined her brothers and sisters at Rhyl, and awaits overhaul.

The Bug, restored from derelict condition, stands at New Romney in 2009. *P. Green*

soldiered on until 1957, after which *The Bug* slowly disappeared beneath tons of scrap metal in an Anderstown scrapyard. In another of the miracles of preservation, the little engine was rediscovered by Sir William McAlpine in 1972 and restored to its original condition and home at New Romney in 1978, from which it makes occasional excursions to suitable venues.

While the tentative re-opening of the **Sutton Coldfield Railway** by Pat Collins in 1923-24 remains rather shrouded in mystery, there is no doubt about its triumphant revival in 1938. The Collins family owned the Great Yarmouth Pleasure Beach, and immediately on hearing that the **Yarmouth Miniature Railway** had closed, the showman bought the equipment and commissioned the elderly Harold Parkinson (then in his 80s) to move it to Sutton Coldfield and extend the original line, running from Crystal Palace to Wyndley Pool, into a 1,000-yard balloon loop, much resembling the track layout used at Great Yarmouth; the line was to be known for the next few years as the **Crystal Palace Railway**. It re-opened in March 1938, the 'Little Giant' Class 10 locomotive *Prince of Wales* temporarily retaining its Yarmouth name and lettering; certainly, no one then recognised that this was none other than *Mighty Atom*, which had been sold away from Sutton to G. V. Llewelyn at Southport in 1919.

Although our story is concerned almost exclusively with the 15-inch-gauge lines, it has to be mentioned – as an interesting general trend – that pleasure railways of wider gauge

were emerging in the course of the 1930s. The **North Bay Railway, Scarborough**, was in fact planned in 1930 as a 'conventional' 15-inch-gauge development, and might even have enjoyed Greenly-designed 2-8-4 tank engines as projected for Sand Hutton, but when constructed in the following year it was to the unusual gauge of 20 inches, running for two-thirds of a mile northwards from Peasholme Park. This line was the test-bed for the innovative and highly successful 'steam outline' diesel-hydraulic locomotives built by Hudswell Clarke of Leeds; the firm used its spare capacity in the Depression years to explore the market for new, larger-scale miniature railways.

In 1934 a line of 1,200 yards was laid on the 21-inch gauge within the confines of the **Blackpool Pleasure Beach**, only a stone's throw from where the seaside miniature railway story had begun 30 years earlier. Again, Hudswell Clarke engines were used – as also on the similar line, but of 20-inch gauge like Scarborough – opened by the same proprietors within the **Morecambe Pleasure Park** in 1953, using equipment from the former **Golden Acre Park Railway**, an over-ambitious scheme (1932-38) at Bramhope, north of Leeds, which had extended to a circuit of a mile and a quarter. The mile-long **Jaywick Railway** in Essex, built by the Miniature Railway & Specialist Engineering Company of Eastbourne in 1936, went for the 18-inch gauge, largely inspired by the availability of the 'Stirling Single' 4-2-2 locomotive from Fairbourne; the Jaywick venture lasted only four years, and its luxurious enclosed coaches were sold on to Tommy Mann's **Fairy Glen Miniature Railway** at New Brighton.

Almost in a class by themselves were the **Lilleshall Abbey and Woodland Railway** in Shropshire, built by the Duke of Sutherland in 1928, the **Wicksteed Park Railway** in Kettering, Northamptonshire, built by Charles Wicksteed in 1931, and the **Trentham Park Railway** of 1935 alongside Trentham Lake, south of Stoke-on-Trent. Although undoubtedly of 'miniature' character and appearance, all three were built to the 2-foot gauge, using equipment from the well-established firm of Baguley of Burton-on-Trent, which – like Hudswell Clarke – had seemingly found a niche market during the Depression years. Only Wicksteed Park runs in its original form today, although the Lilleshall equipment saw further use at **Alton Towers**, Staffordshire, from 1953.

Railway history is littered with 'might-have-beens', and we might revisit the **Llewelyn Miniature Railway** at Southport for a good example. During the late 1920s Griffith Llewelyn was becoming increasingly reliant on the services of a local engineer, Harry N. Barlow, to maintain his two 'Little Giant' Class 20 locomotives, so frequently renamed that it is hard to cite their identities in any particular year! The trackbed was leased from Southport Corporation as owners of the foreshore, and

when Llewelyn went into liquidation in 1933 the Corporation sought a lessee to rebuild the line to 20-inch gauge and extend it into a circular route all round the Sea Bathing Lake (opened by the Corporation in 1928) and Princes Park. No one came forward, so Barlow (as the biggest creditor) took over the lease of the existing line and renamed it the **Lakeside Miniature Railway** to preserve the 'LMR' initials. The end could very easily have come in 1938 when a night-time fire at the engine shed, possibly caused by a defective battery charger used for electric light in the outsized glass coach or 'Royal Saloon', badly damaged both the working locomotives. But Barlow was made of sterner stuff, and his contribution – to Southport and to other 15-inch-gauge railways – fittingly falls into the later parts of the story.

Second World War – the end of an era?

In an unfortunate piece of timing, a completely new 15-inch-gauge line was proposed for the Mill Hill area of North London in 1939, with a fresh design of 2-6-0 locomotive from Henry Greenly's drawing board. Inevitably it was abandoned in June 1940, and many of the seaside lines that had flourished during the 1930s had already closed at or before the outbreak of war. Holidays were much curtailed, but the lines at Rhyl and Southport (and the inland Sutton Coldfield venue) continued to

The original (1911) Princes Parade station building of Llewelyn's Miniature Railway still stands below Southport Pier.

The replica Second World War armoured train, complete with camouflage netting, at New Romney.

operate brief summer seasons, and stone traffic continued at Ravenglass.

The **Romney, Hythe & Dymchurch Railway** took on an entirely new role, first moving civilians away from the coastal defences and operating troop trains for incoming army personnel. Under the control of the War Department, specifically the Royal Engineers, the railway belatedly fulfilled the dreams of Sir Arthur Heywood 60 years earlier for the wartime use of 15-inch-gauge railways. Two of the ex-Eskdale ballast hoppers and the locomotive *Hercules* were converted to form an armoured anti-aircraft gun unit, which patrolled the marshes and shingle banks ready to wreak vengeance on the German aircraft that so frequently attacked the coast. The intrepid crew claimed to have 'downed' a Dornier bomber, and at this distance of time the author would not like to cast even a shadow of doubt on the heroes' achievement; others have less kindly suggested that the Romney Marsh rabbits were the chief gunfire casualties, destined for the troops' cookhouse. The small scale of the railway did undoubtedly prove to be the downfall of one Luftwaffe pilot who, imagining that he was attacking a full-sized train, came in too low and crashed on the shingle. Fifty years later Derek Smith and the Romney coachbuilder Colin Bunn re-created a replica of the train (with plywood 'armour'), which aroused considerable interest; its firepower included a real Boyes anti-tank rifle, delivered by car round the M25 motorway during a terrorist alert!

Much more important to the war effort was the preparation in 1943-44 of the oil supply pipeline for the D-Day landings, 'PLUTO' (Pipe Line Under The Ocean), which was welded into 300-foot sections at New Romney and moved to Lade on carriage chassis from which the bodies had been removed. As the project became more and more urgent, crawler tractors were used with consequent wrecking of the railway track. But with so much of the coastline, at Romney and everywhere else in Britain, under military control and out of bounds to the public, it would have taken a brave person in 1945 to predict any kind of future for the miniature railway.

2. History of the 15-inch-gauge, 1945-2011

The 1950s : a new 'Golden Age' for some...

The **Romney, Hythe & Dymchurch Railway** returned to Captain Howey's control in July 1945, when he set about restoring it with all his old energy and – fittingly – some compulsory help from German prisoners-of-war; the New Romney to Hythe section re-opened in March 1946. Locomotives were overhauled, some by the Southern Railway at Ashford Works; new and improved coach bodies were built; and the line to Dungeness was ceremonially re-opened by Laurel and Hardy in March 1947. The event was recorded on newsreel film and gave the Romney line world-wide publicity.

Just as the Duffield Bank equipment had given the Ravenglass & Eskdale Railway a much-needed boost in 1916, so the Eaton Railway – closed by the Duke of Westminster in 1946 (the Cuckoo's Nest branch) and 1947 – provided coaches and a 'Simplex' petrol engine for New Romney, together with 21 sets of points and more than 5,000 yards of track. Fresh from the Railway Operating Division of the Royal Engineers came a new General Manager, Terence Holder, and a new Senior Driver, George Barlow, adding the former occupations of stockbroker and journalist respectively to the varied ranks of 15-inch-gauge personnel! Passenger numbers increased dramatically as the Kent coast attracted crowds of holidaymakers, and all the outstanding debt on the line was quickly paid off. Captain Howey continued to lavish money on his 'pet' steam locomotives, which were progressively fitted with superheated boilers, but only the bare minimum was done to the railway's underlying infrastructure. Greenly had fulfilled, only too well, his commission to build a line to last for the Captain's lifetime, and when Howey died in September 1963 (his ashes are in a rockery opposite the New Romney signal box) his successors were to inherit a huge maintenance backlog.

In Cumbria, the **Ravenglass & Eskdale Railway** had ended the war just about in working order, with the steam locomotives stored and granite traffic (for main-line railway ballast) worked by Muir-Hill tractors from Beckfoot to Murthwaite, then onwards to Ravenglass on the 'gauntleted' standard-gauge track. After Sir Aubrey Brocklebank's death in 1929, neither his son nor his business partner Henry Lithgow had been inclined to make significant new investment in the quarry or railway, and following Lithgow's death in 1948 the concern was sold to the Keswick Granite Company. To its credit, the new owner carried on the summer passenger service that Lithgow had reinstated in 1946-47, and a final and 'king-sized' blasting of 60,000 tons of stone at Beckfoot in August 1949 gave another 2½ years' work to the quarrymen. The worn-out condition of the Murthwaite crushing plant was a factor in the company's decision to shut down the mineral operation in 1953, though a more significant reason was perhaps its ambition to secure in its core business the highly lucrative contract to supply aggregate for construction of the Calder Hall Atomic Power Station. With only open coaches, two steam locomotives at best, and little publicity, it is hardly surprising that the passenger numbers at Ravenglass stagnated in the 20,000s in the 1950s, and the service made an annual loss. For some years this could be offset against profits in the owners' quarrying business, but the 1957 Finance Act was to close this convenient loophole and place the railway under threat.

At Southport, Harry Barlow's **Lakeside Miniature Railway** had continued to operate, in a small way, during the wartime summers, giving Merseysiders the chance of familiar pleasures at the seaside away from the wartime realities of the city. In 1947-48 it achieved a small part of its pre-war potential by extending with a sharp seaward turn under a footbridge and the famous Southport Pier to a new station named Peter Pan's Pool; both platforms had run-round loops, and a turnstile allowed promenaders on the Pier to exit via a flight of steps down to the station. With similar improvements at the Pleasureland end of the line, three trains could be operated simultaneously – one in motion while the others disgorged and reloaded passengers at the rate of 1,000 per hour. The author has childhood memories of crowds queuing at the ticket booths and surging up and down the platforms. Barlow proudly claimed that the railway carried around half a million passengers each year, employing up to 16 staff. The additional motive power that had been urgently needed was supplied by the ingenious engineer's acquisition of Fordson tractor engines and redundant wartime searchlight generators; forcibly combined into generator and motor units, these powered the formidable 'Barlow Pacifics' with stylised body outlines suggesting, rather than slavishly imitating, the Gresley 'A4' 4-6-2 world speed record-holder *Mallard*. Ten examples were built at Barlow's works in Upper Aughton Road for Southport and other lines, and their reliability and simplicity were so appreciated by miniature railway operators that it is believed that no fewer than six still survive.

Without fuss, the **Rhyl Miniature Railway** resumed its role as a valuable adjunct to Rhyl Amusements, the owners far-sightedly rebuilding the station with a concrete roof and providing a brick engine shed in which the four Barnes 'Atlantics' received expert maintenance during their winter slumbers. Under the same ownership was the site of a pioneering miniature electric tramway development in Voryd Park, operated by Charles Lane from

Golden Jubilee of 1963 propels a typical articulated pair of coaches on the 1947 extension to the Lakeside Miniature Railway.

1951 to 1954 as a test-bed for his larger-scale developments at Eastbourne and, more recently, Seaton in South Devon.

The **Fairbourne Miniature Railway** had declined steadily during the 1930s, with the track badly damaged by storms and flooding in 1927 and 1938-39, and *Count Louis* abandoned in its shed after a coupling rod broke – water still in the boiler, and the remains of the last fire cold in the grate. Wenman Bassett-Lowke paid a final visit to Fairbourne in 1943 to visit his old friend John Wills, and was greatly saddened by what he saw of the railway. Further damage was done by military equipment churning up the sandhills during practice for the Normandy landings, and it is amazing that anything survived to be rescued in 1946. John Wilkins, Managing Director of Wilkins & Mitchell of Darlaston in the West Midlands (best known for its associated washing machine firm Servis), had his enthusiasm for 15-inch-gauge railways aroused by visits to the Hardwick Manor Railway and its successor, the Sutton Miniature Railway, then in course of revival by his friend Thomas G. Hunt of Hunt Brothers, the Griffin Foundry, Oldbury. John Wilkins visited New Romney, where Captain Howey offered him the chance to own and drive his own engine, but Kent was too remote from the Midlands for this to be a practical invitation. Doubtless knowing of the Fairbourne line from pre-war holidays, Wilkins decided to buy the railway in partnership with his brother, Philip, and Tom Hunt.

The investment that John Wilkins poured in can be compared only to that made by Captain Howey in the 1920s at New Romney. The track was relaid and extended in 1978 to a new terminus close to the Barmouth Ferry landing point; Fairbourne acquired a greatly extended station and workshop; coaches were purchased from Hardwick Manor and nine new ones built; and no fewer than three new steam engines (from designs by Ernest W. Twining) and three internal-combustion engines were purchased. Passenger numbers soared at the railway, though ominously little other development of facilities in the neighbourhood took place apart from some residential housing of a largely 'retirement bungalow' character, and the prosperity of the local holiday industry would decline markedly in the 1970s. Prior to 1940 the operation had possessed some semblance of a commercial operation, albeit on a 'shoestring'; from 1946 to 1983 it was a rich man's hobby, to be enjoyed – in due course – together with a holiday home at Borthwnog, a steam yacht, and a Rolls-Royce car. Naturally the resources of Wilkins & Mitchell were drawn upon for locomotive overhauls and track components, and the railway's full-time staff was supplemented by volunteers hand-picked by the owner. John Wilkins also gave unstinting help, not always reciprocated, to some early railway preservation movements – notably the Talyllyn Railway, just down the coast at Tywyn, the Ffestiniog Railway at Porthmadoc, and the Welshpool & Llanfair Light Railway, for which he bought back one of its original locomotives, *The Earl*.

The Dunn family of Bishop Auckland, already collectors of 15-inch-gauge equipment, promoted a number of new lines on the North East coast, the most important being the **Saltburn Miniature Railway**, which extended for three-quarters of a mile from the seafront at Cat Nab to Valley Gardens. Its motive power included Greenly's veteran petrol locomotive *Blacolvesley* from Blakesley Hall, renamed firstly *Yvonne* then *Elizabeth* and fitted with a pair of unlovely smoke deflectors. The line passed to a Mr Pickering in 1950, and ten years later to Saltburn Motor Services, which purchased a 'Barlow Pacific', *Prince Charles* (soon renamed *Prince of Wales*) as its mainstay. Following changes of local government and transport ownership in 1974-75, the line closed and suffered considerable vandalism, but reconstruction began in 1980 and the railway is still very much in operation in the 21st century. A new track alignment was opened in 2003 to replace damage caused by flooding in November 2000. In later years the Dunn family had operations at **Seaton Carew** near Hartlepool, and at the **Whorlton Lido**. The **Ocean Park Railway** at Seaburn, north of Scarborough, was a local authority venture, which, interestingly, began life with a Cagney-type 4-4-0 locomotive pulling three open coaches acquired from the Blakesley Hall Railway.

Left: Many shades of green: *Prince Charles* and train in the Valley Gardens at Saltburn on 10 August 2012. *D. Holroyde*

Below: Heraldic animals: Fairbourne used a dragon and Sutton a griffin, while the Romney Hythe & Dymchurch Railway boasts the white horse of Kent.

Developments in the Midlands

The **Crystal Palace Railway** at Sutton Coldfield, which had limped through the war years in a somewhat run-down condition, came to the notice of Thomas G. Hunt of Oldbury in 1946 when he was called upon to inspect the venerable *Prince of Wales* (Bassett-Lowke's original *Mighty Atom*). Already a co-director of the Wilkins brothers in their Fairbourne adventure, he lost no time in buying the Sutton line from the Collins family for redevelopment by himself and his son, Bill Hunt. By another of the remarkable coincidences that appear in the story of 15-inch-gauge railways, the equipment that the Hunts desperately needed became available exactly at the right moment: Douglas Clayton, the owner of the **Hardwick Manor Railway**, died in September 1947 and his two locomotives based on the Bassett-Lowke Class 30 'Little Giant' design (one complete, the other a set of unfinished parts), three coaches and track went from Bredons Hardwick to the newly renamed **Sutton Miniature Railway**. Even if the Hunt family investment was not quite on the scale of that of John Wilkins at Fairbourne, there was money enough to rebuild and improve *Sutton Belle* and *Sutton Flyer*, to build four new open coaches and three more closed ones (identical to the ex-Yarmouth set), and in 1957 to completely rebuild the terminal station. At the same time that the Fairbourne

trains acquired a heraldic device featuring a cheerful Welsh dragon, the Sutton coaches displayed a highly coloured griffin bearing a shield – an unobtrusive reference to the owners' family business at the Griffin Foundry. With passenger numbers soaring, the line should have been set for a certain and prosperous future.

Completing a trio of miniature-railway-minded Midlands industrialists was Trevor Guest (1906-86), a partner in a family building firm at Amblecote near Stourbridge. As a young man his sporting interests extended to motor car and speed boat racing – exactly like Captain Howey! In the mid-1930s he and a neighbour (one Captain Saunders) decided to build a 10¼-inch-gauge locomotive designed for them by J. N. Maskelyne, and formed a company, G. & S. Light Engineering of Stourbridge, for the purpose. In 1938 the 10¼-inch-gauge line was established along a hillside ledge within the **Dudley Zoological Gardens**, and it continued to operate throughout the Second World War. By 1946 Guest had also seriously caught the '15-inch-gauge bug' and relaid the line to that gauge using concrete sleepers made at the family building firm. Initial motive power was a Morris petrol locomotive outwardly resembling a GWR streamlined diesel railcar (later, and today, part of the Sutton Collection). Soon, the Dudley Zoo line became a proving ground for steam engines designed by the innovative Ernest W. Twining, most of which passed in due course to Trevor Guest's close friend John Wilkins at Fairbourne. Diesels then took over the Dudley operation; the 0-4-2 steam-outline locomotive *Clara* today operates at the Rhyl Miniature Railway, and a larger diesel now does valuable work at the Windmill Farm Railway. The later history of the Dudley operation was somewhat complex, being sold to the Zoo itself in 1968 and sharing in a gradual run-down; it finally closed in 1992.

Battersea Park, London

In the London area, a miniature line in the vicinity of Alexandra Palace, Muswell Hill, had operated fitfully before 1950 when it was regauged to 15 inches and extended to circle the boating lake, being powered by a 'Barlow Pacific'. It had a life of 20 years, but was overshadowed by the activities in Battersea Park from 1951, when the Festival of Britain site was home to – one can safely say – the most bizarre 15-inch-gauge railway ever conceived, the **Far Tottering & Oystercreek Railway**, which brought to life the wildest fantasies of the cartoonist Rowland Emett. Only a third of a mile long, and running at the back of the pavilions, it nevertheless operated three locomotives created by S. & B. Engineering of Southport, of which *Neptune* outwardly resembled a paddle-steamer and *Wild Goose*

(originally to have been called *Air Service*) a hot-air balloon, while *Nellie*, predictably, had some affinity to an elephant! Under the amazing bodywork built by Lancaster Metalcraft in Southport – and decorated by Emett himself – for those with ears to hear, there clattered and rumbled 'Barlow Pacifics' with their reliable tractor engines.

The line paid off its initial costs in the first three weeks of operation and lasted well into 1952, carrying more than 2 million passengers, its success having been marred only by a head-on collision in July 1951 resulting in one fatality. It was then relaid in more conventional form in 1954 alongside the East Carriageway in Battersea Park itself, running the 900 yards from 'Queens Circus' to 'Chelsea Bridge' station. Some of the articulated coaches from the Festival, shorn of Emett enhancements, made their way back to Southport to supplement the stock of the Lakeside Miniature Railway. The Park line is believed to have used two of the Festival locomotives, rebuilt by Barlow to his usual outline (*Princess Anne* and *Princess Margaret*) and to have closed about 1975; the locomotives later met an undeserved fate in the liquidation of the Medina Valley Railway project. Seemingly, it was through an encounter with *Nellie* at Battersea Park in 1951 that the late Terry Martin, at the tender age of four, began a lifelong love-affair with narrow-gauge railways culminating in his two-volume study of the Darjeeling Himalayan Railway, *The Iron Sherpa*. Few other miniature locomotives can have inspired such a monumental achievement! The young architect Robin Butterell also visited Battersea Park and was disappointed not to find live steam in use – but nevertheless went on to a lifetime of devotion to miniature railways.

A period of change: the beginning of 'preservation'

At the close of the 1950s it seemed as if the historic **Ravenglass & Eskdale** line was living on borrowed time. No longer able to write off its losses against Corporation Tax, its owner offered the railway for sale in September 1958 and again in August 1959. It seemed possible that the assets would go for scrap, and faced with the loss of a valuable (if underdeveloped) tourist attraction, a local movement to save the railway came into being headed by Douglas Robinson, Clerk to Muncaster Parish Council. At the same time, railway enthusiasts were coming together to form the Ravenglass & Eskdale Railway Preservation Society. The railway preservation movement, so commonplace today, was of course then in its infancy and almost entirely focused on the Welsh narrow-gauge lines; standard-gauge preservation, at the Keighley & Worth Valley Railway and Bluebell Railway, would not happen until the mid-1960s. Public recognition of the historical value of the Ravenglass line was important in itself, and the moment on 10 August 1960, when Douglas Robinson raised his hand with the winning auction bid of £12,000 to save the railway, surely marks a turning point in the story of 15-inch-gauge railways.

The Society had raised a creditable £5,000 on its own account and the balance came from a Birmingham stockbroker, Colin Gilbert, supported by Sir Wavell Wakefield, MP for Kendal. Under enthusiastic new management, the Ravenglass line blossomed forth with fresh investment on a scale almost comparable with John Wilkins's indulgence at Fairbourne: a new locomotive, *River Mite* – very similar to Greenly's *River Esk* – new coaches, and a realignment of the worst curve on the route at Hollingshead into 'Gilbert's Cutting', funded by the same generous benefactor. Passenger numbers soared, so much so that a small operating profit was made in 1964, the first for 70 years! Enjoying the business acumen of the Wakefield family, whose other Lakeland interests include the historic Ullswater passenger vessels, and the active support of the Preservation Society, the railway has seen continuous improvement, notably the provision of new station buildings at Dalegarth for Boot in 2007 and the even more recent rebuilding of the fine terminal station at Ravenglass.

The appearance of stability at Sutton Coldfield was quickly to prove illusory, due to the fact that the site of Tom Hunt's **Sutton Miniature Railway** – like so many others – was only leasehold, not freehold. Local politics reared their head in 1960 with a decision by Sutton Town Council that amusements would disappear and most of the Park would revert to a natural state after the leases expired in 1962. The site of the railway would become the Wyndley Leisure Centre. The closure of such a well-known line, in October 1962, was regretted by the enthusiast fraternity as well as by many local residents: the fine new station building had been used for only five years before it was dismantled! All might so easily have been dispersed or destroyed, had Bill Hunt not had the foresight to place all the equipment in safe storage. As we have already mentioned, miracles can and do happen in the world of miniature railways – assisted by the National Lottery Heritage Fund – and the Sutton Collection has woken like 'Sleeping Beauty' to its new life at Cleethorpes in the 21st century.

The following year, 1963, brought another turning point with the death of Jack Howey at New Romney. His widow, anxious to return to London, lost no time in putting the **Romney, Hythe & Dymchurch Railway** up for sale. The appearance of profitability to potential purchasers actually masked a long-standing lack of maintenance and investment, except of course on the Captain's favourite locomotives. Furthermore, the whole character of the coastal area was changing rapidly to one of residential, virtually suburban, housing, which not only made the journey less visually attractive but also brought a significant danger of collisions at the 13 level crossings. These recurrent incidents, in which road vehicle drivers wilfully ignore even the latest and most advanced warning signals, have had tragic, fatal consequences for two of the line's locomotive drivers: Kevin Crouch on *Hercules* in August 2003 and Suzanne Martin on *Hurricane* in July 2005.

Purchased by two retired bankers in 1964 for just £1 per share, the railway was to change hands again to a group of 21 local businessmen four years later. Considerable expenditure took place in response to professional reports on the condition of the bridges and the carriage stock, but there seemed little hope of the outlay being recovered, let alone of the railway ever returning to profit. Shortening of the line was considered and rejected, as was complete transfer to a new location on the (closed) Paignton to

The undistinguished surroundings of parts of the present-day Romney, Hythe & Dymchurch Railway, typified at Seaview Road level crossing. *J. Cleaver*

Kingswear standard-gauge route – but that was successfully taken over and preserved as 'main-line' steam. (As an aside, the author sometimes wonders what we might perhaps have seen if the Porthmadog to Caernarfon route of the erstwhile Welsh Highland Railway had been available, 30 years before its rebuilding by the Ffestiniog company – *Green Goddess* speeding across the Glaslyn marshes; the 'Canadian Pacific' engines bursting out of the Aberglaslyn Pass tunnels for all the world as if in the Rockies; the eight-coupled engines raising the echoes as they climb up through the Beddgelert Forest – even diesel-powered shuttles from Dinas to the centre of Caernarfon – all the stuff of winter evening dreams!)

Carefully 'leaked' suggestions that the owners might be forced to close the railway produced the desired effect in the formation of a group of 32 investors headed by Sir William H. ('Bill') McAlpine, prepared to purchase the assets for £100,000 without any great expectation of a financial return. A Supporters' Association of enthusiasts had been formed in 1967, initially with an emphasis on history and research, and this has since gone on to become a major shareholder in the company as well as a source of volunteer labour and practical assistance. In the last 40 years the railway has been quietly transformed back to a condition that Howey would have been proud of, with new and rebuilt coaches, two additional steam

locomotives, a diesel-hauled daily train for local schoolchildren, vastly improved station facilities for visitors, and a variety of special gala events for enthusiasts. Not least, the Romney locomotive fleet has been seen far and wide on visits to other railways, most notably at the Liverpool International Garden Festival in 1984 and the opening years of the Bure Valley Railway in the early 1990s.

The problems of operating on a leasehold trackbed came to a head again at the **Rhyl Miniature Railway** in 1969, with the owners of Rhyl Amusements (Trust House Forte Leisure Ltd) being unwilling to invest in the somewhat run-down Marine Lake site without a new, long lease from the Borough Council. When this was refused, Trust House Forte decided to vacate the site completely; the track was lifted in 1970 and several of the locomotives were dispersed. Perhaps as a gesture of contrition, *Billy* was purchased and preserved locally by the Council. Local government reorganisation in 1974 transferred responsibility for the site to the Rhuddlan Borough Council, which made some tentative improvements at the Lake, and was prepared to reinstate the railway for operation by a contractor. The proposal was taken up by Alan M. Keef in 1978, to provide useful work for his firm during the summer months; in retrospect he came to regard it as 'a total and unmitigated disaster [which] should have brought the company down'. Estimates of passenger numbers (200,000 annually) proved to be hopelessly optimistic, though with only one steam engine (*Michael*) and an ex-Dudley Zoo diesel available, capacity was in any event extremely limited. More serious were problems with the reinstated track leading to a prolonged dispute with the Council; in 1979 only 35,000 visitors were carried, and the line was then sold to a Rhyl businessman, Les Hughes, who set about bringing home as many of the original Barnes locomotives as possible.

Temporary closure of the line in 1997 for the construction of a flood relief 'tank' and a huge pumping station proved a blessing in disguise, as the track was lifted, then relaid to a high standard by Alan Keef Ltd in April and May 1998. Subsequently the railway was put into the care of the Rhyl Steam Preservation Trust (Les Hughes being Chairman) and operated by Ken Dove and its Friends organisation. The preservation movement may have come to Rhyl slightly late in the day, but reaped its reward in grant funding for the magnificent new Central Station building opened in 2007. *Billy* resides in splendour in a well-presented museum display, and the centenary of the railway was celebrated in style in May 2011, with all six of the Barnes locomotives being brought together for the very first time, and the much rebuilt *Red Dragon* making a guest appearance under its 1911 identity as *Prince Edward of Wales*.

New lines for old: converting closed standard-gauge routes

The extensive closures of branch lines, many in areas attractive to tourists, as a result of the 'Beeching Plan' (*The Re-shaping of British Railways*) in the 1960s offered obvious possibilities for the building of pleasure lines by enthusiast societies or local entrepreneurs. Unfortunately, few of the early schemes were to succeed, for a variety of reasons. Some routes were seized upon for road improvements. British Railways naturally wished to sell trackbed land at a commercial price, with the purchaser taking over responsibility for maintaining large structures such as standard-gauge bridges and tunnels. In all cases, a promoter would have to obtain a Light Railway Order to operate a line carrying fare-paying passengers and crossing highways and footpaths, and would have to meet current legal and safety regulations. However, some local authorities gave considerable encouragement to tourist railway schemes, notably Meirionydd County Council, which purchased sections of the Bala to Morfa Mawddach (Barmouth Junction) line to facilitate the 2-foot-gauge **Bala Lake Railway**, and offered the route alongside the Mawddach estuary to John Wilkins of the **Fairbourne Railway**. For whatever reason, the latter offer was allowed to lapse and the route has subsequently become an attractive 'railway walk'.

Red Dragon briefly resumes its 1911 identity at the Rhyl Miniature Railway Centenary. The builder's plate refers to the 1991 reconstruction – incorporating original parts – at Southport.

So far as the 15-inch-gauge is concerned, the first serious proposal was to reconstruct the Axminster to Lyme Regis branch line on the borders of Devon and Dorset. Les Andersen's ambitious 1973 plan for the **Axe & Lyme Valley Railway** would have reconnected the resort to its main-line junction, with the possibility of regular local traffic, but there was also opposition by local residents to the use of the (still intact) original terminal station. The structural condition of Combpyne Viaduct was also a potential worry and, although about a mile of track was laid, the project failed to attract financial backers and local authority support. In 1976 the scheme was abandoned and the equipment was dispersed, much going to the **Lappa Valley Railway** in Cornwall. The route near Axminster has since been severed by a by-pass road, while the Lyme Regis station building has taken on a new existence at New Alresford on the preserved standard-gauge Watercress Line. Mr Andersen next tried to establish a mini-tramway for commuter traffic on the 15-inch-gauge between Sandsfoot and Westham, through Rodwell Tunnel, on the former Weymouth to Portland branch. It was a pioneering idea for 1980, but one that was beset by road access problems and the perceived risks of electrification. A prototype 'Rapido Rail' unit, with power generated on board, was built in 1983 by the operator of the Dudley Zoo Railway and tried out successfully there, and subsequently at Rhyl. It might have been developed as a useful form of transport to link the new concept of shopping malls to their car parks, bus and rail stations.

One of the most interesting proposals, which certainly deserved to succeed, was the **Medina Valley Railway** planned for the Isle of Wight in 1980. The proprietors had support from both the Isle of Wight County Council and the Tourist Board for their proposal to convert a 3-mile section of the Cowes to Newport line (closed in 1964), and successfully obtained a Light Railway Order, but the task of raising £350,000 proved time-consuming and ultimately unsuccessful. Rolling stock was widely sourced, negotiations being opened with Mr Tom Tate to purchase equipment from his North Eastern Railway at Haswell Lodge – some of which actually moved to the island – and with John Wilkins to acquire the complete **Fairbourne Railway**, which might in the event have been transported from Wales to the island by ship! Also acquired from storage in Portsmouth were two of the 'Barlow Pacifics' previously used on the Battersea and Alexandra Park lines, which are believed to have been scrapped after it became clear that the scheme could not move forward. Given its scenic location in an extremely popular tourist area (the promoters hoped to attract 12% of the island's 2½ million annual visitors) the failure was little short of tragic. It is perhaps just a slight compensation that the route today forms a well-promoted cycle path.

At the opposite end of Britain, the **West Buchan Railway** planned in 1983 to re-open a section of line inland from Banff, closed by British Railways in 1964. Local residents of the Scotstown Road in Banff strongly opposed the interference with their garages and washing lines 'squatting' on the old trackbed, and another landowner refused consent outright, forcing a deviation of 400 yards. In the event, only 1½ miles of line were completed to Swordanes, with an intermediate halt serving a hotel at Banff Springs; the hoped-for extension to Whitemills never happened. The Scottish Tourist Board gave a substantial grant, and the railway duly opened in June 1984 with Wilhelm van der Heiden's Dutch-built 0-4-0 steam locomotive *Chough* – already at its fourth home! – and a Severn-Lamb 'Rio Grande' internal-combustion engine; coaches were from a closed line at Fleetwood. It quickly became clear that insufficient thought had been given to likely tourist numbers in such a remote location, despite operating for a 12-hour day. Matters became desperate in 1985, with only 5,000 passengers using the line against a forecast of more than 25,000. The owners appealed for the District Council to take over, but more strident opposition from the Scotstowners put paid to that idea, and the railway closed with considerable debts. The resilient little *Chough* went on to further adventures, finally migrating across the Atlantic in 1996 to the Bear Creek Park Railway on the outskirts of Vancouver, British Columbia.

An interesting minor variant on the theme was to appear as late as 1991, with Mr

The much-travelled *Chough*, seen at Vancouver, Canada, in 2007. *P. Ashworth*

Albert Hart's plan to revive the Stepaside to Wiseman's Bridge section of the long-defunct **Saundersfoot Railway** in Pembrokeshire. This had been purely a mineral line, laid to the gauge of 4 feet (which was often used in the 18th and 19th centuries for such lines). A temporary 400-yard circuit was opened at Stepaside with the much-travelled *Chough* to stimulate public interest but, as so often happened, sufficient finance could not be raised. The Saundersfoot Steam Railway did indeed obtain its Light Railway Order in 1991, but three years later its equipment was repossessed by its bankers and sold.

From such a sorry tale of 'might-have-beens', it is a relief to turn to schemes that actually succeeded, including of course one of the finest of all the 15-inch-gauge lines, the Bure Valley Railway in Norfolk. Perhaps we should admire all the more the determination of its promoters! We might first visit Cornwall, where the trackbed of the former Great Western Railway's Newquay to Chacewater branch had run close to East Wheal Rose lead mine, and the tourist potential of this historic industrial site inspired the **Lappa Valley Railway** to take over the 1¼-mile section from Benny Halt to the visitor centre. No less than five years of negotiations were required to acquire the trackbed, and to persuade the local authority to take on the maintenance of a large road overbridge (which would have been a prohibitive liability for the miniature railway) before the line opened in 1974. Using both steam and diesel traction it is, happily, very much alive today.

Moving as far east as Norfolk, we find the striking example of cooperation between a local authority, Tourist Board and private enterprise that created the 9-mile-long **Bure Valley Railway**, linking the attractive market town of Aylsham to the slightly less attractive tourist centre of Wroxham, which is nevertheless a 'Mecca' for cruising on the Broads and still benefits from a frequent train service between Norwich and Sheringham. The line up the Bure Valley had originally extended inland to the remote County School Junction and was later altered to provide a freight link southwards to Lenwade and Norwich; passenger traffic had ceased as long ago as 1952, and local goods in 1974. The potential for re-opening clearly lay east of Aylsham, where the gentle river valley scenery, and villages such as Coltishall, are enticing to visitors. The scheme's stroke of genius lay in the adoption of the 15-inch-gauge, with the rails laid at one side of the standard-gauge trackbed; trains of modern carriages hauled by powerful locomotives offered great carrying capacity, while allowing a footpath and cycle path to be built all along the route, securely fenced and giving access to and from other local roads and paths.

It is a characteristic of the '15-inch-gauge bug', to which the author has often referred, that it infects its victims with an exuberance in spending money, clearly reflected in the magnificent new station buildings – with shop, restaurant and Tourist Information Centre – and parking facilities provided in 1989 at Aylsham. Two and a half million pounds were invested, and construction involved the refurbishment of several bridges and tunnelling under the new Aylsham by-pass road. The permanent way was substantially laid for

The Bure Valley footpath is to the left of the fence, as *Spitfire* thunders towards the camera. *G. Sutton*

heavy locomotives at speed, and a fleet of (eventually) 31 coaches was provided, usually running as nine-coach trains. From the Bure Valley's opening day on 10 July 1990, it was clear that the Romney, Hythe & Dymchurch had a new rival to the title of 'Main Line in Miniature'! Wisely, engines were hired in from New Romney and elsewhere at the outset until experience suggested an ideal design for the demands of the route. This proved to be a half-scale version of the 2ft 6in (760mm)-gauge British-designed 'ZB' Class locomotives used in India and Pakistan. Among the most powerful machines ever to run on the 15-inch-gauge, *Spitfire* and *Blickling Hall* have truly been a triumph of design and building. In its early years the Bure Valley ran up heavy losses by operating only with salaried staff (the 'top brass' even enjoying company cars!); however, following a change of ownership in 1995 the line has learned to live within its means and gained extensive volunteer support from its Friends organisation.

Hard on the heels of the Bure Valley came the **Kirklees Light Railway** in South Yorkshire, a most enterprising private promotion by Brian and Doreen Taylor, who lived close to the former Shelley to Clayton West branch line. They had experience of building and operating a 10¼-inch-gauge miniature railway in Shibden Park, Halifax, from 1983, using a 1/6th scale Ivatt 'Atlantic', and had also considered taking on part of the closed Wadebridge to Padstow line, where their plans were defeated by planning and environmental issues.

The Clayton West branch line had originated in the complex railway politics of the Yorkshire coalfield, and never progressed beyond providing a single-track link of 2½ miles to Clayton West. It lasted until 1970 for goods and (heavily subsidised) 1983 for passengers, and its original ambitions to reach Barnsley are still reflected in the double-track-sized earthworks and the impressive 500-yard-long Shelley Woodhouse Tunnel (the longest on any 15-inch-gauge railway!) The Taylors were able to lease the trackbed from Kirklees Council, and duly obtained a Light Railway Order in 1991. Starting with just a mile run to a halt called Cuckoo's Nest, the line progressively extended with help from European Union funding to reach Shelley in 1997. The railway was sold to the Hurd family in 2005, and future developments may yet include an interchange with the Huddersfield to Sheffield standard-gauge line. The Kirklees Light Railway provides both a family attraction (with a Visitors' Centre, and play and picnic areas) in a well-populated catchment area, and also a highly interesting venue for enthusiasts, including an elevated model engineers' track. The late Brian Taylor (who sadly died in April 2009) designed all four of the steam locomotives around narrow-gauge prototypes.

Garden Festival railways:
Liverpool and Gateshead

All of the five Festivals held in Britain since 1984 have included some type of railway system as an essential means of moving large numbers of visitors around their sites, and two are directly relevant to our theme. Indeed, the **Liverpool Garden Festival Railway** was one of the finest 15-inch-gauge lines ever conceived, since it was built to the highest standards and demonstrated the full potential of the 'minimum gauge'. The 1984 Liverpool Garden Festival was the first of its kind in Britain, and the only one to have held International status. The objective was the reclamation of 250 acres of derelict industrial land at Dingle, south-east of the city, locally known as the 'Cast Iron Shore', and involved the movement of 3 million tons of material. The finished landscape and the gardens are still remembered with affection and pride 25 years later. There were in fact two railways on the site, one providing a shuttle service from the Herculaneum entrance (the northernmost point) to the centre, rather dismissively described in the official handbook as 'for the use of disabled and elderly people, and mothers with prams', and a main line circling the various garden areas. Passengers changed lines by footbridge at stations named 'Play Centre' and 'Festival Hall', adjacent to the impressive, moated central building.

Planned by civil engineers and garden designers, the route of the main line made few concessions to conventional railway engineering, thus providing major challenges of curvature and gradients (1 in 70) to which the builders (the Ffestiniog Railway Company) and the operators rose magnificently. From his vantage point on the footplate of *River Irt*, Peter van Zeller saw the route as 'the worst bits of the "Ratty" [Ravenglass & Eskdale] put together in an attempt to outdo Duffield Bank'! Consisting of a double balloon loop, nearly 2 miles in length, with a short section of double track past the International Themes Gardens, the railway had stations at Dingle, Fulwood and The Mill, as well as the Festival Hall. Trains of nine carriages, carrying up to 170 passengers, ran on a 10-minute headway under full colour-light signalling and radio control. Naively, the organisers expected that visitors would ride only from one stop to the next but – travel being free – the '15-inch-gauge bug' spread like a pandemic. Most visitors made the whole circuit at least once (or, in the author's case, several times!). It is doubtful whether any other railway system could have risen to the occasion and coped with the crowds – up to 16,000 per day riding on the trains.

Motive power came from the Romney, Hythe & Dymchurch and the Ravenglass & Eskdale railways. The former provided Greenly's 4-8-2 *Samson* (originally intended for freight haulage) and Roland Martens' 4-6-2 *Black Prince* (originally *Fleissig Lieschen* from Düsseldorf), optimistically accompanied by the Krauss 0-4-0 *The Bug*, which once again proved useful for construction trains but was outclassed on passenger work. Ravenglass sent

The greatest of all the 'lost' 15-inch-gauge lines? Crowds throng the 1984 Liverpool International Garden Festival; *Black Prince* heads the train.

both the newly overhauled and re-boilered 0-8-2 *River Irt*, to take the place of *The Bug*, and the 4-6-4 diesel *Shelagh of Eskdale* (both incorporating parts of earlier Heywood locomotives), and also a newly built a four-car diesel railcar unit in the latest British Rail 'executive' livery for the Herculaneum shuttle. Rolling stock was mostly built new by the Steamtown Museum at Carnforth – 21 coaches including three with disabled access – supplemented by six further vehicles from the Romney, Hythe &

Dymchurch Railway. Some comments in the contemporary railway press suggested that the Festival management were not too keen on railway enthusiasts, but the author was enthralled by the whole experience, not least the wholehearted engine driving to be heard right across the site – 'everything forward, and trust in the Lord!' When the Festival closed on 14 October 1984, nearly 2 million passengers had been carried, about 40% of them on the Herculaneum shuttle. The final circuit was a lap of honour, double-headed by *Black Prince* and *River Irt*, and surely the ghosts of Sir Arthur Heywood, Henry Greenly and Roland Martens must have jostled for space on their footplates.

Visitors to the Festival area of Liverpool now can only weep over what could, and should, have been saved as a priceless public asset. What might it have contributed to the 2008 Capital of Culture celebrations? The railway was dismantled almost immediately, the track, station buildings and most of the coaches going to the ill-fated **Britannia Park Railway** at Shipley near Ilkeston in Derbyshire. True, a small part of the river

'Cinderella' at her first ball! – *Samson* draws away from Fulwood station at the Liverpool International Garden Festival. *R. Ruffell, Silver Link Publishing Collection*

Spartan interior: the 'Romney' layout of wooden seats in a 'Liverpool' coach.

frontage at Herculaneum became valuable open space, new housing arose at Fulwood, and a commuter relief road snaked through the site. But the greater part, mired in Liverpool political in-fighting and closed to public access by concerns about methane under the 'made' ground, was allowed to fall derelict until even the Festival Hall itself was demolished as unsafe. Not until the summer of 2012 was a small area of the gardens re-opened for public enjoyment.

The venue for the 1990 **Gateshead Garden Festival** had much in common with the 1984 Liverpool event, being reclaimed industrial land on the south bank of the River Tyne, though it was slightly smaller in size (200 rather than 250 acres). The Festival opened for 157 days between May and October 1990, attracting more than 3 million visitors to a wide variety of cultural and sporting events as well as the garden displays. The site, which had cost £37 million to develop, was largely re-used for housing after the Festival closed. The transport facilities included a monorail line, a road train and electric tramcars, as well as a 15-inch steam railway in the form of a double balloon loop with a bridge across the River Team at its central point, linking the 'Riverside' and 'Dunston' areas of the Festival. Construction and much of the rolling stock were provided by the Ravenglass & Eskdale Railway, which sent the steam locomotives *River Irt* and *Northern Rock* as well as the diesel-hydraulic *Shelagh of Eskdale*. Twenty carriages were provided, ten being ex-Liverpool Festival vehicles and five each coming from the Ravenglass & Eskdale and the Romney, Hythe & Dymchurch fleets. Notable among them were the capacious steel-bodied 'maxi' design built for Ravenglass, and still to be seen running there today, demonstrating the inherent stability of 15-inch-gauge vehicles.

Country parks, wildlife and theme parks

Although on a smaller scale than the Garden Festivals, numerous railways have been built since 1965 within parkland settings, sometimes as attractions in themselves, and sometimes just as a means of transporting visitors within the site, especially in locations such as wildlife parks where the public cannot be allowed to roam on foot without some danger of being eaten! Here again, the 15-inch-gauge has demonstrated its very practical value in combining a high carrying capacity with a small, low-visibility 'footprint', and a tolerance of sharp curves and inclines. The railway-minded intending visitor must remember that in many cases travel on the train first requires payment of the site entry fee for the principal activity. No slight is intended in saying that many of these lines follow a similar pattern, and are described only briefly below, since all provide a pleasant ride and facilitate enjoyment of the parks for the less able-bodied; but some have special railway interest and so merit a little more detail.

The first such line was opened at **Longleat Park**, adjoining the mansion of the Marquis of Bath, in 1965 and was initially operated by Les Andersen as a precursor to his Axe & Lyme Valley proposals. Steam locomotives designed by David Curwen were introduced in 1967 and 1970, and the track was extended from half a mile to 1 mile in length. The main station has interlocked signalling and there are full workshop facilities. The current steam engine, an 'Exmoor' Class 0-6-2, was at first named after the railway's operator, *John Hayton*.

Next came the **Whorlton Lido Railway**, opened by Raymond Dunn at a popular outdoor venue east of Barnard Castle in 1971. His ambitions to extend further along the River Tees were thwarted by planning objections to the use of steam traction, the initial motive power being the ex-Southport 'Little Giant' *King George*, which for many years retained its previous identity. Later acquisitions included a fine quarter-scale model of *Flying Scotsman* and the Barnes 'Albion' Class *John* (dispersed from the Rhyl fleet by way of static display at Alton Towers), but by 2000 the operation was reduced to a Colby-Simkins diesel and the line closed in May 2005. Now privately owned, a small group began to rebuild the Lido railway in 2012 and hope to reopen it on a limited basis in 2013 as the Thorpe Light Railway.

Also in 1971 the Earl of Derby commissioned the **Knowsley Safari Park Railway** at Knowsley Hall near Prescot, running for 800 yards just outside the Park as an early example of what would become

The rural 15-inch-gauge: agricultural buildings form the depot of the Waveney Valley Railway at Bressingham Steam Museum.

a popular genre. In 1972 the **Blackpool Zoo Miniature Railway** was built within the zoo park itself, linking 'Dodge City' to 'Wells Fargo' with a Severn-Lamb 'Rio Grande'-type engine, appropriate enough in its context.

The late Alan Bloom, equally famous as a plantsman and a locomotive collector, was already establishing the steam museum at Bressingham Gardens in Norfolk, and in 1973 the **Waveney Valley Railway** opened, straddling the Norfolk/Suffolk county boundary. A notable piece of opportunism was his seeking out and purchasing of two of the 4-6-2 locomotives built by Krüpp of Essen in 1937 to the design of Roland Martens (*Rosenkavalier* and *Männertreu*), together with 19 steel-bodied coaches of unmistakably German *parkeisenbahn* appearance.

In 1976 a short line opened at the **Paradise Park** Bird Gardens near Hayle, Cornwall (including the distinction of a tunnel!), and at the opposite end of Britain the 10¼-inch-gauge railway within **Craigtoun Country Park** near St Andrews was rebuilt on the 15-inch-gauge, initially as an end-to-end run and altered 20 years later to circuit around the lake. A similar regauging took place at the **Blaise Castle Miniature Railway** at Henbury near Bristol in 1978, which extended the scope of 15-inch-gauge technology to battery-powered railcars, created from former Axe & Lyme Valley project coaches by incorporating milk-float electrics!

The **Lightwater Valley Theme Park** near Ripon in North Yorkshire built a 1,300-yard circular line round a small artificial lake in 1979, and has included steam traction in the handsome shape of *Yvette*, a scale model of an LNER 'Shire' Class 4-4-0 begun in 1942 for the private line of a Mr Younger at Ponteland. The **Safari Express** within the West Midland Safari Park near Bewdley also began operation in 1979, ferrying visitors between the entrance and the leisure area. The **Pixieland Miniature Railway** of 1980, in the fun park of the same name at Kilkhampton near Bude, can claim to be one of the shortest 15-inch-gauge lines ever built – just 200 yards cut into a steep hillside – but nevertheless acquired an 'Exmoor' Class steam locomotive in 1997.

Openings of country and theme park railways came thick and fast in the 1980s and 1990s, many of course on gauges smaller than the 15 inches to which we are confining ourselves. One of the results of this 'miniature railway mania' was an emerging market for new locomotives and carriages of practical, easily maintained designs, and firms such as Severn-Lamb, Alan Keef Ltd and the Exmoor Steam Railway were quick to take advantage of the opportunity. Just as the 'Barlow Pacifics' supplied a niche demand in the 1950s, Severn-Lamb's 2-8-0 'Rio Grande' Class of petrol, gas or diesel engines with their distinctive 'Wild West' steam-outline appearance and embellishments were built in quantity, in various gauges; they caught the imagination of younger passengers – and of at least some enthusiasts – wherever they appeared.

1985 saw the creation of an 800-yard line within the **Cricket St Thomas Wildlife Park** incorporating a substantial steel viaduct 20 feet above a stream, being in fact one of the largest structures on any 15-inch-gauge railway. Built and equipped by Alan Keef for John and Stephen Taylor, initially with equipment retrieved from the Rhyl fiasco, it has recently operated with a modern push-pull train driven from both ends, thus requiring no time-consuming 'running round' between trips. Unfortunately, it did not operate during 2012 and was expected to be dismantled early in 2013.

The dispersal of equipment after the Fairbourne Railway was regauged in 1985, described more fully below, inspired at least two new lines in 1986. The **Haigh Railway** was the creation of Gilbert Swift, a former Leisure Director of Wigan Borough Council, running through 250 acres of woodland and past the walled garden and lake at the Haigh Hall Country Park north of Wigan. Two locomotives came from Fairbourne, Ernest W. Twining's *Katie* and the petrol shunting engine *Rachel* becoming *Haigh Hall* and *W. Brogan MBE* respectively at their new home. In Berkshire, the new owner of **Littlecote House** near Hungerford, Peter de Savery, commissioned a line to facilitate visitor access around the property. It was built by Alan Keef Ltd and mainly powered by Twining's *Siân* – once the identical sister of *Katie* – then hideously 'Americanised' by John Ellerton and still bearing the former Fairbourne telephone number, 362, as its running number. The Littlecote Railway proved to be short-lived, as the house was closed to the public around 1990 and the equipment was dispersed.

The hasty dismantling of the **Liverpool Garden Festival Railway** was due, in part, to a plan to establish a new line at the projected 390-acre **Britannia Park** at Shipley near Ilkeston, Derbyshire. Over-optimistic at best, the scheme was promoted by a firm called KLF, opened in a blaze of publicity in June 1985 but lasted only ten weeks before the receivers were called it, to discover debts of £9½ million. After a three-year investigation, and

a marathon fraud trial, the promoters reaped their reward in the form of prison sentences. Using the diesel locomotive *Shelagh of Eskdale*, the initial line had covered a route of just half a mile. Ownership of the site then passed to Grenada Leisure and opened as the **American Adventure Theme Park**, with the railway being remodelled several times by successive owners. Ultimately, despite refurbishment in 2005-06, the decision was taken to close the park at Shipley and the railway equipment, together with some of the other rides, has been transferred to the **Twinlakes Theme Park** near Melton Mowbray, Leicestershire, where it reopened in late 2008.

Openings of new lines continued relentlessly in the following years. 1987 brought the **Oakwood Miniature Railway** of 1,100 yards at the theme park near Narberth in Pembrokeshire; the **Marwell Wildlife Railway** of 900 yards at the Marwell Zoological Gardens near Winchester; and a 700-yard line at **Paulton's Park** near Ower in Hampshire. Three more lines appeared in 1989 – **Gulliver's World Railway**, 500 yards, at the theme park at Old Hall, Warrington; the **Combe Martin Wildlife Park Railway** in Devon (soon afterwards extended from 150 to 500 yards); and the interesting **Markeaton Park Light Railway** on the outskirts of Derby. This has a run of 1,400 yards from the main entrance and car park to 'Mundy Halt' at the opposite corner of the site, and houses some ex-Fairbourne coaches; the 'Exmoor' Class steam engine *Markeaton Lady* was used until 2009.

The Colley family's purchase of two locomotives built by K. Hardy was the inspiration for their creation of the **Sherwood Forest Railway** in Nottinghamshire, which first opened in 2000 and soon extended to 800 yards between Loxley and Welldale stations. The adjacent Farm Park attraction unfortunately closed at the end of the 2010 season, but the railway has continued in operation at the site. Although the pace of building has slowed somewhat, the Gulliver's Land theme park at Milton Keynes also acquired **Gulliver's Railroad** of 600 yards in 1999, and as recently as 2010 the **Billing Aquadrome Miniature Railway** has been instated on the trackbed of a former 2-foot-gauge line in the water park near Northampton – the 15-inch-gauge returning to one of its 'spiritual homes' from which Bassett-Lowke and his partners promoted miniature railways. Less successful, unfortunately, was the short-lived **Powderham Castle Steam Railway** in Devon, which opened in August 2001, offering a ride of 400 yards in two ex-Fairbourne closed coaches. The locomotive *Earl of Devon* was built by Prestige Engineering of Abbotskerswell, based on an interesting prototype – the GWR 'Dukedog' Class 4-4-0.

For the enthusiast, two of the most substantial and interesting recent creations are the Windmill Farm Railway and the Evesham Vale Light Railway, which both have important museum roles underlying their everyday operations. The **Windmill Farm Railway** near Burscough (just north of Ormskirk in Lancashire) was set up in 1997 by Austin Moss; a dedicated preservationist, he has brought together a substantial collection of locomotives at his '15-inch-gauge Heritage Centre', including E. W. Twining's first freelance design, *Katie* (previously used at Fairbourne, Haigh Hall and Cleethorpes), and no fewer than three of the surviving 'Barlow Pacifics'. Most notably, he has taken a leading part in the preservation of the 1909-built 'Little Giant' Class *Red Dragon*, which proclaims its identity in a striking scarlet livery wherever it travels for exhibitions and steam galas.

Running for 1¼ miles through the country park just north of Evesham, with two stations,

the **Evesham Vale Light Railway** was built by Jim and Helen Shackell to restore, house and operate their collection of locomotives. It was home to – among others – E. W. Twining's 4-6-2 *Prince William* (formerly *Winston Churchill*); the Barnes 'Albion' Class *John* (which we last encountered at Whorlton Lido); and the 'Exmoor' Class *St Egwin*, and was until the end of the 2012 season, the base for the privately-preserved 'Little Giant' Class *Count Louis*. This historic machine, which began life on the Higham Railway in 1924, has been restored to its full splendour, succinctly described in the enthusiast press as 'a Gentleman's light sporting locomotive'. The railway has grown quickly from small beginnings in 2002, with a balloon loop opened in 2003 and a new tunnel completed in December 2004. It may be extended further in future years as the (currently rather underdeveloped) parkland hopefully receives fresh investment.

Changes at the seaside

The long reign of Harry N. Barlow at Southport's **Lakeside Miniature Railway** ended in 1969, bringing about the end of regular steam operation. The railway was operated by the late John Spencer until August 2001, when the present owners took charge, but has retained much of its traditional character in the face of significant alterations – much for the worse,

A lifelong friend of the author finds the perfect viewing position at the Windmill Farm Railway!

in the author's opinion – in its surroundings. Beachside leisure facilities and the open-air pool have given way to a retail park, and even the famous Pleasureland Amusement Park is no more. Barlow's last creation, named for the railway's *Golden Jubilee* in 1961, has since been joined by two other diesel-hydraulics, one designed by David Curwen (*Princess Anne*) and the other by Austin Moss (the 'steam outline' *Jenny*), demonstrating the faith of the owners in the line's future. Steam made a dramatic comeback in March 1983 when examples of the three sizes of Bassett-Lowke's 'Little Giants' – *George the Fifth*, *Princess Elizabeth* and *Synolda* – returned for a single weekend. Austin Moss's reconstructed *Red Dragon* made occasional appearances on Saturdays in the 1990s, on one occasion being photographed with the 91-year-old Harry Barlow himself.

Cleethorpes has enjoyed no fewer than six miniature railway operations going back as far as 1948, but our story very nearly starts in 1972 when the Borough Council reconstructed the existing 10¼-inch-gauge line alongside the boating lake. 'Very nearly', because the contractor mistakenly measured the 15-inch distance between the rail centres, not the inner edges, resulting in a totally unique 14½-inch gauge demanding specially adapted rolling stock! This line closed in 1990 for reconstruction to the proper gauge under the ownership of Chris Shaw, and as the **Cleethorpes Coast Light Railway** it has gone from strength to strength. A new viaduct and station, 'Kingsway', have been built at the 'Town' end of the line, and the other original station, 'Lakeside', has been transformed by the arrival of buildings from the Sutton Miniature Railway.

More recently, in 2006-07, the route has been extended by a sweeping curve from a new platform at 'Lakeside' to climb for 900 yards to 'North Sea Lane', almost on the Meridian Line, with extensive views across the (sometimes windswept) Humber Estuary to Spurn Point. The locomotive fleet includes a replica of Heywood's first engine, *Effie*, a freelance 0-4-0 *Mountaineer* by the Dutch engineer W. van der Heiden, which once worked in Tasmania, and a model of an LNER 'Shire' Class 4-4-0, *Yvette*, first used on the private 'Redlands' railway at Ponteland. To all this must be added the locomotives, coaches and artefacts of the Sutton Collection, which, with the recent establishment of the Miniature Railway Museum at Lakeside, truly makes Cleethorpes one of the premier venues for the 15-inch-gauge enthusiast.

Unfortunately, not all seaside lines have had the success of Cleethorpes. At **Fleetwood** on the Lancashire coast, a line was opened in 1975 from the car park at Mount Road to the boating lake at Laidley's Walk; for part of its course, below the Esplanade, it paralleled an earlier 10¼-inch-gauge track. At a time when the resort did not have too many competing attractions, it should have been an ideal location, but regrettably the railway fell prone to vandalism and closed in 1982, the Severn-Lamb locomotive and five coaches reappearing two years later at the equally unsuccessful **West Buchan Railway** at Banff. A novel venture in 1994 was a battery-electric tramcar service running from Princes Parade to Tower Esplanade in **Skegness**, its double-decked vehicle looking somewhat precarious on the 15-inch-gauge, but the line fell victim to road improvements and closed in 1998.

On the South East coast, the **Dreamland Miniature Railway** at Margate ran exactly as in the 1930s, the 'Albion' Class *Billie* being the staple motive power in a smart livery of Southern Railway green and fitted with smoke deflectors. The veteran *Prince Edward of Wales* was less and less used, largely superseded by a petrol-mechanical engine that R. H. Morse had built (in 1939, originally for the Dean's Mill

Railway near Haywards Heath), which came to Margate in 1959. *Prince Edward of Wales* – the erstwhile *Red Dragon* – was sold to Robin Butterell and William McAlpine in 1968, after *Billie* had been overhauled with a new boiler. During the mid-1970s the railway was operated on a concession basis, and seemed secure enough with the track being re-sleepered throughout and the 'Magic Garden' station rebuilt in 1979. But without warning the line closed completely in 1980, and the assets were sold to the new owner of the **Rhyl Miniature Railway**; *Billie* is now preserved in private ownership. The Dreamland site was drastically modernised with new rides in the 1980s, but did not survive the rapid decline of traditional holiday resorts, being completely closed in 2003. Only a small portion of the railway trackbed remains visible, and any hope of its revival must be linked to the valiant efforts being made to preserve the remains of John Iles's famous Scenic Railway – as the oldest surviving roller-coaster in Britain, now a listed structure – and to install other historic fairground equipment from the now-closed Pleasureland at Southport.

The **Fairbourne Railway** (the word 'Miniature' was dropped at the height of its prosperity under John Wilkins) had by the mid-1970s established itself as one of the leading 15-inch-gauge operations, with a peak passenger figure of 112,000 in 1973 and a new extension to Penrhyn Point opening in May 1976. Below the surface, however, problems were mounting: the railway's debts were about to exceed its then value, and although most of

The new Kingsway terminus at Cleethorpes has a fine lantern roof to light the interior.

the debt was notional (money invested by John Wilkins) there was some real indebtedness to its bankers – a trading loss was recorded each year from 1975 to 1981. As age began to catch up with the owner, it became clear that some form of sale had to be considered, and a time-consuming process of buying up the remaining leasehold pieces of land was a necessary preliminary. A revaluation of the railway by John Milner in 1979 produced a reassuringly high figure, but that in turn raised a price barrier in front of any interested purchaser. The most promising scenario would have been for the Fairbourne equipment to have been transferred completely to the Medina Valley (Cowes to Newport) venture in the Isle of Wight; we can be certain that John Wilkins would have been keenly interested in its future. But as we have seen, finance could not be obtained. Nothing came of other tentative enquiries, and by 1982 passenger traffic was less than half the 1973 record. With hindsight, we may wonder why no preservation association was formed until April 1983, rather too late in the day to be effective; the answer seeming to be that the voluntary helpers at Fairbourne were all recruited individually by John Wilkins. Several were assisted with travel and accommodation costs, and indulged with money to carry out projects of mutual interest, but there was never any sense in the owner's mind that the volunteers formed a corporate body, or had input into the management of the line.

At the end of 1983 a young Anglo-American businessman, John de Vries Ellerton, made a dramatic entry onto the scene. He already knew the Barmouth area, and had been a somewhat 'larger than life' contemporary of the author at university in North Wales; friends have recalled his endearing trait of writing off expensive cars! His first foray into miniature railways had been the 12¼-inch-gauge **Réseau Guerlédan Chemin de Fer Touristique**, opened in 1978 on the Mur-de-Bretagne to Caurel section of the former metre-gauge Réseau Breton. The author finds it hard to understand what, apart from the acquisition of a French wife, had encouraged the young entrepreneur to believe that a British – and specifically Welsh – type of half-scale narrow-gauge railway, planted in a remote part of Brittany, would attract popular support, but in the event the only 'British' characteristic of the local populace turned out to be a penchant for vandalism, such as lifting the rails. The line finally closed in September 1979 after a serious attempt by *les saboteurs* to derail a loaded passenger train. A number of ideas for relocation were considered, including the Afan Valley near Port Talbot, the faltering Medina Valley scheme in the Isle of Wight, parts of the former Lynton to Barnstaple and Welsh Highland routes – and even a site in Bermuda – but as John Ellerton was well acquainted with John Milner (a former aircraft engineer, builder of two of the half-scale engines at his workshop at Higher Kinnerton near Chester, and also John Wilkins's agent for the sale of the Fairbourne Railway), it was perhaps natural that his attention should turn to Fairbourne after the collapse of his hopes at the Réseau Guerlédan.

With two locomotives in hand, two more stored in England, and no fewer than 30 carriages retrieved from France, it is not surprising that conversion of the Fairbourne Railway to the 12¼-inch gauge seemed an obvious solution, especially as the existing Wilkins-era rolling stock could be sold piecemeal to a number of newly emerging 15-inch-gauge lines. Despite his losses in France, there was money enough for John and his father, the late Dr Sydney Ellerton, to write a cheque 'on the spot' at Fairbourne in January 1984, and subsequently to invest around £1 million in redevelopment by his new company, North Wales Narrow Gauge Railway Ltd. What the author, and many others, find it hard to forgive is the short-term 'Americanisation' of the working locomotives in the last two years of the 15-inch-gauge, the formerly elegant *Siân* acquiring hideous black steel cladding as Sea Train, No 362 – actually the railway's telephone number! The gauge conversion was completed by Easter 1986, and thereafter the equipment so lovingly brought together by John Wilkins was gradually sold away. Two locomotives were retained for a while, and both remain in preservation today – the veteran *Count Louis*, as already mentioned, currently at the Evesham Vale Light Railway, and the 'Pacific' *Ernest W. Twining* far away at the Shuzenji Romney Railway in Japan.

Hugely on the credit side, of course, is the financial investment made during the six years of the Ellerton regime, not least the splendid new station facilities at both Fairbourne and Penrhyn Point. The carriages, of a traditional Welsh narrow-gauge outline, are certainly more at home on the Cambrian coast than in Brittany, and the surplus units that ran temporarily on 15-inch-gauge bogies in 1984-85 have since become welcome additions to the fleets at Markeaton Park, Evesham Vale and elsewhere. And what steam enthusiast can stand today by the splendid half-scale Darjeeling 'B' Class engine, *Sherpa*, without an almost irresistible urge to get on the footplate and take the regulator? But in that curiously cyclic way in which history at Fairbourne seems to repeat itself, traffic failed to reach the hoped-for levels and in 1990 the railway was again advertised for sale, though it was another five years before it was purchased by Prof and Mrs Atkinson and Dr and Mrs Melton. They in turn invested heavily in their new company, North Wales Coast Light Railway Ltd, without drawing any share income, in order to secure its future. From February 2009, in an even more remarkable act of generosity, the ownership of the railway was transferred to a charitable body and it is now supported by the Fairbourne Railway Preservation Society. Let us hope there are no more downturns in the future.

Private railways since 1945

A wonderfully diverse set of railways have appeared (and in some cases, unfortunately, disappeared) since the Second World War, ranging from lines built almost regardless of expense with brand-new equipment to a home-made operation that literally outgrew a suburban back garden into a stretch of 'green belt' woodland. It would be virtually impossible to document all such ventures, but through the wonders of the Internet fascinating discoveries can be made in sites such as the 'Miniature Railway World Forum'. For the present book, a small selection must suffice.

Around 1942 a certain Mr Younger (who also operated a miniature railway at Town Moor, Newcastle-upon-Tyne) established a private 15-inch-gauge line at his house, 'Redlands', at Ponteland using the American Herschell-Spillman locomotive formerly at Southend and a scale-model LNER 'Shire' Class 4-4-0 named *Yvette*, and this operated until about 1950. The **North Eastern Railway** was to be the home for a collection of equipment brought together by Tom Tate after his rescue of the original *Little Giant* from an amusement park at South Shields in 1963, and his purchase of the historic *Blacolvesley* (rather heavily disguised as the 'streamlined' *Elizabeth*) from Saltburn. His line ran for 800 yards down

Fairbourne at the end of its 15-inch-gauge era: the author's daughter tries to divert his attention from *Ernest W. Twining* in 1983.

the drive of the derelict Haswell Lodge country house, with a passing loop at Central station, and incorporated some genuine (standard-gauge) NER signals and a signal box; the rolling stock included a splendid working steam crane. Built between 1968 and 1971, it sadly survived for only about a decade before vandalism made its continuance impossible. The Medina Valley project was to be the intended beneficiary, but after its failure the locomotives transferred to the Lightwater Valley Miniature Railway in North Yorkshire.

Other private lines of this period included the extensive garden railway of the racing motorist Mr Lemmon Burton, at Paynesfield near Allbourne in Sussex, and the **Jacot Railway** linking the house of the miniature railway writer, Michael Jacot, to his engineering workshop at Handsworth near Birmingham. The former used an American-style 0-4-0 shunting engine, of generous proportions, built by R. H. Morse (a retired main-line railway engineer), while Mr Jacot's rolling stock including the internal-combustion locomotive *Redgauntlet* of 1964, later purchased by Sir William McAlpine and

moved to New Romney, and some very early Heywood goods vehicles, two probably being from the 9-inch-gauge line that the youthful pioneer had set up at Dove Leys in the 1860s.

At Liphook in Hampshire, Mr Charles Lane, the enterprising landlord of the Royal Anchor Inn, exceeded the example of George Tonner at Warburton by building no fewer than three railways of different gauges, and by amassing a huge collection of model and miniature locomotives. Mr Lane's own design of diesel locomotive, *Royal Anchor* of 1956, incorporated a hydraulic transmission derived from naval gun mountings. Rather under-powered, it nevertheless ran with reasonable success on the Ravenglass & Eskdale Railway and was later used at the Steamtown Museum line in Carnforth; it is now preserved in the United States.

The charming **Rhiw Valley Light Railway** was built by the late Jack Woodroffe around the meadows between his house at Manafon near Berriew (between Welshpool and Newtown) and the River Rhiw. Exactly as Heywood had done a century earlier, he began by calculating

The rural delights of the Rhiw Valley Light Railway at Manafon, Powys, on one of the occasional public open days.

the size of his passengers and the space they would need, before first settling on the 10¼-inch gauge. However, a visit to the Severn-Lamb works at Stratford-upon-Avon in 1971, in search of motive power, brought the builder face to face with the David Curwen-designed 0-6-2 *Dougal* under construction for the Longleat Railway – resulting in the Rhiw Valley opening in 1973 on the 15-inch-gauge, with an almost identical locomotive, *Powys*! The track was lightly laid following the natural surface of the land, but has proved to be durable; the work of hauling the four home-built vehicles is shared between *Powys* and *Jack* (the latter begun by the owner, and completed in 2003 by TMA Engineering). For some while the railway carried passengers on summer Sundays, but this was lately confined to a single weekend, usually early in September, coinciding with a nearby Garden Railways Exhibition and the 'gala' event at the Welshpool & Llanfair Light Railway. However, the line has exciting expansion plans in the pipeline, including more public openings, and the support of a new Friends organisation.

The availability of new designs of locomotives from builders such as Alan Keef and the Exmoor Steam Company since the 1980s has encouraged a further generation of private railway owners. The recent **Wotton Light Railway** at Wotton Underwood near Brill, Buckinghamshire, has come to possess an example from both manufacturers, the diesel locomotive including a heated cab for the comfort of the owner's railway-minded cat. The public were occasionally permitted to travel, on occasions such as village fetes.

The shortest-lived private line was probably the half-mile circuit built by Derek Parnaby at **Whitworth Hall** near Spennymoor, the birthplace of 'Bobbie Shafto' of ballad fame. Converted in 1994 from a 9½-inch-gauge line, it was to operate only during the summer of 1995 before the family decided to sell the property, which is now a (railway-less) hotel.

One of the finest of private lines has been constructed within new gardens at Raphoe in County Donegal in 2002 for Sir Gerry Robinson. The closed carriages of the **Difflin Lake Railway** are styled after those of the

3-foot County Donegal Joint Railways, but are usually hauled by an 0-4-0 diesel locomotive. The route is on two levels round the upper and lower lakes, through woodland and a paddock, giving the impression of a much larger site, and the buildings are in a Swiss style.

A few years earlier, in 1998, the Duke of Westminster decided to re-create a 1½-mile section of the **Eaton Railway** at Eaton Hall, a century after its first building; the line starts from some of the surviving railway buildings and makes a grand circle through the park and past the cricket meadow. It was opened to the public for the first time in September 2004. The truly beautiful replica of Heywood's 0-4-0 *Katie*, built by FMB Engineering in Hampshire, pulls a set of equally handsome coaches and brake vans (originals and replicas), all correctly numbered as in the original fleet. The line is very popular with visitors on the three or four Sundays each year when the Duke opens his gardens for charity, and in some years there has also been an enthusiasts' 'Steam at Eaton' event when historic locomotives from other venues have been put through their paces. Particularly noteworthy was the August 2007 visit of the replicas of *Effie* and *Ursula* with the Heywood rolling stock from the Perrygrove Railway.

At the opposite end of the spectrum, as it were, was the **Woodland Railway**, which began in the 1970s in the garden of a suburban house in Ditton, Kent. Not to be confused with its much earlier namesake on the Isle of Grain, the line moved to green belt land at Roger's Wood near Brands Hatch and grew to a half-mile loop with a wooden viaduct across a Second World War bomb crater. Rail was salvaged from industrial sites and any source of scrap timber provided the sleepers! Ultimately there were two home-made petrol locomotives based on car components, a motor trolley powered by a lawnmower engine (!), three coaches, and sundry wagons for hauling timber to be used for firewood and garden work. It was all great fun for the owners and their friends, but had to be abandoned in about 1996 when the site became overgrown and the family moved to Cornwall. It is thanks to the builder, Chris Mace, that the story of such a truly English adventure came to be recorded in 'The Narrow Gauge' (No 115), and more recently it has been recalled by his son on the 'Miniature Railway World Forum'.

The glories of replica-building! *Katie* and her train are seen at Eaton Hall in May 2010.

The Steamtown Miniature Railway: lost but not forgotten

The Steamtown Museum at Carnforth was established in 1967, as a restoration and display centre for main-line steam locomotives at a time when it seemed that preserved locomotives would have little or no access to the national network. Dr Peter Beet and Sir William McAlpine played important roles in its earlier years, but after 1990 it became the base for Carnforth Railway Restoration & Engineering Services and West Coast Railways.

In 1975 a short length of 15-inch-gauge railway from the 'Locomotion 150' celebrations at Shildon was brought to Steamtown and set up on the east side of the car park. Soon afterwards it was moved to the west side of the main site, and through a Job Creation Scheme in 1978-79 it was extended to a mile run from the northern entrance of Steamtown (Keer End), through the main engine shed to Crag Bank at the southern extremity, where there was an interchange with the standard-gauge passenger line. In the early 1980s McAlpine proposed building an extension for 3 miles along the shore, past Bolton-le-Sands, to a terminus by Happy Mount Park at Bare (the northernmost part of Morecambe), but eventually decided not to force the issue in the face of local opposition.

Morecambe soon entered a rapid decline as a holiday destination and, with the benefit of hindsight, the 15-inch-gauge railway might have been greatly to its advantage.

Around 1990 McAlpine sold his controlling interest in Steamtown to David Smith, and public access to the main site ceased in 1997 due to the greatly increased commercial activity and movements of main-line equipment. The 'writing was on the engine shed wall', so to speak, for the 15-inch-gauge line, but the operation struggled on at weekends until July 2000. The entire equipment was then sold by Bonhams Auctioneers, most being purchased by an American enthusiast, Francis Ford Coppola, by whom it has been carefully preserved, overhauled and – from time to time – displayed in public in California.

The steam locomotives used at Carnforth comprised the 'Class 10' Little Giant *George the Fifth*, rescued from Belle Vue, the 'Class 20' *Princess Elizabeth* from the Lakeside Miniature Railway, and Twining and Guest's 4-6-2 *Prince William*. These were supplemented by three diesel locomotives including *Royal Anchor* built by Charles Lane at Liphook, Hampshire. The sudden demise of the railway, which was very well known to enthusiasts, and the inability to raise sufficient funds instantly to retain more engines in Britain, are still widely regretted.

A relic of the Steamtown line, displayed at the Windmill Farm Heritage Centre.

Bunty meanders peacefully past lush vegetation on the bank of the River Till on the Heatherslaw Light Railway.

In a class of their own:
Heatherslaw and Perrygrove

The final two lines on our journey are at diagonally opposed corners of England but, at least to the author, typify the character and spirit of the 15-inch-gauge railway. The **Heatherslaw Light Railway** links the mill and visitor centre at Ford Forge near Cornhill-on-Tweed with the attractive ruins of Etal Castle. Just 2 miles in length, it meanders unpretentiously along the banks of the River Till (a tributary of the Tees), past woods and fields in this picturesque, relatively little-known part of Northumberland. The line was built by the late Neville Smith in 1989 – the track being completed in two weeks! – and its first steam locomotive, *The Lady Augusta* (named after a former philanthropic owner of the Ford and Etal Estate) was ordered from Ravenglass & Eskdale Engineering and completed by Brian

Taylor of the Kirklees Light Railway. She has recently been joined by a partner, to share the work of hourly trips during the summer. The new *Bunty* was begun by Mr Smith and given his wife's nickname, the construction being finished by Alan Keef Ltd. Heatherslaw station boasts two platforms with an overall roof, and trains of up to eight coaches can be operated. The use of offcut timber from the estate's sawmills as fuel has saved costs and, having regard to environmental issues, substantially reduced its 'carbon footprint'. Neville Smith died in 2009, and the line is now owned and operated by his son Paul.

Our journey began in earnest at Duffield Bank near Derby, and it is appropriate that it should end at the **Perrygrove Railway** just south of Coleford in the Forest of Dean – the line that perhaps today bears the closest resemblance to Sir Arthur Heywood's vision, and houses the magnificent Heywood

Collection of preserved and replica vehicles. The site is the remaining portion of what was once a larger farm, including ancient woodland and the site of an iron-ore mine, the Oak Iron Pit, and was discovered by Michael and Frances Crofts in 1992 after a nationwide search. Tiring of the world of corporate 'big business', their vision of an ideal lifestyle was to create a classic 15-inch-gauge railway as the centrepiece of a range of family attractions in a beautiful rural setting. How magnificently they have succeeded, after investing literally all the money they possessed! Construction of the railway began in 1995, the line climbing the steep hillside in elongated S-shaped loops, with two sections of 1 in 30 gradients. Two intermediate halts – one appropriately named 'Heywood' – are passed on the way to the present upper terminus at 'Oakiron', with the possibility of a short future extension.

Opened in 1996, Perrygrove is surely the 'Duffield Bank Experimental Railway' brought into the 21st century, combining pleasure with a serious purpose – in this case, to preserve and re-create historic equipment. The extent of the Heywood Collection is summarised in the later account of museums, but what could compare to riding in the re-created Duffield Bank dining carriage, or the Eaton Hall saloon coach, while a replica of the 0-6-0 *Ursula* pounds triumphantly up the final 1 in 30 to Oakiron at a vintage trains afternoon? *Ursula*, built by James Waterfield (a friend of the line's owners) over seven years, was inaugurated by Sir Peter Heywood, the present Baronet, and normally resides at Perrygrove, but her active social life frequently involves visits to her friends at other railways. Usually she takes along one or two historic vehicles for company, such as the Duffield Bank 'dynamometer carriage' or the Eaton Hall brake van, and becomes the centre of attention wherever she goes.

Normal train operation at Perrygrove is by the 'Exmoor' Class 0-6-0 *Spirit of Adventure* or the powerful 2-6-2 *Lydia* built by Alan Keef Ltd in 2008, truly one of the most impressive machines to appear in the new millennium, and even more recently provided with matching coaches. By no means the least of the achievements of the operating company, Treasure Train Ltd, is their employment of local young people as operating staff, who receive valuable training and work experience as well as income.

Sir Arthur Percival Heywood, were he alive today, would surely be overjoyed by the Perrygrove Railway. What more can one say?

Re-created: *Ursula* at the Perrygrove Railway, driven by her builder James Waterfield.
G. Sutton

Right: The 'Exmoor' Class *Spirit of Adventure*, the initial motive power of the Perrygrove Railway. *G. Sutton*

Below: The best of modern practice at the Perrygrove Railway: *Lydia* and new coaches by Alan Keef Ltd.

3. 15-inch-gauge locomotives

Setting the scene

Locomotives have already featured largely in our tour through the history of 15-inch-gauge railways, because they have taken centre stage in the minds of both railway operators and the public. The longevity of some of the pioneering designs, and the ease with which they passed from one line to another, gives us the opportunity to see and experience almost the complete story from surviving and replica examples.

We have seen that from the outset two traditions of engineering have been combined: the simple, robust 'industrial' locomotive differing little from those built for the 2-foot or larger tracks and, on the other hand, the scale model of a main-line prototype (one-quarter or one-third full size). In the last few decades, a third strand has been added – locomotives scaled down not from standard-gauge engines, but from the types evolved by British manufacturers for export to countries where long-distance routes had been built on gauges as narrow as 2ft 6in. The builders of 15-inch-gauge machines have sometimes been pioneers, introducing radical design concepts and novel types of wheel arrangement for steam locomotives. This is still true at the beginning of the 21st century as the ideas of the last generation of steam engineers – such as Livio Dante Porta's 'gas-producing' boilers – have been incorporated into new locomotives. Steam building is still alive and flourishing, and long may it so continue.

The term 'scale model' perhaps needs a word of qualification. The rail gauge of 15 inches is generally taken as one-quarter of standard-gauge (56½ inches), though even this is not, of course, precisely correct. Many fine model locomotives have been built as closely as possible to quarter-scale, but practical factors inevitably demand that certain components are 'over-sized'. Track and pointwork are rarely laid to such exact tolerances that true-to-scale wheels and flanges will run at speed without derailing, and structural framing, brake gear, bearings and springs have to be able to withstand hard usage. Most importantly, boilers must be constructed with the barrel, firebox and tubeplates of sufficient thickness to withstand much the same steam pressure as in a full-size locomotive. It was quickly recognised that engines with a small trailing axle behind the driving wheels had the advantage of allowing a wide firebox to extend outside the frames, and after 1912 boiler sizes began to increase visibly; the logical conclusion, in Greenly's classic designs for Ravenglass and New Romney, was that, although the track was *one-quarter scale*, the locomotives needed to be constructed to *one-third scale*.

Whatever the attractions of steam, we should not overlook the contribution of internal-combustion technology, some of its very earliest applications to rail traction having been on the 15-inch-gauge. It was petrol or diesel power (sometimes lurking under 'steam-outline' bodywork) that enabled many lines to survive and prosper in the 1930s, 1940s and 1950s, and encouraged the growth of country park and theme park railways from the 1970s to the present day. Robust, cheap to operate, and relatively simple to drive and maintain, they support operations at venues where steam would simply not be affordable or justifiable.

Pearl: the earliest British 15-inch-gauge locomotive?

It seems possible that the very first 15-inch-gauge locomotive ever built was a demonstration model constructed by the Norris Locomotive Works of Philadelphia, USA, in 1854. Almost nothing is known, except that it was taken to Yokohama in that year in a fruitless

attempt to create railway interest within the Empire of Japan. About seven years later Peter Brotherhood of Chippenham built the handsome quarter-scale 2-2-2 engine *Pearl*, still preserved today at the Strand campus of King's College, London. Born in 1838, Brotherhood had been educated at King's College School between 1852 and 1855. His father had a large engineering works at Chippenham and had been a contractor for parts of Brunel's Great Western Railway; Peter Brotherhood himself worked under Daniel Gooch at Swindon for two years, before entering his father's works.

Whether built as a tool for practical instruction, or simply for pleasure, *Pearl* generally resembled a standard-gauge (4ft 8½in) rather than a broad-gauge (7ft 0¼in) passenger engine; a typical prototype would have been those of the Midland Railway in the late 1850s. The boiler was of iron with 12 tubes and a conventional firebox; working at 50psi and with cylinders of 4 inches by 5½ inches driving 1ft 8in-diameter wheels, she would have generated considerable power. Completed by 1862, *Pearl* was apparently redundant by March 1868 when the builder offered her to King's College.

By 1958 *Pearl* needed complete restoration, which was carried out by Sidney A. Leleux and other members of King's College Railway Club in the college workshops between 1959 and 1961; however, the work raised as many questions as it answered. The mechanical components had clearly been meant for use, yet the cylinder, valve and pump glands had never been packed. Limescale in the boiler, and the fitting of a well-tank underneath, suggested it had been steamed many times, but there was no tender or other provision for a driver to control *Pearl* on the move. Nevertheless, repainted in her original royal blue with red frames and buffer beams, she is today as impressive as ever on the college staircase, having once enjoyed an outing to New Romney in 1987 for the 60th anniversary celebrations there.

It is quite possible that some of the early garden railways used steam power, though there is much uncertainty. Charles Fildes's railway at Far Sawrey in Cumbria apparently used a

The venerable *Pearl*, 150 years old, still holds pride of place on the staircase at King's College in the Strand. *King's College London*

2-2-2 named *Lavinia*, presumably quite unlike *Pearl* in having a steam-launch boiler and engine unit that may have been made by Isaac Watt Boulton of Ashton-under-Lyne. George Callender's line at Ardkinglas in the 1870s had an 0-4-0 with a tall chimney and a boiler lagged with wood; Callender was certainly known to Arthur Heywood, so the similarity to Heywood's first design, *Effie*, should perhaps not be ignored.

The 'Heywood' designs at Duffield Bank and Eaton Hall

Much has been published on Sir Arthur Heywood's work, and the present brief summary cannot hope to do full justice to the research of Mark Smithers, James Waterfield and others. The steam enthusiast cannot do better than to enjoy the replicas of *Effie*, *Ursula* and *Katie* built in recent years, or to travel behind *River Irt* (built on the chassis of Heywood's *Muriel*) at Ravenglass.

The Duffield Bank workshops seem to have been set up on a small scale in 1873, and by 1875 their first locomotive was completed and at work on the initial 300 yards of railway. *Effie* was a simple 0-4-0, not very different from the little 18-inch-gauge Crewe Works engines, with Stephenson valve gear between the frames; she was used for construction work and with the first two carriages, but was quickly superseded. Her movements after about 1890 are an

enduring mystery and later 'sightings' of her – it has been well remarked – have something in common with those of the Loch Ness Monster! However, an official publication of the Grosvenor Estate states that *Effie* was hired for 13 months for construction of the Eaton Railway, and as Sir Arthur almost immediately afterwards inherited Dove Leys from his father, it is possible that she was returned there rather than to Duffield, ready for the next grand plan to create a Dove Bank Railway. Certainly, a long-serving servant of the family later insisted that there had at one time been a steam engine at Dove Leys.

Heywood's principal aim was to produce an engine capable of pulling a useful load up a gradient of 1 in 12 and round a curve of a radius as tight as 25 feet. To achieve this he concluded that the engine must have three or four axles, all connected by cranks; that the wheels of the outer axles should be free to swivel around curves; and that the total weight (including coal, water, and even an allowance for the driver) must be spread equally across all the axles. These requirements sprang to life in the 0-6-0 *Ella* of 1881. To avoid the unbalanced weight of a conventional firebox behind the rear driving axle, a circular 'marine-type' firebox was contained entirely within the 2ft 1in-diameter boiler, supplied by Messrs Abbott of Newark – boilers were the only major component that could not be manufactured at Duffield Bank. The front and rear axles had inner and outer

The second replica of Heywood's *Effie* of 1875, partially built, at Cleethorpes Coast Light Railway workshops in 2010.

elements, the fixed inner shaft (which was driven by the cranks) being linked by ball-joints at its centre point to the cone-shaped outer axles that carried the wheels. These radial axles were cross-connected by a system of hoop-shaped links, by means of which *Ella* and her later sisters guided themselves smoothly around curves. This particular invention has stood the test of time, since a broadly similar plan patented by the German engineers Klein-Lindner in 1892 was used extensively on locomotives with four coupled axles in continental Europe, the last built as recently as 1987.

Heywood's inventive capability was not yet exhausted. Unable (because of the complex axle arrangements between the frames) to use valve gear driven by eccentrics, he devised his own variant of Brown's valve gear, first used on Swiss tram engines. This worked outside the engine frames using rods, links and pins attached between the driving crank and the rear crank. When he later encountered the Brown/Heywood valve gear at Ravenglass, Henry Greenly thought it had too many joints and pins to transmit a wholly accurate setting to the steam inlet valves – but the rebuilt *Muriel/River Irt* largely retains her original mechanics to this day. Interestingly, this type of valve gear had features in common with that of the pioneer engineer Timothy Hackworth; although almost forgotten in Heywood's own day, modified versions of Hackworth's valve gear have been fitted to some recent 15-inch-gauge locomotives. Springing at Duffield Bank was by an early application of rubber blocks.

One of the most noticeable features of all the Heywood engines was the complete lack of any cab for the driver apart from a largely ornamental 'spectacle plate' carrying the pressure gauge, and a polished handrail at the rear; the designer thought that an enclosed cab would hinder escape in the event of a water-gauge glass bursting, or any similar mishap, and that a stout mackintosh would be the driver's best weather protection! All the engines built at Duffield Bank were finished in a dark holly green, fully lined out in red and gold, with vermilion buffer-beams and all the brass and copper fittings highly polished. The ladies of the Heywood family gave their names to the Duffield Bank fleet, while the ladies of the Grosvenor family of the Duke of Westminster appeared at the Eaton Railway.

In all, the Duffield Bank works produced six locomotives:

Effie (0-4-0) 1875 At Duffield Bank until
?1894; later history uncertain; probably to
Eaton Hall to 1896, then to Doveleys
Ella (0-6-0) 1881 From Duffield Bank to
Hill Bros 1916; to Ravenglass 1917;
withdrawn 1926 and frame re-used for
internal-combustion loco No 2 (wrecked
1928); some parts further re-used

Heywood's design of outside valve gear is prominent in this view of *Ursula* at Perrygrove.

Muriel (0-8-0) 1894 On loan to Eaton Hall 1900-02; modified with new boiler 1908-10; from Duffield Bank to Hill Bros 1916; to Ravenglass 1917; converted to 0-8-2 with new boiler 1928; reboilered 1987; still in operation as *River Irt*

Katie (I) (0-4-0) 1894-96 From Eaton Hall to Ravenglass 1916; to Southport 1919; to Fairbourne 1923; withdrawn 1926, frame used as rolling stock and later stored – currently at Ravenglass.

Shelagh (*Katie* (II)) (0-6-0) 1904 To Eaton Hall; renamed *Katie* 1916; scrapped at Balderton 1942

Ursula (0-6-0) 1916 To Eaton Hall; scrapped at Balderton 1942

The technical details of the six locomotives, so thoroughly analysed by Mark Smithers, indicate steady enlargement of the cylinder dimensions, boiler lengths, steam pressure, and the number of fire tubes used. In general terms, the three six-wheeled versions seem to have been the most successful in their original forms: *Ella* was thoroughly tested in 1894 pulling a load of 35 tons on the level, and almost her own weight on the 1 in 12 incline. She was able to run for 50 miles at an average of 7½mph, given hourly stops for water, and managed 1½ hours non-stop on one full tank.

Muriel represented a final attempt by Heywood to interest the Royal Engineers in the use of a heavy eight-coupled machine. But it was the little *Katie* (I) that acquired something of a legendary status in her later life; already well used when sold to Ravenglass, her enduring image is of being stopped for lack of steam on the climb into Eskdale, John Wills patiently sitting on the rear handrail while passengers gather round offering well-meant advice and others drift off to pick lineside flowers! The author remembers seeing her frame, given a lick of grey paint, at the back of the Fairbourne workshops in the 1960s, and we may soon see a rebuilding (rather than a 'replica') on this authentic component at Ravenglass. In the meantime, the replica constructed by FMB Engineering delights visitors to the Eaton Hall gardens open days each year. Other examples are believed to have been completed to 'rolling chassis' stage, so the little 0-4-0 design may well be seen further afield in future. Work has also begun on a replica of the 0-6-0 *Ella* as running before 1900, to further enhance the Heywood Collection at the Perrygrove Railway.

Miniature locomotives for the masses: the Cagney design

The four Irish-American Cagney brothers began trading in their own name in 1894, selling small locomotives to fairground and amusement park operators all over the world; a nickel-plated example was sold to the King

'Age shall not weary them': Heywood's *Muriel* of 1894 is still the chassis of the much-rebuilt *River Irt*, seen at Ravenglass in 2008. *P. Green*

of Siam! The Cagneys used just one prototype – the New York Central Railroad 4-4-0 No 999 – which was claimed in 1893 to have reached a speed of 112¼mph hauling the 'Empire State Express'; the claim was, and still is, hotly disputed on this side of the Atlantic. However, no attempt was made to copy the fine detail of the original; the emphasis was on robustness and simplicity. Many working parts were considerably over-sized, but the overall dimensions were small enough for the same basic design to be built for track gauges between 12⅝ and 22 inches, the 15-inch-gauge version being known as the 'Class D'. Before 1900 all were built by the Cagneys' uncle, Peter McGarigle, at his McGarigle Machine Co at Niagara Falls. In later times the newly named Miniature Railroad Company had many locomotives built by the Herschell-Spillman Co of North Tonawanda, New York – which fitted a distinctive 'wagon top'-shaped boiler – and for this reason the Cagneys are often referred to as 'Herschell-Spillman locomotives'. A few may have come from other contractors, including Captain Boyton's Glasgow Exhibition example of 1901, which a contemporary report curiously attributed to the Baldwin Locomotive Co of Philadelphia.

The total number of 'Cagneys' built has been the subject of varied estimates – certainly as high as 1,300, even possibly more than 3,000. It must surely count as one of the most successful locomotive designs of all time, on any gauge. The good times came to an abrupt end in 1926 following legislation, adopted in most states, that required locomotives used in public to be manned by certified engineers enjoying union pay and conditions. Such an increase in labour costs was prohibitive to the owners of fairgrounds and amusements, and thereafter the locomotives' use was largely confined to museums and private sites, although the Cagney brothers continued in the railway business until switching to war work after 1942.

The Cagney presence in Britain, though interesting, was never large – perhaps a maximum of five locomotives. They appeared at a number of temporary exhibition lines before 1910, and in later years there was one at Southend (the Kürsaal), and the example at Ettrick Bay in Bute. After restoration by Laurence Brooks in

the 1960s, this historic locomotive has been preserved at the **Strumpshaw Steam Museum** near Norwich. Traditionally identified as Charles Bartholomew's 'own' locomotive, this may well be the contemporary, near-identical machine seen at Blakesley Hall in 1904-06. The original Blakesley machine is probably lost, having been spirited away from Dean's Mill around 1943 by some Canadian troops from Burgess Hill on the pretext of repair, never to be returned.

In recent years, the breed has reappeared 'in captivity' at the **Rhyl Miniature Railway** in the shape of Cagney No 44, built at Jersey City about 1910, from the Lancaster & Chester Railway (not 'Railroad') in South Carolina. A standard-gauge line of just 29 miles, the Lancaster & Chester had a wonderful flair for public relations: not only did employees operate their 'Narrow Gauge Division' miniature railway for children in the Springs Recreation Park near Fort Mill at weekends, but the company also enlisted a cast of 29 'celebrities', one for each of its miles, as its Vice-Presidents! The famous striptease impresario 'Gipsy Rose Lee', who had a special responsibility for 'unveiling', visited in 1952 and travelled on the line but – apparently resistant to the '15-inch-gauge bug' – declined to drive the engine. Brought to England in 1999, and with its gauge now reduced from 16 inches back to the original 15 inches in the course of restoration at the **Windmill Farm Railway**, this 'Class D' Cagney is truly a revelation for anyone who might doubt the sheer pulling power of such a pocket-sized machine, as it sprints away from Rhyl Central station and circles the Marine Lake without pausing for breath. Other, similar, engines have been imported from Peru in 2001 and from Canada in 2006, and can be found making occasional special appearances at steam galas.

Before finally leaving the Cagney design, if imitation is the sincerest form of flattery it is perhaps appropriate to mention the American-style 0-4-0 'switcher' (shunter) built in 1950 by the retired engineer Mr R. H. Morse of Potter Heigham in Norfolk for his short private railway. Numbered as Pennsylvania Railroad No 712, it was a robust little machine and was once considered by John Wilkins for use at

Fairbourne. It was sold in 1956 to Mr Lemon Burton for his private line at Paynesfield in Sussex, and acquired in 1998 by the **Evesham Vale Light Railway**, where it currently (2012) awaits overhaul.

'Perfection in Miniature': the Bassett-Lowke 'Little Giant' Classes

Wenman Bassett-Lowke's mantra can surely be applied, without hesitation, to the 4-4-2 (or 'Atlantic') tender locomotives designed by Henry Greenly and built in the new workshop attached to J. T. Lowke's engineering business in Northampton. Built as one-quarter full size, they seem to have had no single prototype, although resembling some of the most up-to-date express locomotives of 1905. To the author's eye, the cab outline is suggestive of the London & North Western Railway, which did of course run through Northampton and liked to call itself 'The Premier Line'. The 'Little Giant' locomotives have already made their appearance in the complex story of the lines built by Miniature Railways of Great Britain Ltd and its successor, Narrow Gauge Railways

Cagney pleasure: No 44 sprints round the Marine Lake at Rhyl on 30 May 2012.

Double Cagney pleasure! No 1904, recently imported from Peru, was built for the 1904 World Trade Fair in New York and is seen with No 44 from Rhyl at the Kirklees Light Railway on 10 September 2009. *D. Verity*

Ltd. As with the Heywood locomotives, the present book can only summarise an extremely complex story, and it is most unfortunate that John Milner and Robin Butterell's monumental research work, *The Little Giant Story*, is now (2012) out of print, and second-hand copies are extremely scarce.

The first series to be built, 'Class 10', seems to have comprised eight actual locomotives, all of which carried several names during their lives, while two (Nos 10 and 11) were also briefly renumbered 14 and 13 respectively at different times. Having limited machine tools at his disposal, Bassett-Lowke formed many of the working parts of the early engines from cast steel or iron, even the main frames being laboriously cut and finished by hand. Small improvements were made as the engines were built, *Mighty Atom* for example having a higher steam pressure than *Little Giant*.

Perhaps, having mentioned most of the class in the historical survey, it is best here to concentrate on the five examples that survive today:

No 10 *Little Giant*

1905	to Blackpool (South Shore) after trials at Eaton Hall
1910	to Halifax Zoo
From 1910 to 1914	ran as *Little Elephant*
1914	returned to Bassett-Lowke, Northampton
1923	to Sunny Vale Railway, Hipperholme
From 1923	ran as No 14 *Baby Bunce*
1948	to Raymond Dunn, Bishop Auckland
1952/53	to Mr Noble (showman) South Shields
From c1953	ran as *Robin Hood*

1957	derelict at a fairground in South Shields
1966	purchased and restored by Mr Tom Tate, Haswell
1980	privately purchased, used briefly at Lightwater Valley and intended for Medina Valley, IoW
1997	visited Saltburn Miniature Railway
2000	exhibited at North Road Station, Darlington
2004	transferred from Darlington to York
2012	displayed (on loan) in National Railway Museum, York

No 11 *Mighty Atom*

1908	to Sutton Park, Birmingham
1909	used briefly at Nancy Exhibition, France as No 13 *Ville de Nancy*
1919	sold to Llewelyn's Miniature Railway, Southport
From 1919	ran as *Prince of Wales*
1929	sold to Great Yarmouth Miniature Railway
1938	transferred to Sutton Park
1953	withdrawn from regular use
1957	last steamed at Sutton Park
2007	to Sutton Collection at Cleethorpes Coast Light Railway, awaiting restoration

Greenly's original *Little Giant*, displayed at the National Railway Museum... *J. Murgatroyd*

...while sister engine *Mighty Atom* awaits restoration at Cleethorpes.

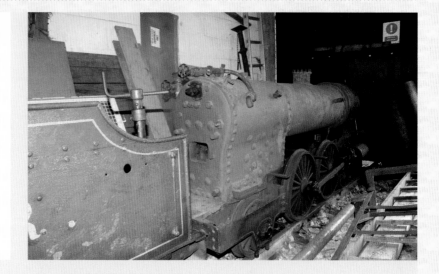

No 15 *Red Dragon*

1909	to White City Exhibition, London
1911	to Rhyl Miniature Railway
From 1911	ran as *Prince Edward of Wales*
1920	sold to Dreamland Miniature Railway, Margate
1968	bought by Robin Butterell as donor machine for rebuild of No 18 *George the Fifth*
1983-91	reconstructed by Gordon Walker and Austin Moss at Southport and Scarisbrick; new frames and boiler and some parts from No 18
1991-98	operated at Lakeside Miniature Railway
2010	at Windmill Farm Railway, Burscough
2011	ran at Rhyl Centenary event (as *Prince Edward of Wales*)

No 18 *George the Fifth*

1911	to Llewelyn's Miniature Railway, Southport
1912	sold to Rhyl Miniature Railway
1922	sold to a 'Mr Bond' at Skegness
1930	sold to Southend Miniature Railway
1936	sold to Belle Vue, Manchester; derelict by 1955
1965	bought by Robin Butterell and John Milner; preliminary restoration
1976	rebuilt by Roger Marsh at Hinckley with tender from No 15 *Red Dragon*
1977	tested at Longleat Railway and formally renamed by Greenly's daughter, Elenora Steel
1979	bought by Sir W. McAlpine for use at Steamtown Miniature Railway, Carnforth
2000	purchased at auction by Francis Ford Coppola; exported to USA
2009	displayed at Reedley Railfest, California, USA
2010	owned by Francis Ford Coppola in USA; renovation in progress

No 19 *Bert Whynne*

1912	to Luna Park Exhibition, Geneva
1913	to Mr M. Meinhardt of Budapest for English fair in 'Angol' (later Vidam) Park

From 1913	Ran as *Hungaria*

1975	last seen in use, with large extended 'windscreen'
1990	on static display at Zanka on shore of Lake Balaton
c1998	owned by Hungarian National Transport Museum and displayed on station platform in Budapest

The story may yet continue into the future, as frames have recently (2011) been laid down for a brand-new Class 10 to be built by volunteers at the **Rhyl Miniature Railway**, as resources permit, truly a wonderful tribute to the lasting appeal of Henry Greenly's design of more than a century ago.

The second series, 'Class 20', or the 'Improved Little Giant' Class (with higher boiler pressure), comprised three locomotives, and it is probable that all survive today. However, almost nothing is known of No 20, which was supplied to the King of Siam (Thailand) – who already had a nickel-plated Cagney locomotive – for the pleasure of the Royal Princes, of whom there apparently were enough to require a complete train. The affairs of the Thai Royal Family are, down to the present day, surrounded by extreme privacy, and it will be very interesting to see whether future researchers can obtain some definite information on what would be a fascinating survival.

No 20

1912	to Royal Palace, Bangkok, with complete train

No 21

1913	to Llewelyn's Miniature Railway, Southport
From 1914	ran as *G. V. Llewellyn*
From 1920	ran as *Lloyd George* (may also have run as *Duke of York*)
From 1930	ran as *Prince of Wales*
From 1933/34	ran as *Princess Elizabeth*

1938	rebuilt by Mr H. N. Barlow after fire damage
1969	sold at auction of Lakeside Miniature Railway
1970	bought by Mr W. McAlpine
1975	operated at Shildon, then to Blenheim Palace
1976	to Steamtown Miniature Railway, Carnforth
2000	purchased at auction by Francis Ford Coppola; exported to USA and restored 2003
2009	displayed in steam at Reedley Railfest, California, USA
2010	owned by Francis Ford Coppola in USA

No 22 *Prince Edward of Wales*

1916	to Fairbourne
1919	overhauled at Northampton
1922	leased back to Ferry Co for use at Fairbourne
1923/24	sold to Llewelyn's Miniature Railway, Southport, and cab modified
From 1924	ran as *Sir Albert Stephenson*
During 1930s	ran as *King George* V, later without the 'V'

1938	rebuilt by Mr H. N. Barlow after fire damage
1969/70	sold to Mr Mason, then to Mr R. Dunn
1976	at Whorlton Lido Railway
1988	at Lightwater Valley Railway
1994	sold to private owner, Derbyshire

The 'Class 30' or 'Sans Pareil' series again contained three actual examples completed by Bassett-Lowke, though it seems that the major parts for five had been put in hand by the outbreak of the First World War in 1914. The general scale was increased from '3 inches to the foot' to about '3¼ inches to the foot', but the key improvement from the two earlier series was the wider firebox extending over the frames, giving a 30% increase in power over the first 'Class 10s'. It is a moot point to what extent the Barnes 'Albion' Class and the two 'Clayton' engines ought to be considered, for all practical purposes, as further developments of the 'Class 30' 'Little Giants'.

The two 'Class 30s' that survive today are detailed below. The third, No 31, may have been tested at Rhyl and worked briefly at the Oslo Exhibition (as *Prins Olaf*), then at Ravenglass as *Sans Pareil* from 1915 to 1926, some parts possibly being re-used in the hybrid *River Mite* (I). Its front bogie survived at the back of Ravenglass shed to do further duty as the trailing unit under the Muir-Hill 'passenger tractor' of 1938.

No 30 *Synolda*

1912	to Sir Robert Walker, Sand Hutton Hall
1922	stored at Sand Hutton and elsewhere
Identity lost	
1930	bought by Southend Miniature Railway from unknown source
1938	sold to Mr H. Dunn, Bishop Auckland
c1942	sold to Belle Vue, Manchester
From c1950	ran as *Prince Charles*
1978	donated to Ravenglass & Eskdale Railway; since fully restored and on display; Frequent visits to numerous locations to date

Synolda, built for Sand Hutton, leads *Sutton Belle* into Lakeside station at Cleethorpes. *P. Green*

No 32

1924	to Count Louis Zborowski, Higham Park
1925	sold to Fairbourne Miniature Railway

Ran as *Count Louis* from 1925

1935	overhauled by Bassett-Lowke, Northampton
1939-45	stored in damaged condition
1947-71	extensively repaired and altered by Mr J. Wilkins (new enlarged tender 1953)
1975	exhibited at 'Rail 150', Shildon
1977	visited Romney, Hythe & Dymchurch Railway
1984	on static display at Fairbourne
2002	to Birmingham Railway Museum, Tyseley, and
	TMA Engineering for restoration by Little Giant Trust Ltd
2009-12	based at Evesham Vale Light Railway

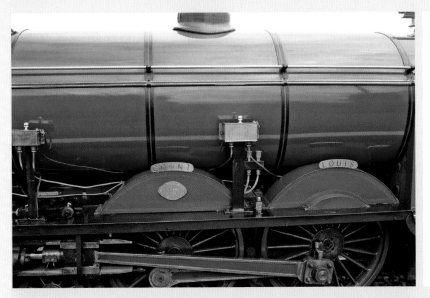

Surely the acme of 'Perfection in Miniature': *Count Louis* at the Evesham Vale Light Railway.

The 'Gigantic' or 'Colossus' Class

Although only the first of these was built by Bassett-Lowke, the two machines were very similar and ended their lives in conjoined form, as the chassis elements of the articulated *River Mite* (I) at Ravenglass. Greenly designed No 60 at the instance of Captain Howey, though in the event war intervened and the engine rarely if ever ran at Staughton Manor. *John Anthony* was tested on the Eaton Railway in 1914 by courtesy of the (second) Duke of Westminster, and doubtless appealed to his taste for speed – he shared with Howey a love of power-boat racing and fast cars. The young railway writer Cecil J. Allen was present at the trials and recorded much technical information until, at 35mph, holding on to the tender took priority over note-making! The significance of the design lay in its being – following the Great Western Railway's *The Great Bear* – only the second British engine built to the 4-6-2 or 'Pacific' wheel arrangement. As it was originally intended for high speed on a private line, the rather light framing of the 'Little Giants' was retained in *John Anthony* – the name was quickly changed to *Colossus* after 1916. Had any further orders been forthcoming, it seems that Bassett-Lowke would have referred to the 'Class 60s' as 'Gigantic'.

It was natural that Sir Aubrey Brocklebank, a Director of the Great Western Railway, should purchase a similar locomotive for himself on becoming interested in the Ravenglass & Eskdale Railway. He commissioned a private consulting engineer, William Cauchi, formerly of the South Eastern & Chatham Railway; seemingly Cauchi approached Bassett-Lowke to use that company's 'Class 60' drawings, but was warned off by Greenly in no uncertain terms. Typically, Greenly then partially relented and allowed Cauchi to 'design up' from the 'Class 30' engines, as he himself had done. The result was an engine with a boiler enlarged to the proportions of a continental rather than a British prototype, and working at higher pressure. This, in turn, may have influenced Greenly to move towards his further enlarged 'one-third-scale' designs of the 1920s.

Sir Aubrey Brocklebank was constructed by Hunt & Co of Bournemouth, better known for marine than for railway engineering, but doubtless happy to oblige the eminent Chairman of the Brocklebank Line and Director of Cunard, with an eye to future business. The new locomotive was tested at Ravenglass in 1919, in the presence of both Greenly and Cauchi – the latter a somewhat shy individual, who withdrew each evening to the safe haven of the Furness Abbey Hotel at Barrow. Henry Greenly himself clearly made a good impression on the owner, being retained as a locomotive designer until he resigned in 1924. There is a wonderful social vignette of the age in the account of Greenly being summoned on one occasion to discuss technical matters with Sir Aubrey – his arrival throwing the Irton Hall footman into consternation as to whether a 'mere engineer' could be admitted at the front door, or should be directed to the Servants' Hall! On that occasion, at least, Greenly's sense of the ridiculous triumphed over any injury to his dignity.

The Barnes 'Albion' Class locomotives, and the Clayton examples

Before moving on to Greenly's work in the 1920s, it is appropriate to return briefly to the **Rhyl Miniature Railway** after its sale in 1912.

A Barnes 'Albion' on home ground: *Joan* at Rhyl Miniature Railway.

The new owners of the railway (and of Rhyl Amusements Ltd), the Butler family of Leeds, recognised its potential and made good use of the local fairground equipment company, the Albion Works. The manager, Albert Barnes, had a background in structural engineering and the locomotive design produced for him by Henry Greenly in 1919 (newly freed from his wartime responsibilities at the Royal Aircraft Factory) was again for a 4-4-2 'Atlantic'; it was very similar to the 'Class 30' 'Little Giants', but able to traverse sharper curves, had an improved trailing axle design, and was slightly easier to service. The close similarity of the designs is evidenced by two of the 'Albion' Class, *John* and *Railway Queen*, having in recent years been fitted with new 'Little Giant'-type boilers. As built, the 'Albion' Class had straight splashers, but two of the six have since acquired the curved type; all have cabs resembling those used on Maunsell's designs for the South Eastern & Chatham Railway. Remarkably, all six engines have survived to the present day.

No 101 *Joan*

1920	to Rhyl
1969	sold to Belle Vue, Manchester
1978	returned to Rhyl; since reboilered
1997/99	visited Windmill Farm Railway
2011	in regular service at Rhyl

Above: The Stephenson valve gear arrangement of 'Albion' Class *Michael*, under restoration in 2010.

Left: A Barnes 'Albion' abroad: *John* at the Evesham Vale Light Railway with driver in 'racing pose'. *P. Green*

'After you, *Billy*.' 'No, no, after you, *Michael*.' All six 'Albion' Class locomotives are shunted into date order at the Rhyl Centenary Gala.

No 102 *Michael* (I)

1921	to Woodland Miniature Railway, Kent (though possibly intended for Margate)
1924	to Saracen's Head, Warburton, Cheshire
From 1925	ran as *George V. Junior*
1928	to Belle Vue, Manchester
From 1928	ran as *Railway Queen*
1949	reboilered by Oxley Engineering
1980s	purchased by Les Hughes
1994	on static display at Llanfair PG, Anglesey
2007	returned to Rhyl for restoration

No 103 *John*

1922	to Rhyl
1969	placed in storage
1978	sold to Alton Towers (mainly on static display)
1985	bought by R. Dunn for Whorlton Lido
?	stored at Lightwater Valley
1996	sold to D. Hibbert; stored at Ravenglass
2011	at Evesham Vale Light Railway

No 104 *Billie* (named after a girl)

1922/23	to Dreamland Miniature Railway, Margate
1968	reboilered
1979	withdrawn from service at Margate
1980	purchased by Les Hughes
1982	overhauled, then used at Dudley Zoo
1984	returned to Rhyl
1993	sold to private owner in Kent
2011	displayed (unrestored) at Rhyl Centenary

No 105 *Michael* (II)

1925	to Rhyl
1969	placed in storage
1978	sold to Alan Keef and returned to use
1980	bought by Les Hughes and used at Dudley Zoo until c1982
1984	returned to Rhyl
1994	on static display at Llanfair PG, Anglesey
2007	returned to Rhyl
2010/11	full restoration to working order

No 106 *Billy* (named after a boy**)**

1930	to Rhyl
1969	placed in storage
1978	purchased by Rhyl Town Council
1981	operated at Rhyl on loan from Council
1982	last steamed at Rhyl
1985/86	restored by Gratton Engineering
2007	exhibited in 'Albert Barnes Room', Rhyl

The two locomotives built by Douglas Clayton complete the tally of 'Little Giant'-type machines. The major castings were supplied by Bassett-Lowke between 1912 and 1914, but assembly did not start until 1930, by which date neither Bassett-Lowke nor Henry Greenly had retained a full set of drawings. The work commenced in Douglas Clayton's private workshop at Coseley Hall, and was completed in the Cannon Ironfounders' fitting shop at Deepfields, Coseley, under the superintendence of Arthur Aston in 1933. The result was a handsome, partly freelance design, which ran so successfully at Hardwicke Manor that work began on the second machine in 1938 using slightly smaller driving wheels. Unfinished at Douglas Clayton's death in 1947, it was assembled by Tom and Bill Hunt and entered service at Sutton Coldfield in 1952. Both locomotives now operate at the **Cleethorpes Coast Light Railway**.

Greenly's work at Ravenglass

With Bassett-Lowke effectively withdrawing from involvement with 15-inch-gauge locomotives after 1919, Greenly's later commissions reached him by different routes. His attention first turned to machines for freight haulage, when Sir Robert Walker of Sand Hutton obtained outline sketches for a 2-8-4 tank locomotive and a 2-6-2 tender version,

the latter in some respects anticipating the *Northern Rock* design produced at Ravenglass two generations later. In his journalistic work, Greenly – like Sir Robert – 'ploughed a lonely furrow' by advocating 15-inch and 18-inch railways for the modernisation of agricultural estates. In 1922 he travelled to Berlin, meeting Dr Walter Strauss (who in 1938 wrote his German work on *Liliputbahnen*, mainly describing British lines with gauges between 2½ and 21 inches), and also visiting the Krauss locomotive works at Munich, where he undoubtedly found a kindred spirit in Roland Martens, and possibly selected the Krauss design of 'pony truck' to be used as the leading axle on *River Esk*.

At Ravenglass the need was for year-round haulage of granite combined with higher-speed working of summer-season passenger trains, and neither the existing scale model engines nor the Heywood designs were entirely suitable – Greenly had expected more of *Ella* and *Muriel* than they were able to deliver. An entirely new design was conceived, the first British locomotive with a 2-8-2 wheel arrangement and the first 15-inch-gauge example built to one-third scale, the driver being seated on the tender but entirely protected within the extended cab roof. With a steam pressure of 180psi, the new machine was to have twice the power of *Colossus* and *Sir Aubrey Brocklebank*. Considered by many, including this author,

Greenly's masterpiece? *River Esk* rests outside Ravenglass locomotive shed. *P. Green*

as Greenly's all-time masterpiece, *River Esk* was very much a collaboration with the firm of Davey, Paxman at Colchester; Greenly had already worked with the firm on the 'Peache' high-speed steam engine used for power stations. Davey, Paxman's experience of Lentz poppet-valve cylinders in refrigeration plants did not, in the event, transfer too happily to railway application, and the same was true of the Paxman patent valve gear but, when these 'innovations too far' had been replaced by conventional designs, *River Esk* settled down as the mainstay of the Ravenglass fleet for 40 years. There could be no higher compliment than the design being almost exactly reproduced in 1965 when the Preservation Society sponsored *River Mite* (II).

River Esk was delivered at the end of 1923, but despite the evident need for more motive power there was to be no funding for sister locomotives. In June 1923 the Locomotive Superintendents of the 'Big Four' main-line companies visited Ravenglass, and Greenly was subsequently elected an associate member of the Institution of Locomotive Engineers. But for the next few years Greenly's energies would

be concentrated at New Romney, and he gave up his active involvement both at Ravenglass and with Bassett-Lowke early in 1924.

In his remaining years Sir Aubrey Brocklebank instigated a policy of rebuilding the best of what he had. A flurry of activity in 1927-28 in partnership with the Yorkshire Engine Company saw the erstwhile *Muriel* transformed with an extended frame, a trailing axle, a conventional firebox and boiler, and a new tender and cab to become the squat but practical *River Irt* – to be rebuilt again, with a much more attractive outline, in 1984. As already related, the chassis units of the two 'Pacifics' were coupled back-to-back under a massive new boiler and supporting frame to become the first *River Mite*, surviving in this form until 1938. Some of its mortal remains were said to have been purchased by Harry Barlow at Southport for re-use, but their ultimate fate is not known to the author. Even *River Esk* was not immune from well-meant 'improvements', the fitting of conventional Walschaerts valve gear in 1927 being accompanied by a supplementary steam engine in the tender; the Yorkshire Engine Company was the licensed user of Poultney's patent for auxiliary power. Since the steam supply to the main cylinders had to be limited in order to feed the powered tender, the whole arrangement was suggestive of 'robbing Peter to pay Paul' and was removed in 1931. The Directors were already very well aware of the potential of internal-combustion power to handle mineral traffic, and to supplement *River Esk* and *River Irt* at times of high passenger demand.

Greenly's work at the Romney, Hythe & Dymchurch Railway

We have already seen that Henry Greenly played a crucial role in the birth of the 'Main Line in Miniature'. At New Romney the emphasis was first and last to be on the appearance and performance of the locomotives from the perspective of the owners and drivers; the experience of the passengers in uncomfortable, four-wheeled open-sided coaches was a relatively minor consideration.

Count Zborowski (who ordered the first two locomotives) and Captain Howey had a very definite prototype in mind: the Class 'A1' (later Class 'A3') 'Pacifics' of the London & North Eastern Railway, represented today by the preserved *Flying Scotsman* in the National Collection. Their designer, Nigel Gresley, shared Howey's enthusiasms and was to become a regular visitor to New Romney. The first to be

finished, *Green Goddess*, took her name from a contemporary West End stage success by William Archer and was tested at Ravenglass in June 1925, the first time that Captain Howey had driven for ten years. She proved the equal of *River Esk* in its original form and touched 35mph – the 'scale equivalent' of about 105mph on the main line!

The first three locomotives were of conventional (for the 15-inch-gauge) construction with two outside cylinders. In Nos 4 and 5 Howey's wish to be true to the prototype brought about a three-cylinder design, emitting the correct six beats per wheel revolution at the chimney. Almost inevitably, the fitting of a crank axle and Greenly's valve gear in the confined space between the frames led to lubrication problems, breakdowns and ultimately a seizing-up; the experiment was reluctantly abandoned in 1935-36 and the wheels were re-quartered on the axles to run with just two cylinders.

For use on stone ballast trains, and with a view to the steep gradients on a possible branch line to the Southern Railway station at Sandling, Greenly had been commissioned to produce an eight-coupled locomotive. Having regard to Howey's penchant for reckless speed, and perhaps also to his dislike of things German, a four-wheeled front bogie was substituted for the Krauss 'pony truck' as used on *River Esk*, resulting in a unique (for Britain)

A timeless scene at New Romney, as Zborowski's *Green Goddess* awaits departure towards Hythe in 1995.

The Captain's engine: a classic view of *Hurricane* at New Romney on 30 May 2010. *J. Cleaver*

4-8-2 (or 'Mountain') wheel arrangement. The ballast traffic never reached the expected level, and while *Hercules* was allowed to haul the inaugural passenger train on 16 July 1927, for some unaccountable reason the Captain took a marked personal dislike to the unfortunate *Samson*, which languished out of use for many years. Passenger numbers after the Second World War demanded a recall to service, and the story had a happy ending – 'Cinderella did go to the ball', not once but twice, to the Liverpool International Garden Festival in 1984, and to the Bure Valley Railway in 1990. A lady friend of the author's family, not naturally an enthusiast, phoned him to say that she had just seen 'the most beautiful, perfect little steam engine' heading through the Liverpool suburbs on a lorry (rather than Cinderella's glass coach!), bound for the Garden Festival site.

The story of the Canadian Pacific-inspired locomotives has already been related, because it is central to the tangled relationship between Greenly and Howey, ending in the engineer's precipitate departure from New Romney. Although very different in appearance from the earlier 4-6-2s, they were mechanically similar except for the enforced use of Krauss-built boilers designed by Roland Martens. The steam locomotive fleet then remained unchanged until relatively modern times; interestingly, the more

recent additions have been one of Martens's own 4-6-2s built by Krupp of Essen, and the rescue and return home in 1978 of *The Bug* first used in construction.

In summary form, the Greenly locomotives to be seen today at New Romney are:

No 1 *Green Goddess* 4-6-2
(Davey, Paxman, 1925)
No 2 *Northern Chief* 4-6-2
(Davey, Paxman, 1925)
No 3 *Southern Maid* 4-6-2
(Davey, Paxman, 1927)
No 5 *Hercules* 4-8-2 (Davey, Paxman, 1927)
No 6 *Samson* 4-8-2 (Davey, Paxman, 1927)
No 7 *Typhoon* 4-6-2 (Davey, Paxman, 1927)
No 8 *Hurricane* (*Bluebottle* 1939-46) 4-6-2
(Davey, Paxman, 1927)
No 9 *Winston Churchill* (*Dr Syn* until 1946)
4-6-2 (Jackson, Rigby and Yorkshire
Engine Co, 1929-31)
No 10 *Dr Syn* (*Black Prince* until 1946) 4-6-2
(Jackson, Rigby and Yorkshire Engine Co,
1929-31)

From the 1950s onwards the Romney locomotives have been extensively modernised with superheated boilers and some experimental use of oil-firing, but it is a wonderful tribute to their designer and to the skilled drivers and engineers at New Romney that all are still in service, to be seen and enjoyed today in a wide range of liveries. Drivers traditionally kept to a single locomotive, and had some influence in the choice of colour and decoration. *Hurricane* was always Captain Howey's choice, Eric Copping drove *Typhoon* for eight years and, in what must surely be a world record, George Barlow drove *Green Goddess* for no fewer than 31 years before taking on the role of Operating Manager. It seemed only fitting that on completion of 30 years on the footplate (and after finishing his day's shift!) his colleagues presented him with 30 bottles of Guinness.

The Romney locomotives are frequent visitors to other 15-inch-gauge railways; indeed, it could almost be said that no steam gala is complete without one making an appearance. Running on lines such as the Ravenglass & Eskdale and Bure Valley allows their performance to be evaluated against that of the home fleets.

'Germany's Greenly': the locomotives of Roland Martens

Martens has already been briefly mentioned in our story, but deserves a place of his own as three of his splendid 4-6-2 designs (and of course, *The Bug* at New Romney) have been brought to England. He was mainly trained at the Maffei works in Munich, but seemingly had enough main-line experience to have qualified as fireman and driver. After 1906 he worked as a consulting engineer, first for the German Government then for a chemical firm in Alsace. Clearly something of an Anglophile, he built 1/24th-scale models of several British locomotives, and by 1912 was sufficiently well-off to buy a 9½-inch-gauge Bassett-Lowke model of a Great Northern Railway 4-4-2 – then costing around £300! – with his own initials, 'RM', rather than 'GNR' on the tender.

By 1923 Martens was back in Munich as Oberingenieur of the small locomotive department of Maffei's sister firm, Krauss (the two later merged), and was well known to his 'dear friend' Henry Greenly. In 1923-25 he was commissioned to build locomotives for a 381mm (15-inch) line at the Deutsche Verkehrs Ausstellung in Munich, later operated in a pleasure park at Dresden; similar *parkeisenbahnen* – often connected with exhibitions – appeared in subsequent years in Leipzig and Köln (Cologne) in Germany, at Cork in Eire, at Toulouse in France and also at Seville in Spain.* He used no exact prototype, but with a marvellous eye for outline and

The boiler of a Roland Martens 'Pacific' – as used at New Romney (and Bressingham) – rests among the autumn leaves on the Wiener Liliputbahn in November 2011.
W. Parkes

* Three of the four Spanish examples built in 1929 have survived, now believed to be in private ownership and preserved since 2002 at the F. C. del Maresne near Barcelona. The fate of the French engines remains a mystery.

Martens highly modified: *Black Prince* on Hythe turntable.
P. Green

proportion designed a one-third-scale version of a typical German main-line *schnellzüglokomotiv* of the period, capable of taking curves with a radius as sharp as 20 metres. Greenly was consulted on many aspects, and all the Krauss-built 4-6-2s incorporated his preference for smokebox steam driers and used the British type of double, rather than the German single, slide bars. But the large, free-steaming boilers with their copper fireboxes should certainly be credited to Martens, and, as we have seen, Krauss later supplied two examples to rescue Captain Howey's Canadian Pacific design from the doldrums. In 1949 another engine was supplied to the Tata works in India, and survives today at the Bal Bhavan Children's Railway in New Delhi, although out of use for several years.

At least 15 engines were built by Krauss – the last three as late as 1950 – but the examples now in Britain, exceptionally, were built by Fried Krüpp AG of Essen in 1937, for use at a trade exhibition at Düsseldorf and a garden exhibition in the Gruga Park at Essen. How good it is to think of these beautiful, pleasure-giving machines emerging from the firm so often associated with the Third Reich's militarism! After the Düsseldorf line closed, it was intended that they would run at a Transport Exhibition in Köln in 1940, but war prevented this and fortunately the three locomotives and 35 coaches were safely stored, well outside the city. They were retrieved and overhauled for exhibition events in 1951, 1953 and 1957, then stored again until 1972, when Alan Bloom of Bressingham – plantsman and steam enthusiast extraordinary – learned 'on the grapevine' (so to speak!) that their owner might be willing to sell. In the event, only two – works numbers 1662 and 1663, named *Rosenkavalier* and *Männertreu* in 1957*, with 19 coaches – were available, but in 1973 the first section of the **Waveney Valley Railway** at Bressingham Gardens was opened.

Three years later the owner of the remaining engine decided that this too could be sold, and it was the Romney, Hythe & Dymchurch Railway that became the proud possessor of Krupp's No 1664 *Fleissig Lieschen* (*Busy Lizzie*).

---

* The original names had been *Donner* and *Blitz*, but these were discarded by a visitors' poll!

Originally the livery had been Prussian blue but, whereas the Bressingham engines had been repainted in dark green with white and black lining, New Romney transformed its engine into contemporary German main-line black with red wheels, and re-used the name *Black Prince*. Practical modifications included a lower position for the driver within the cab, giving better protection from the Dungeness weather, new injectors and water gauges, and of course the standard Romney couplings, buffers and vacuum brake. Recent alterations including a high running plate have still further altered the appearance, for better or for worse, according to personal taste.

Internal-combustion power to 1939

Some of the earliest applications of petrol engines to rail traction appeared on the 15-inch-gauge. Exactly as with steam locomotives, two distinct types quickly appeared: the 'no frills' industrial-type machine, which in its earliest forms tended to resemble a wooden box on wheels, and the 'steam-outline' version, which pretended to its passengers to be a model main-line locomotive with dummy boiler, cylinders and chimney.

As early as 1905 Charles Bartholomew recognised the potential of 'instant power' to deliver supplies to Blakesley Hall, especially coal for electricity generation. As the owner

of a Humber car, with an estate engineer who was a competent motor mechanic, he had no difficulty in producing *Petrolia*, a 4-4-4 unit with a twin-cylinder, horizontal water-cooled engine, a three-speed bi-directional gearbox – and a 6-foot-tall chimney to carry the exhaust fumes clear of passengers! It could haul six coal trucks up to the Hall, reach 30mph on a downhill trip with the passenger coaches, and run well enough to be substantially rebuilt by Bassett-Lowke in 1910. Its ultimate fate is unknown, though some components were probably used in the machine assembled by R. H. Morse for use at Dean's Mill in Sussex in 1937.

Henry Greenly's *Blacolvesley* was one of the most remarkable and handsome of his early designs and the first example of 'steam-outline' petrol power. Some castings and fittings were identical to the 'Little Giant' engines, but the boiler casing concealed a narrow 12hp NAG car engine connected to the driving wheels by a three-gear Wicksteed patent gearbox and separate reverse; cleverly, the exhaust passing up the chimney pulled cooling air through a radiator concealed within the smokebox. The external appearance was of a 4-4-4 tank locomotive, and the author is tempted to see both London & North Western (Bassett-Lowke) and Metropolitan Railway (Greenly) influences in the perfectly proportioned body outline.

Greenly's *Blacolvesley* formed the centrepiece of the 'Rails to the Sands' exhibition at Cleethorpes.

Blacolvesley passed to Charles Bartholomew's secretary in 1919, who kept it to remind her of 'many happy hours spent on the railway' until 1943; it was then purchased by Mr Younger of Ponteland, fitted with an Austin Seven engine and renamed *Yvonne*. A few years later Raymond Dunn acquired it for use at **Saltburn**, and around Coronation Year (1953) the name changed again to *Elizabeth* and a wholly unsuccessful attempt was made to streamline the appearance. Fortunately, the historic machine was recognised by Tom Tate of Haswell in 1968 and purchased for restoration; magnificently restored to its original name and livery, *Blacolvesley* is now owned by Dr Robert Tebb, and in 2010-11 it fittingly formed the centrepiece of the 'Rails to the Sands' seaside railways exhibition at the **Miniature Railway Museum** at Cleethorpes.

Surprisingly little use was made of internal-combustion power in the years just after the First World War, despite the numbers of 'Simplex'-type engines built for the 2-foot-gauge trench supply railways, which could quite cheaply have been re-gauged. In the early 1920s Ravenglass experimented with lightweight motor trolleys, which had to be manually turned to face the direction of travel, until a bogie locomotive based around a Ford T car – with a wooden-planked body – appeared in 1925 and promptly claimed the line's speed record for the downhill trip! Shortly afterwards, the chassis of the worn-out Heywood 0-6-0 *Ella* was fitted with the mechanics of a Lanchester car and proved able to match the pulling power of the steam locomotives on mineral trains. Even more successful were the heavy-framed Muir-Hill tractors using Fordson petrol/tvo engines, one of which acquired a trailing bogie and steam-outline body in 1933 and undoubtedly played a major role in keeping the Ravenglass & Eskdale passenger service a viable operation until the end of the 1950s. As overhaul of the **Eaton Railway** steam locomotives had proved difficult after Sir Arthur Heywood's death in 1916, the Duke of Westminster bought a new 'Simplex' engine from the Motor Rail & Tramcar Co in 1922 and another in 1938, enabling the line to carry on throughout the Second World War.

The interesting designs built by Commander Parkinson of Sheringham for use at Great Yarmouth and Southend have already been briefly mentioned. The Southend example was a 2-4-0 of 'steam-outline' type and, like the later Barlow design, had the petrol engine in the tender; it later ran briefly at Saltburn (1947-48). The Great Yarmouth machine resembled a North Eastern Railway centre-cab electric locomotive and was powered by a 10hp Chapuis Dornier motor. More remarkable still was the twin-coach Austin Seven petrol-electric railcar set, which delivered acceleration to rival a contemporary Tube train. On the opposite side of Britain, the **Porthcawl** line used 'steam-outline' petrol locomotives from its outset in 1932, while the **Fairbourne Railway** acquired a lightweight Lister Blackstone-type RT tractor in 1935 (with no pretensions at bodywork until rebuilt in 1955), which did at least keep a service of sorts running through to 1940, and possibly just tipped the balance in favour of the line's survival.

Miniature railways on wider gauges, emerging in the 1930s, have universally used internal-combustion power; the operations using the 20-inch and 21-inch gauge generally favouring diesel-hydraulic units by Hudswell Clarke of Leeds, while the 2-foot-gauge lines at **Lilleshall Abbey**, **Alton Towers**, **Wicksteed Park** and **Trentham Gardens** used only petrol or diesel locomotives by Baguley of Burton-on-Trent until very recent years.

The 'Barlow Pacifics'

Harry N. Barlow of Kew Road, Southport, took control of the Lakeside Miniature Railway in 1933, and faced a motive power crisis five years later when both the 'Little Giant' 'Class 20' steam locomotives were badly damaged in an engine shed blaze. (Exactly how much of the originals survived is a mystery, and the author is tempted to speculate whether Barlow's purchase of the remaining parts of *Colossus* and *Sir Aubrey Brocklebank* from Ravenglass in 1939 was in some way connected with their resurrection.) At all events, it was clear to him that after the Second World War those miniature railways that had survived would be in urgent need of new, economical motive power.

Wartime surplus equipment offered the

The unmistakeable outline of the first 'Barlow Pacific', *Duke of Edinburgh* from 1948, restored at Windmill Farm Railway.

best, perhaps the only, source of engines and transmissions in the form of diesel tractor engines and searchlight electric generators. The power was generated in the 'tender' unit on which the driver sat, and transmitted to a second searchlight unit acting as traction motor, geared down to the 'locomotive' driving wheels. Beginning in 1948 with a single machine for his own **Lakeside Miniature Railway**, Barlow's workshop at Upper Aughton Road, Southport, went on to produce eight examples for the 15-inch-gauge and two for the 2-foot gauge 'Silver Belle' streamlined train on Southport Pier – which crossed over their siblings on the Lakeside line several times each hour. The final example, *Golden Jubilee*, built for Lakeside in 1963, utilised an advanced form of hydraulic, rather than electric, transmission. Its bodywork was inspired by the English Electric 'GT3' prototype gas-turbine locomotive, which – had it been successful – might have been used to convert hundreds of 4-6-0 steam locomotive chassis about to be withdrawn by British Railways. The Pier locomotives, and *Golden Jubilee* – like the recently built *City of London* – were actually of 4-6-0 wheel arrangement, suggesting that the trailing pony truck on the other examples may have been a troublesome feature.

Most of the locomotives have moved to several locations during their lives, and have enjoyed (or endured) changes of name along the way – to say nothing of the bizarre bodywork carried by the three Festival of Britain units

Latter-day 'Barlow' design: *City of London*, at Windmill Farm, incorporates wheels from a former Southport Pier (2-foot-gauge) train.

in 1951! Uniquely, the 1948-built *Duke of Edinburgh* had just two bands around its streamlined casing, while the later machines all had five, so its wanderings can more easily be traced in photographs; as Michael Caine might have said, 'Not many people know that!' Six of the originals have survived, and the author gratefully acknowledges the pioneering research of Lawson Little (published in *The Narrow Gauge*, No 176) and the help of Mr Austin Moss and several enthusiasts in supplying information for the following summary, which he hopes will be as accurate as possible:

[No 1] 4-6-2 *Duke of Edinburgh* (I)

1948	to Lakeside Miniature Railway, Southport
1956	to Lytham St Annes as *Princess Anne*
1962	to Butlins, Skegness
1974	to J. H. Rundle, dealer
1976	to Bird Paradise, Hayle
1984	to Haigh Hall, Wigan
1987	to Jubilee Miniature Railways, Southport
1990	privately purchased for preservation
1998	to Windmill Farm, Burscough

[No 2] 4-6-2 *Duke of Edinburgh* (II)

1950	to Alexandra Palace, North London
1971	to Knowsley Safari Park as *Sir Nigel Gresley*
1994	privately purchased for preservation
1997	to Windmill Farm, Burscough
2008-10	at Lakeside Miniature Railway, Southport; name restored

[No 3] 4-6-2 *Princess Anne*

1951	to FT&OR, Battersea Park, as *Nellie*
1953-54	rebuilt at Southport
1954	to (new line in) Battersea Park as *Princess Anne*
1975	to Powell Dyffryn, Portsmouth
1977	to Medina Valley Project, IoW
c1982	scrapped

[No 4] 4-6-2 *Princess Margaret*

1951	to FT&OR, Battersea Park, as *Neptune*
1953-54	rebuilt at Southport
1954	to (new line in) Battersea Park as *Princess Margaret*
1975	to Powell Dyffryn, Portsmouth
1977	to Medina Valley Project, IoW
c1982	scrapped

[No 5] 4-6-2 *Prince Charles*

1951	to FT&OR, Battersea Park, as *Wild Goose*
1953-54	rebuilt at Southport
1954	to (new line in) Battersea Park as *Prince Charles*
c1960	returned to Southport
2006	at Windmill Farm, Burscough
2010	at Lakeside Miniature Railway, Southport
2012	at Windmill Farm, Burscough

[No 6] 4-6-2 *Prince Charles*
1954	to Saltburn Miniature Railway
1960s-1989	ran as *Prince of Wales*
1987	overhauled at National Engineering Training Centre, Stockton-on-Tees
2004	re-engined with Perkins 1004 diesel
2012	in service at Saltburn Miniature Railway

[No 7] 4-6-0 *Silver Belle* (1) (2-foot gauge)
1954	to Southport Pier
1976	reserve locomotive for new train
c1982	scrapped

[No 8] 4-6-0 *Silver Belle* (2) (2-foot gauge)
1954	to Southport Pier
1976	to Steamport, Southport
c1982	scrapped

[No 9] 4-6-2 *Princess Anne*
1956	to Lakeside Miniature Railway, Southport, as *Duke of Edinburgh* (III)
c1962	renamed on return of No 1 from Lytham St Annes
2012	at Windmill Farm, Burscough

[No 10] 4-6-0 *Golden Jubilee 1911-1961*
1963	to Lakeside Miniature Railway, Southport
2012	still in service at Lakeside

Remarkably, as recently as 1987 the wheels and some other parts of the *Silver Belle* (2) unit have been rebuilt by Jubilee Volante into a new 15-inch-gauge 4-6-0 version of the type, resembling the LNER's streamlined 'B17' Class engine No 2870 *City of London* used on the 'East Anglian' express service from London to Norwich – a fitting tribute to Harry Barlow's pragmatic and workmanlike design of nearly 40 years earlier. After spending some time at Windmill Farm, this unique machine may now (2012) be sold on.

Ernest W. Twining, Trevor Guest and the 'freelance' movement

Ernest W. Twining (no relation to the famous family of tea merchants) was born in 1875 and was thus a contemporary of Sir Arthur Heywood as well as W. J. Bassett-Lowke and Henry Greenly. He played an important role in reinventing the idea of 'freelance' rather than scale model building in the 1930s. He was first apprenticed to the Western Counties & South Wales Telephone Co and studied at the Bristol Fine Art Academy, where his hobbies included photography, then worked in the telephone industry in Glasgow from 1901 before moving to London in 1904. He established his own firm, Twining Models, at Hanwell – building some of the earliest model aeroplanes – before moving to premises at the rear of J. T. Lowke's works in Northampton and specialising in architectural and showcase models. The firm continued until 1965, although Twining himself sold his interest in 1940. Interestingly, Twining had done much of the detailed work on the 'scaling up' of Greenly's 'Class 30' 4-4-2s into the 'Class 60' 4-6-2 *John Anthony/Colossus*, being instructed to retain as many 'Class 30' components as possible to save cost.

His scale-model locomotive designs began around 1932 with a 9½-inch-gauge 4-6-2 for a line at Mablethorpe. This was followed by a 10¼-inch-gauge 4-6-0 for Trevor Guest in 1938, used on the first line at Dudley Zoo.

After the Second World War a scale model of an LMS Class 5 4-6-0 in 15-inch-gauge was designed by E. W. Twining and J. N. Maskelyne; it operated at Dudley Zoo from 1949 to 1960, then at the Fairbourne Railway, where the limitations of its narrow firebox and fine-scale wheel flanges became only too apparent. *Prince Charles* was rebuilt in 1968 as a 4-6-2 with a wider firebox, and renamed *Winston Churchill* then, more recently, *Prince William*, it led a useful life at the **Blenheim Park Railway**, **Steamtown (Carnforth)** and **Windmill Farm**, then passing to the former owners of the **Evesham Vale Light Railway**.

The next locomotive was built as a wide-firebox 4-6-2 from the start. *Ernest W. Twining* was completed in 1950 and after the obligatory decade at Dudley Zoo transferred to Fairbourne in 1961. Proving ideal for the line, it was subsequently modified with a light blue livery,

a cowcatcher, and shutters to the cab windows giving a distinctively 'colonial' appearance. It fortunately survived the 1984-85 changes at Fairbourne and has been preserved since 1987 in Japan – though not currently in working order – on the Shuzenji Romney Railway at Niji-No-Sato south of Tokyo. Strange and wonderful things can happen in the world of small locomotives; who can say whether, one day, *Ernest W. Twining* might be repatriated to Britain?

It is probably for his sister 2-4-2 machines, *Katie* and *Siân*, that Twining will be best remembered. Clearly developed from ideas for 18-inch-gauge 0-4-2s and 0-6-2s that he had published in 1934, these were simple, practical 15-inch-gauge machines with high-pitched boilers, generous fireboxes, tall chimneys for good steaming, and frames outside the driving wheels, as used by Heywood. Twining died,

The classic Trevor Guest 0-4-2 diesel *Clara* of 1961, restored and at work on the Rhyl Miniature Railway.

Another Guest design – the powerful eight-wheeled diesel-hydraulic used at Dudley Zoo and later at Cricket St Thomas, now at Windmill Farm.

aged 80, just at the time *Katie* was completed in 1956 for Dudley Zoo and named after Trevor Guest's mother (no reference to the earlier *Katie* of Eaton Hall and Fairbourne). After only a year of use, *Katie* was seen and purchased by the eccentric Captain Vivian Hewitt of Cemaes Bay, Anglesey, a collector of all things mechanical, who intended to set up a 15-inch-gauge railway on his West Indies coconut plantation! In the event the Captain died before his scheme was realised and *Katie* subsequently joined her younger sister at Fairbourne. Intended for Fairbourne from the outset, *Siân* was ordered by John Wilkins at the end of 1962 and was equipped wherever possible with sealed bearings, to overcome the perennial problem of wind-blown sand. One economy measure was the use of a steel, rather than copper, firebox in the boiler. After their sale from Fairbourne, both locomotives led an itinerant life with time at the Bure Valley, Haigh Hall, Littlecote Park, Kirklees and Cleethorpes – and possibly other venues! – before being reunited at the **Windmill Farm Railway** for restoration.

The role of Trevor Guest was perhaps more as a railway operator and locomotive builder, with his designs focussing on internal-combustion locomotives; petrol was the favoured fuel where commissions for Fairbourne were concerned, John Wilkins having a personal aversion to the noise and smell of diesels. The G&S Light Engineering Co (later called Engineering and Maintenance) had been formed by Trevor Guest and his friend Raymond Saunders in the 1930s, based in the Guest family's sand quarry at Stourbridge. A 15-inch diesel locomotive resembling a Great Western streamlined railcar was built in 1946 and sold from Dudley Zoo to the Sutton Miniature Railway in 1957. Its replacement was a petrol-mechanical engine, which survived to be sold to Alan Keef in 1978 and later ran at the Cricket St Thomas Wildlife Park, heavily disguised as a (moving) thatched cottage! G&S provided a handsome new body for the Fairbourne Railway's *Dingo* in 1954 and built the 0-6-0 *Rachel* and the twin-cab bogie *Sylvia* to further enhance John Wilkins's fleet. A variation on the theme was the steam-outline 0-4-2 *Clara*, also of 1961, which remained at Dudley until sold to Alan Keef in 1978 for use

in his Rhyl project. *Clara* has remained at Rhyl to the present day, receiving a new engine in 1996 and another in 2012.

Perhaps the most interesting G&S product was the 'hybrid' *Tracy-Jo*, named after Trevor Guest's daughter and based on the 2-foot-gauge Vale of Rheidol 2-6-2 tank engines. She had been ordered by Captain Hewitt, but the order was cancelled before a boiler has been constructed and *Tracy-Jo* emerged in 1964 as a petrol-mechanical machine. She ran briefly at Fairbourne in this form before being stored at Dudley in 1966-67, then pursued an itinerant existence at New Romney, Blenheim Palace, the Lightwater Valley, Carnforth (Steamtown) and Kirklees. The story ended happily, as Winson Engineering converted the chassis back to steam with a new boiler in 1991, and – renamed *Wroxham Broad* – she is today a valuable member of the **Bure Valley Railway** locomotive fleet, owned by a specialist preservation group.

Modern locomotive designs for the 15-inch-gauge

We have seen that the half-century since 1960 has been remarkable both for the proliferation of new lines and for the preservation of classic ones by enthusiasts. This has encouraged new and highly talented designers to come onto the scene; specialist locomotive building firms have found miniature railways to be a valuable 'niche' market; and some of the railway companies themselves have branched out into locomotive manufacture. This has flourished since the 1980s against a background of decline in the wider British manufacturing and engineering industries. It may even be, paradoxically, that the availability of large quantities of second-hand machine tools and equipment, suitable for miniature locomotive work, actually encouraged the process. While the following account cannot be comprehensive, it may serve as an appreciation of a wonderfully productive period, which has equipped 15-inch-gauge railways in the early 21st century with a varied and interesting range of modern designs, running alongside lovingly preserved historic machines.

David Curwen

Born in 1913, and widely recognised as a doyen of the miniature railway world, David Curwen's early engineering experience was with motor cars and flying boats – the latter with Short Brothers of Rochester-upon-Medway. In 1946 he began building steam locomotives in gauges up to 10¼ inches; his first large-scale model was an 18-inch-gauge 4-4-2 for Tommy Mann's Fairy Glen Miniature Railway at New Brighton. He designed more than 50 locomotives to be built at his own workshop at All Cannings near Devizes, or by commercial manufacturers. Notably, the firm of Severn-Lamb built more than 36 examples to his designs, with no fewer than 18 of the

company's standard 'Rio Grande' steam-outline 2-8-0s with petrol, gas or diesel power units being for the 15-inch-gauge. He enjoyed an extremely long and fulfilling life until his death in June 2011.

While some enthusiasts regard Curwen's 10¼-inch and 12¼-inch designs – such as the half-scale *Jubilee* and *Beddgelert* narrow-gauge engines built for John Ellerton – as his finest work, a listing of his own 15-inch-gauge output reveals his remarkable range of talent. The reference numbers are those used in the Narrow Gauge Railway Society's comprehensive catalogue of his work, edited by Lawson Little and David Holroyde.

48 0-6-0 *Muffin*

1967	built by Berwyn Engineering for Longleat Miniature Railway; tested at Blenheim Palace
1976	to Lappa Valley Railway
1991	rebuilt by N. J. Tambling

49(e) C-C *Princess Anne* (diesel-hydraulic)

1971	built by Severn-Lamb for Lakeside Miniature Railway
2003	repaired by Alan Keef Engineering
2006	repaired by Austin Moss

50 4-C-4 *Shelagh of Eskdale* (diesel)

1969	completed by Severn-Lamb Ltd for Ravenglass & Eskdale Railway
1984	ran at Liverpool Garden Festival
1990	ran at Gateshead Garden Festival
1998	rebuilt at Ravenglass
2004	re-engined

51(a) 0-6-2T *Dougal*

| 1970 | built by Severn-Lamb Ltd for Longleat Miniature Railway |
| 2005 | to Evesham Vale Light Railway |

51(b) 0-6-2T *Powys*

| 1973 | built by Severn-Lamb Ltd for Rhiw Valley Light Railway |

51(c) 0-6-2T *Zebedee*

| 1974 | built by Severn-Lamb Ltd for Lappa Valley Railway |
| 1990 | rebuilt as 0-6-4T by N. J. Tambling |

George Woodcock

Perhaps best known for his writings on 'The Development of the Miniature Steam Locomotive' (*Railway World*, November 1961)

and other topics, he was apprenticed to the Great Eastern Railway and also worked for the Midland and North London railways. From 1928 he lived in Bishop's Stortford and built

The neat and elegant *Powys*, a David Curwen design, built for the Rhiw Valley by Severn-Lamb Ltd.

a total of 34 model locomotives, two being 15-inch-gauge: an 0-4-2 tank engine of 1950 and an 0-6-0 tender engine of 1959. George Woodcock died in May 1979.

Stanley Battison
Stanley Battison lived at Ilkeston in Derbyshire, and rose from humble beginnings to become Works Manager at Tatham's Mill there. He built no fewer than eight miniature locomotives (three in 7¼-inch gauge, one in 9½-inch, one in 10¼-inch and one – his last – in 15-inch-gauge). Each was sold on completion to finance the next project; he never achieved his ambition of a private railway, as he died suddenly in 1959 only three years after moving to a house with a sufficiently large garden. The 10¼-inch-gauge *Royal Scot* was probably his finest work, being completed in 1953 for a model engineering competition; it has more recently been restored at Newby Hall near Ripon in Yorkshire.

The 15-inch-gauge 'steam-outline' petrol-mechanical locomotive was finished late in 1958, the large-format (2-6-4 tank design) being dictated by the availability of a Parkinson lorry engine as prime mover. It ran at Blenheim Palace and at Steamtown (Carnforth), and may also have appeared at Lakeside (Southport), before being preserved with the name *Battison* at the **Cleethorpes Coast Light Railway**.

Wilhelm van der Heiden
Born in 1915, Mr van der Heiden of Rotterdam was one of the founding fathers of model engineering in mainland Europe. He is perhaps best known for his small 7¼-inch engines, but he constructed three freelance 0-4-0 machines (with tenders) in the 15-inch-gauge, one of which remains in Britain at the **Cleethorpes Coast Light Railway** and makes an interesting comparison with the freelance designs of E. W. Twining, David Curwen, and the Exmoor Steam Railway.

We have already met the first of the 15-inch-gauge trio – the much-travelled *Chough* (originally named *Tekkel* after a breed of small dog), tested at New Romney in 1970 and used successively by Mr George Marsh at Acrise in Kent, the Paradise Railway at Hayle, the West Buchan Railway, the Butterfly Farm at Barrow in Suffolk, the Saundersfoot Steam Railway, and the Whitworth Hall Railway near Spennymoor! After overhaul by Alan Keef Ltd, *Chough* migrated over 5,000 miles to the Bear Creek Miniature Railway near Vancouver, British Colombia, in 1996 where she remains to this day.

The second locomotive was built in 1972 and (after modification by Severn-Lamb Ltd) was exported as *Sarah-Kate* in 1985 to the Bush Mill Railway at Port Arthur in Tasmania, a venture that ultimately closed in 2004 on the owner's retirement. Named *Mountaineer* on its return to Britain, the engine is in regular use at Cleethorpes. Finally, at the age of 72 in 1987, Mr van der Heiden completed a third example, again named *Tekkel*, for a line at Ghent in Western Belgium.

Stanley Battison's only design for the 15-inch-gauge, the steam-outline diesel *Battison*, is seen at the Cleethorpes Coast Light Railway on 13 August 2012. *D. Holroyde*

It is perhaps making a fine distinction to treat these individual designers separately from the engine-building companies that have appeared on the miniature railway scene since the 1970s. But the author senses a difference in the scale of activity and commercial opportunity in recent decades, with a wholly new development in the form of working railways – especially the **Ravenglass & Eskdale** and **Kirklees** lines – building new locomotives for their own use and for others.

Carland Engineering Co Ltd, Harold Wood, Essex
The firm's main product was a 1/6th scale (10¼-inch-gauge) 4-6-0 based on the LMS 'Royal Scot' prototype, of which several were exported as far as Australia. However, at least one 'scaled-up' version was built for the 15-inch-gauge line at Sunderland in 1950, and used later at the Lightwater Valley and Cleethorpes before being privately preserved. It had the singular misfortune to be converted to a 'steam-outline' diesel in 1963, but was soon restored to live steam!

Severn-Lamb Ltd
It is tempting to characterise this firm as a latter-day Bassett-Lowke with the energy and ambitions of the Cagney brothers! It was founded by Peter Severn-Lamb (1922-75) at Stratford-upon-Avon in 1948, initially

Wilhelm van der Heiden's *Mountaineer*, returned from the Bush Mill Railway in Tasmania, pictured by the tall signal box at Humberstone North Sea Lane.

building 3-inch-gauge and 5-inch-gauge models. Its later manufacture of leisure railway equipment was just one part of a huge output that included large-scale models of ships and engineering plant; again, the similarity with Bassett-Lowke is striking. The factory at Western Road, Stratford-upon-Avon, burned down and was rebuilt in 1980 and extended in 1990. Additional premises at Tything Road, Alcester, were acquired in 2004 and the firm was reconstituted as Severn-Lamb (UK) Ltd in 2005.

Trains for pleasure lines have been built in gauges from 7¼ inches to 3ft 6in, with a total of 188 locomotives constructed between 1969 and early 2010, according to the valuable catalogue compiled by David Holroyde and Lawson Little for the Narrow Gauge Railway Society. Here we must confine ourselves to the 15-inch-gauge, and in fact the four earliest Severn-Lamb builds have already been described above as the designs of David Curwen: the diesel-hydraulic *Princess Anne* and the three 'Dougal' Class steam engines.

The firm's most successful designs have been steam-outline internal-combustion engines using petrol, diesel or propane power units and hydraulic transmissions. They are characterised by a 'Wild West' American appearance (mainly based on the 3-foot-gauge Denver & Rio Grande Railroad's No 278) and by a superb quality of finish and painting. The 'Pretender' Class was built from 1972 with a 2-8-0 wheel arrangement, ten of the first series and eight of the Mark II design being supplied in 15-inch-gauge. From the mid-1980s a 2-6-0 ('American Mogul') version effectively become the standard model, available in gauges between 10¼ inches and 2 feet; a total of 11 were built for the 15-inch-gauge, two having English rather than American-style bodywork. A significant proportion of Severn-Lamb's output has been for export, and the British examples have naturally been resold, modified and renamed among almost all of the modern leisure and theme park lines, developing a modest enthusiast following in their own right as they have done so.

Apart from the Curwen designs and the company's own standard products, Severn-Lamb Ltd has built four 15-inch-gauge locomotives of special interest. The reference numbers are those of the NGRS catalogue:

[10.2] *Doctor Diesel*

1969	completed for Longleat Railway (work begun by Minirail Ltd)
1974	to Axe & Lyme Valley project
1976	to Blenheim Palace Railway
1982	to Steamtown, Carnforth
2000	sold to F. Coppola, California
to 2005	at Golden Gate Railroad Museum, San Francisco

[10.5] *Lenka* **(diesel railcar)**

1973	to Longleat Railway (some parts from a Lister four-wheel locomotive)
1985	to Oakwood Park, Narberth

[10.24] S.N.C.B. (Belgian-style diesel locomotive)

1984	built and exported to Belgium

[10.54] *Wonderland Express* **(2-6-2 s/o battery-electric)**

1998	built and exported to Greece

Alan Keef Ltd, Lea Line, Ross-on-Wye

Thanks to the extremely detailed, engrossing (and often forthright!) full-length autobiography and company history published by the founder in 2008, this is one of the best-documented of current locomotive building firms. Its origins go back to a pig-farmyard operation and pleasure line in Gloucestershire,

Steam building is alive and flourishing: the new *Lydia* for Perrygrove on test at the Alan Keef Ltd works in August 2008.

through which Alan Keef was drawn into the world of industrial narrow-gauge locomotives in the 1970s. In a sense this was just the right decade, because although industrial railways had entered a slow (and ultimately terminal) decline, there were quantities of equipment in need of renovation available for purchase, and there was also a niche market – for those who knew where to look – for new or repaired locomotives and wagons. The acquisition of the 'Simplex' (Motor Rail Ltd) business became the mainstay of the industrial side of the company, while on the pleasure lines side contracts for the maintenance of various Butlins Holiday Camp lines led towards the rebuilding of the **Rhyl Miniature Railway** in 1978. It was apparently a failure, or even a financial disaster, at the time, but this historic line might otherwise never have been revived to see its centenary in 2011.

In the hands of its multi-talented founder, and now his son and daughter, the firm's output has included some exotic types of guided movement systems such as monorail excavators, lifeboat launching ramps and trolleys, and even a bobsleigh practice run! While 15-inch-gauge equipment has never been the major element of the business, there are some notable achievements in our area to record. The firm's Open Days, usually in September each year, attract enthusiasts from far and wide to see the work in hand: in 2008 visitors saw the newly completed 2-6-2 *Lydia* for the Perrygrove Railway proudly in steam on a short test track, a sight to gladden the author's heart.

'New-build' (or heavily rebuilt) 15-inch-gauge equipment includes the following. The '/YY' of the works number indicates the year of construction:

-- --/77	4w p/m *Redgauntlet* [New frame to M. Jacot loco]
	To Romney, Hythe & Dymchurch Railway
AK 39/79	0-6-2 s/o d/h *Sir Winston Churchill* 'Blenheim' Class
	To Blenheim Palace
AK 41/92	0-6-2 s/o d/h *Gilbert Swift* 'Blenheim' Class
	To Haigh Hall
AK 42/92	0-6-2 s/o d/h 'Blenheim' Class
	To Whitworth Hall 1995;
	to Bear Creek, Vancouver, 1996
AK 51/95	0-6-2 s/o d/h 'Blenheim' Class
	To Cricket St Thomas Wildlife Park
AK 52/96	0-4-0 d/h
	To private railway near Oxford

AK 64/01   4w-4w d/h *Pompey*
               To private railway near Oxford

AK 66/02   0-4-0 d/h *The Earl of Oakfield*   (as AK 52/96)
               To Difflin Lake Railway, Ireland

AK 69/03   2-6-4T *Mark Timothy*
               (rebuild of Winson Engineering No 20)
               To Bure Valley Railway, Norfolk

AK 77/07   2-6-2T *Lydia*
               To Perrygrove Railway

AK 79/07   0-6-0 d/m *Flynn*
               To Longleat Railway

AK 85/10   2-6-0T+T *Bunty*
               (completion of loco started by late N. Smith)
               To Heatherslaw Light Railway

Abbreviations: p/m = petrol-mechanical; d/h = diesel-hydraulic; s/o = steam-outline bodywork; T = tank locomotive (steam); T + T = tank locomotive with tender (steam)

A number of other interesting 15-inch-gauge locomotives have passed through the firm's hands in the course of sale and relocation, including the Barnes 'Albion' Class 4-4-2 *Michael* and the Guest 0-4-2 d/m *Clara* (to Rhyl, 1978); two further Guest p/m engines from Dudley Zoo (to Cricket St Thomas and Blenheim Palace); a Morse p/m engine from Dreamland, Margate (to Rhyl) in 1980; and the historic 4-6-4 p/e (petrol electric) *Silver Jubilee* of 1935 from Coney Beach, Porthcawl (to private owner, 1987).

Winson Engineering Ltd
Although no longer in business, this firm had some notable achievements in the 15-inch and other gauges. It was founded in 1984, though not incorporated until 1990; initially based at Porthmadog Harbour, it moved to Penrhyndeudraeth in 1988 and to Daventry in 1995. The core business was steam locomotive restoration and the building of new machines (up to 30 tonnes weight) for the leisure railway industry. A subsidiary business was Winson Model Technology, established in 1995 and using computer-aided-design technology to produce 5-inch-gauge live steam model locomotive kits for home-building. Unfortunately, the business went into liquidation in 2001.

Gleaming 'ZB' Class locomotive *Spitfire* at the 2009 Bure Valley Railway gala. *G. Sutton*

Winson Engineering's name will for ever be associated with the five steam engines at the **Bure Valley Railway**, four of which are based (as 'half-scale' versions) on the British standard design of 'ZB' Class locomotives for the 2ft 6in (760mm)-gauge railways of India in the 1920s. Some of these magnificent prototypes, intended for working heavy trains at main-line speeds, were at work in Pakistan until quite recently. The Winson Engineering version developed considerably more than half the tractive effort of the full-size 'ZB', thus becoming one of the most powerful 15-inch-gauge types ever built.

Brief particulars of the five locomotives are:

[7]   Bure Valley Railway No 1 2-6-4 tank *Wroxham Broad*
         Built 1964 by G&S Light Engineering; rebuild of internal-combustion locomotive *Tracy-Jo* as live steam, 1992
[12]   Bure Valley Railway No 6 2-6-2 tender *Blickling Hall* As 'ZB' prototype, 1994
[14]   Bure Valley Railway No 7 2-6-2 tender *Spitfire* As 'ZB' prototype, 1994
[16]   Bure Valley Railway No 8 2-6-2 tank *Thunder* Begun by BVR, 1996; external appearance as Vale of Rheidol Railway type, 1998; chassis as 'ZB'
[20]   Bure Valley Railway No 9 2-6-4 tank *Mark Timothy* External appearance originally as County Donegal Railways type, 1999 (rebuilt by Alan M. Keef to Leek & Manifold Railway type, 2003); chassis as 'ZB'

All the 'ZB' locomotives have been modified while in service at the Bure Valley Railway in the light of operating experience, including frame strengthening and alterations to the cylinders and steam passages to facilitate free running and fuel economy.

Before leaving the Bure Valley fleet, it is interesting to remember the half-scale version of an American 2-foot-gauge 2-6-2 that ran there in the early 1990s. The prototype was built by Baldwin in 1919 as Sandy River & Rangely Lakes RR No 24; the miniature version began life as a 12¼-inch-gauge machine at Fairbourne. Even when re-gauged to 15 inches it was a large and impressive machine, and has found a permanent home at the **Cleethorpes Coast Light Railway**.

The Exmoor Steam Railway, Bratton Fleming, Devon

The 12¼-inch-gauge line at Cape of Good Hope Farm was established by the Stirland family in 1990 as a public attraction, after they had spent 20 years in the plant hire and construction business. Ready-made locomotives being scarce and expensive, they decided to use their expertise in welding and machining to build their own – which performed so successfully that orders came in from private customers. In 2001, following devastating effects of the foot-and-mouth epidemic on the local tourist industry, the decision was taken to cease public operation of the on-site railway but to retain it as a test track, to which end an additional half-mile on a gradient of 1 in 28

The joy of speed, as *Wroxham Broad* (the erstwhile *Tracy-Jo*) races 'light engine' along the Bure Valley line. *P. Green*

was brought into use in 2009.

The firm has now built no fewer than 50 locomotives in gauges of 7¼, 10¼, 12¼ and 15 inches – and one example of a 2-foot-gauge Hunslet-type for a railway in Alabama, USA. All have a strong 'family resemblance', but are in fact individually designed for customers by Tony Stirland and erected by Tony and his sister Julie, while their father Trevor Stirland carries out boiler welding, shot blasting and final painting, and mother June handles the administration. The engines are characteristically robust and powerful, quick to steam and maintain, and durable in use. To date, eight have been supplied to 15-inch-gauge lines, the most powerful being equipped with cylinders of 5½-inch diameter and 8-inch stroke:

'Exmoor' Class *St Christopher* (still lettered for the Windmill Farm Railway) celebrates the Queen's Diamond Jubilee at Bressingham. *J. Robinson*

No 295 (1993) 0-6-0T *Spirit of Adventure*
   To Perrygrove Railway, Forest of Dean (with set of carriages)
No 300 (1996) 0-4-2-T *Markeaton Lady*
   To Markeaton Park, Derby (with set of carriages); loco (2012) with previous owners of Evesham Vale Light Railway
No 301 (1997) 0-6-0T *Sandy*
   To private owner, Buckinghamshire
No 302 (1997) 0-4-2T *Dennis*
   To Pixieland Railway, Cornwall
No 311 (2001) 2-6-2T *St Christopher*
   To Windmill Farm Railway, Lancashire; 2011 at Waveney Valley Railway, Bressingham
No 312 (2003) 0-4-0T+T *St Egwin* (with tender)
   To Evesham Vale Light Railway
No 317 (2003) 0-4-2T *The Duchess of Difflin*
   To Difflin Lake Railway, Ireland
No 323 (2004) 0-6-2 *John Hayton*
   To Longleat Railway, Wiltshire

TMA Engineering, Erdington, Birmingham
The main business of the firm is connected with power presses, but it has an important subsidiary activity in the building and repair of locomotives in gauges from 7¼ inches (the 'Romulus' Class of 0-4-0 tank engines) upwards. On the 15-inch-gauge, steam activities have included overhauling *Northern Chief* for the Romney, Hythe & Dymchurch at Lichfield in 1980, building *Jack* for the Rhiw Valley Railway in 2003, overhauling *River Mite* from Ravenglass in 2006-07 and, more recently, restoration work on the privately preserved *Count Louis*. The finely detailed, quarter-scale model of No 70000 *Britannia*, which was

begun by Longfleet Engineering of Poole using the original British Railways drawings, was completed by TMA Engineering in 1988, incorporating a boiler by Gowers of Bedford; it is now displayed in the Conwy Valley Railway Museum at Bettws-y-Coed.

Five new diesel locomotives have been produced for 15-inch-gauge lines. Three identical single-cab diesel-hydraulics were built: two (*John Southland* and *Captain Howey*) for the Romney, Hythe & Dymchurch Railway in 1983 and 1989, and *John Southland II* for the Shuzenji Romney Railway in Japan in 1988. A double-cab version (*Douglas Ferreira*) was completed for the Ravenglass & Eskdale

The splendour of modern power: TMA Engineering's *Douglas Ferreira* at Ravenglass on 10 October 2009. *D. Holroyde*

Railway in 2005. An 0-6-0 locomotive also went to the Shuzenji Romney line in 1988, ready for its opening in 1990.

The Great Northern Steam Company
Founded more than 15 years ago, with its main engineering facilities in Darlington, the company actively builds model, miniature and full-size railway engines and also road locomotives and steam launch machinery. The most prestigious project to date was the full-sized 'new build' LNER 'A1' 4-6-2 No 60163 *Tornado*. In the 15-inch-gauge, the company built the first replica of Sir Arthur Heywood's pioneer design *Effie* in 1998-2000 and has since replicated the design in 7½-inch gauge for general sale.* Currently (2011), Great Northern Steam is working on a 15-inch-gauge, quarter-scale version of LNER No 4472 *Flying Scotsman* in its original form for a private owner in Sydney, New South Wales. The locomotive will be accompanied by three Pullman-style coaches, each seating 12 passengers, and 3 kilometres of running track – it promises to be a wonderful sight.

The Ravenglass & Eskdale Railway workshops
When the Preservation Society financed the

purchase of a new steam locomotive in 1966, the result was the scale model 2-8-2 *River Mite* (II), very similar to the well-tried *River Esk* and built by an outside firm, Clarksons of York. It is remarkable that within ten years the railway became equipped to design and build in its own workshops a class of heavy-duty, freelance 2-6-2 engines. The first, *Northern Rock*, enjoyed sponsorship from the building society of that name and was so successful on its home line that two further examples were built for the Shuzenji Romney Railway, *Northern Rock II* in 1989 and *Cumbria* in 1992. One of the Ravenglass drivers went out to Japan for several months to train the drivers at the Rainbow Park (Niji-no-Sato) in Izu, Shizuoka.

Other interesting projects have included the conversion of a former Kerr, Stuart 2-foot-gauge 0-4-0, donated by Ian Fraser, to the 15-inch-gauge 0-4-2 *Bonnie Dundee* in 1992, a useful machine for lighter trains in winter, and since fitted with a tender. A similar engine, *The Lady Augusta*, was built (in conjunction with Brian Taylor at Kirklees) for Neville Smith's **Heatherslaw Light Railway** in 1989.

The Kirklees Light Railway workshops
One of the most varied, unusual and – one might almost say – futuristic range of steam

---

* The idea of an *Effie* replica originated in 1980, in a discussion between David Humphreys and Mike Satow for a small engine to be built by the Locomotion Enterprises training company at Stockton-on-Tees. No drawings of

Effie existed and, remarkably, the work was later carried out to a General Arrangement prepared by Mark Smithers and dimensions scaled from photographs.

locomotives was designed and built by the late Brian Taylor in his large and comprehensively equipped workshops at Clayton West. Although essentially freelance, they nevertheless typify narrow-gauge prototypes built for export by British manufacturers, and thus enable enthusiasts to experience locomotives that are now scarcely to be seen anywhere else. They incorporate technology from the last generation of main-line steam engineers, still experimental in its day, and have been continuously refined and improved in the skilful hands of Ian Screeton. Four locomotives are in use, the two largest being double-bogie machines of the 'Kitson Meyer' and 'Heisler' types:

Fox (1987-90) 2-6-2T
Based on a Hunslet Engine Co (Leeds) 2-6-4T exported to India; since fitted with enlarged cab and bunker, gas-producer firebox and Lempor multiple-jet exhaust

Badger (1991) 0-6-4T
Based on Kerr, Stuart and Co 'Tattoo' Class saddle tank design; since fitted with Marshall valve gear, gas-producer firebox and Lempor multiple-jet exhaust

Hawk (1998) 0-4-0+0-4-0T
Based on Kitson Meyer articulated engine (with four cylinders) built by Andrew Barclay, Sons & Co for export to Chile; possibly the most powerful 15-inch-gauge machine in the world today! Since fitted with modified frame and multiple-jet exhaust; gas-producer firebox planned for future

Owl (1999) 0-4-0+0-4-0GT
Based on a 1920s design by the Avonside Engine Co of Bristol, this geared (shaft-driven) machine has a twin-cylinder 'V' engine and axles coupled by chains, and was fitted with a gas-producer firebox from new

The workshops have also built a four-wheel 'steam-tram-outline' engine and a larger diesel-hydraulic, *Jay*, which at first made use of a 1947-vintage Dorman 2DL power unit that had seen service in one of the Hudswell Clarke locomotives at the Blackpool Pleasure Beach railway.

The steam locomotives are notable for proving, in relatively compact boilers, the practicality and efficiency of the 'gas-producing' or double-combustion system invented by the

Badger and *Fox* raise steam at the Kirklees Light Railway on 9 September 2011. *D. Holroyde*

Articulated super-power: *Hawk* and *Owl* double-head at the Kirklees Light Railway gala on 12 September 2009. *P. Green*

great Argentinian engineer Livio Dante Porta, whose ideas – had they been given a fair trial – might have produced a further generation of main-line steam towards the end of the 20th century. In essence, coal – which can be of poor quality – is partially burned in a mixture of air and exhaust steam in the lower part of the firebox; the gases given off are then mixed with fresh air admitted through specially shaped vents in the firehole door, and burned fully and cleanly in the upper part of the firebox. Further modifications have been made continually to the engines, with extensive use of sealed roller bearings to improve mechanical reliability, water treatment chemicals to extend boiler life and reduce the need for washouts (another Porta idea), and better steam sanding of the rails in wet weather. With more proposals in the pipeline, Kirklees is surely leading the way to demonstrate just how far the steam locomotive can be modernised and improved –

a technology not of the past, but of the 21st century.

Whither the diesel?

In writing this chapter, the author has been struck by the ongoing identification, in the public mind, of rail traction with the outline – if not the actuality – of the steam locomotive. By far the greatest number of internal-combustion units have concealed their true nature under dummy bodywork, and this continues to the present day in the products of Severn-Lamb (UK) Ltd. Powerful, modern diesels without pretensions have found a toe-hold on the Ravenglass & Eskdale and Romney, Hythe & Dymchurch lines (the latter especially for the year-round school trains), but it may be some time yet before they find complete acceptance in the popular imagination.

4. Carriages and wagons

The sublime and the simplistic...

We saw with locomotives how two schools of design emerged, and to a large extent the same has been true of passenger carriages. On the one hand there were luxury vehicles for private railways at Duffield Bank, Eaton Hall and Hardwick Manor, and on the other simple open trucks for the paying public at exhibitions and seaside pleasure lines. In more recent years there has been a welcome return of the covered, fully fitted-out coach, stretching the ability of the designer, and some fine replicas to accompany the re-creations of Sir Arthur Heywood's *Effie*, *Katie* and *Ursula*.

Little is known of the rolling stock used on the earliest garden railways, although George Callender's line at Ardkinglas had in 1875 'a handsome carriage capable of accommodating two persons'. The story begins in earnest with Heywood's experiments to determine the carrying capacity and margins of stability of the 15-inch-gauge. For more than a century this was established as two adults or three children seated side-by-side; not until the 1990s did the 'maxi' coaches at the Gateshead Garden Festival and the Ravenglass & Eskdale lines 'break the mould' by seating three adults across.

Heywood's first carriage for Duffield Bank in 1875-76 proved a prototype for dozens, perhaps hundreds, of later examples: a simple four-wheeled chassis carrying a wooden body of two compartments, with a total capacity of eight passengers. Superseded by later designs, it was scrapped by 1894. Wood was the favoured construction material wherever possible, for lightness and strength, a policy continued by Miniature Railways of Great Britain (doubtless encouraged by its timber-importing director, Ernest Trenery) and by the Cagney brothers in their exhibition and amusement park trains. The very smallest Cagney four-wheelers seem to have held just one single compartment.

The great leap forward in design came in

'A ton of passengers in a ton of coach': a replica of a wooden open Heywood vehicle at Eaton Hall.

The splendour of the
Duffield Bank dining
carriage, re-created by
James Waterfield at
Perrygrove. The wagon
attached is the rail-
bending machine!

Early 20th-century
luxury: the interior
of the restored Eaton
Railway coach, which
once conveyed King
Edward VII, Queen
Alexandra and
Winston Churchill, at
the Perrygrove Railway.

1881, when Heywood built the first of his
Duffield Bank enclosed bogie coaches; inspired
by the work of Charles Spooner at the Ffestiniog
Railway, the fully roofed compartments
(three in number) were tall enough to seat
ladies and gentlemen wearing their Victorian
headgear. The bogies were supported on raised
end balconies (with open seating), the frame
dropping to within a few inches of the rails in
between; couplings were attached to the bogies
rather than the body headstocks, and to ease
the transition round curves one wheel was free
to rotate independently on each axle. As with
the locomotives, the coach made pioneering
use of rubber block springing. A similar design,
but unroofed throughout, achieved the magic
formula of equating tare weight and payload –
a ton of passengers being carried in a ton of
coach. Interestingly, construction was entirely
of timber, pitch pine being used for the frame
and body and elm for the bogie frames.

An early example of a Cagney two-compartment bogie coach, preserved at Rhyl.

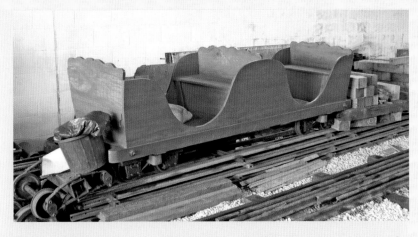

The Duffield Bank and Eaton Hall fleets

The Duffield Bank passenger coaches were joined, by 1894, by two of the most elaborate vehicles ever to run on the 15-inch-gauge. The Dining Carriage seated eight persons in single seats, divided by a central gangway, and the kitchen was equipped with folding work tables, plate racks and a Rippingale paraffin stove; it was a true saloon, entered by end doors from the balconies. The Sleeping Car provided four berths, a dressing table, coat pegs and a folding washbasin as used on yachts. It would have been a tight fit for adults, but provided useful accommodation during house parties for the younger Heywood children, who could doubtless have been lulled to sleep by being whirled round and round the loop lines, over the viaducts and through the tunnels! Dimensions were the maximum allowed by the Duffield Bank tunnels, i.e. 5ft 8in high and 3ft 7in wide. There was also a bogie luggage van with sliding doors, chiefly used for conveying meals to be served to family and guests at the Tennis Ground station, and three further open coaches. The passenger stock passed to the **Ravenglass & Eskdale Railway** after 1915, but tended to receive hard usage there, and regrettably all had been scrapped by 1950. We can, however, see the magnificent replica of the Dining Carriage, constructed by James Waterfield from 1999, complete with dark red plush upholstery and a genuine oil stove, in the Heywood Collection at the Perrygrove Railway – and even ride in it on very special occasions, an experience not to be missed!

The Duke of Westminster, as one of the wealthiest landowners in the kingdom, entertained on the grand scale at Eaton Hall and the initial provision in 1896 of an open carriage and a brake van proved inadequate. A closed coach arrived from Duffield Bank Works in 1904 and another was under construction at the time of Sir Arthur Heywood's death in 1916. This unfinished vehicle migrated to Ravenglass and met the same fate as its siblings, but the Eaton Railway fleet passed to the **Romney, Hythe & Dymchurch Railway** in 1947 and three units (open and closed coach and brake van) survived to be returned in 1980 to Eaton Hall and, maybe, to inspire the reconstruction of the railway.

Other private railways

At **Blakesley Hall**, Charles Bartholomew acquired a set of at least eight four-wheeled coaches to run with his Cagney locomotive, and seems never to have entertained the idea of covered vehicles. However, the carriage bodies were soon adapted to run on new frames made from surplus rails, mounted on wooden bogies – a rare example of one has survived to be restored at the present day – and others were built, or more likely borrowed, for special occasions.

Sir Robert Walker bought four standard Bassett-Lowke coaches, two fitted with vacuum brakes, to run with *Synolda* at **Sand Hutton**, while his estate staff built a four-wheeled brake van and a bogie saloon coach seating ten passengers on reversible garden seats. After

Greenly's substantial *cars de luxe*, around 90 years old, still do exactly what they were built for at Rhyl.

1922, the 'glass coach' (and possibly the other 15-inch-gauge vehicles) went to augment the motley Ravenglass & Eskdale fleet; its life was even shorter than the Duffield Bank stock, and some time after 1927 it became a garden shed at Ravenglass.

Whether Count Louis Zborowski ever had coaches to run with his 'Class 30' 'Little Giant' at the **Higham Railway** seems to be a mystery, but possibly Bassett-Lowke still had one or two spares hanging around at the Northampton works after supplying some – at least for publicity photographs – to Captain Howey at **Staughton Manor**. In later years the **Hardwick Manor Railway** had three heavyweight open bogie coaches with seats in pairs, besides the handsome Great Western-style enclosed compartment coach with photographs of Cotswolds beauty spots, built by J. Wilkes & Sons of Breedon, Worcestershire; all eventually ended up at Fairbourne by 1956. Only the underframe of the compartment coach has survived, awaiting rebuilding to its former glory in the collection of Austin Moss at the **Windmill Farm Railway** in Lancashire.

Fine recent examples of coachbuilding for a private railway can be seen at the annual open weekend at the Rhiw Valley Light Railway in Powys, including a splendidly upholstered Directors Saloon complete with net curtains at the windows!

Passenger-carrying on pleasure lines

The early lines at venues such as Blackpool South Shore and Sutton Park tended to offer only short rides in the simplest of open coaches, and when the weather turned wet – as it surely must have done even in the long Edwardian summers – business presumably had a temporary lapse while the operators sought whatever shelter was available. Lightweight awnings appeared on some of the Bassett-Lowke and Cagney four-wheelers, mainly as a protection against sparks falling onto ladies' dresses and elaborate hats. Equally useful were glass screens on the outer carriage ends to which engines were normally attached, and modern versions of these features are to be seen in some fleets today. Where trains ran backwards and forwards, seats normally faced each other to form compartments with vertical backs, but for lines where the track was a continuous circuit – notably the **Rhyl Miniature Railway** – Greenly designed *cars de luxe* having five seats with comfortable sloping backs, arranged in what we would now term 'aircraft-style'. Eight of these solidly built coaches form the mainstay of the Rhyl fleet to this day, but – with considerable enterprise – the line has also sourced two original Cagney four-wheelers from as far away as Peru to run with its Cagney locomotive. The *cars de luxe* style enjoyed a revival in 1952-56 when four were built for the Sutton Miniature Railway making use of slatted wooden seats from wartime utility bus bodies.

Coaches of the Romney, Hythe & Dymchurch Railway

As already mentioned, expenditure on passenger comforts was some way down Captain Howey's priority list in 1926-27. The fleet of four-wheelers with open sides and ends ultimately

Vintage coaches on an evening Dining Special at Dungeness. The Queen has twice travelled in the Royal Saloon, here coupled next to a saloon from 1934.

numbered 105, up to 20 being marshalled into one train at times of peak demand. Later many were modified to run as articulated sets of five or nine units before the owner decided in 1932 to sell them off. The opening to Dungeness in 1928 brought a great improvement in the shape of eight Greenly-designed saloon coaches, with steam heating, wind-down windows and electric light, built by Clayton Wagons Ltd and immediately dubbed 'Clayton Pullmans'. A new standard design of saloon with metal-clad bodies was constructed from 1934 onwards by the local Hythe Cabinet & Joinery Works, and 54 examples were on the line by the time of the Army's take-over in 1939.

The war years were destructive of the carriage fleet, many vehicles being reduced to their chassis to carry the 'PLUTO' pipeline components, and carriage reconstruction has been one of the most significant challenges facing the railway ever since. The Heywood-designed coaches from the **Eaton Railway** proved a useful stopgap in 1947, though their roofs had to be lowered to pass under the road bridge at New Romney. 'Economy' body renewals in softwood proved to be short-lived in the bracing coastal climate, and the fleet of standard 20-seat coaches introduced from 1970 has used initially varnished hardwood and more recently aluminium-panelled bodywork on new frames, while retaining the bogies and brake gear of earlier, shorter vehicles.

A number of vehicles of special interest have been produced, including two partially streamlined observation saloons, and an eight-seat Royal Coach with gold curtains for the visit of HM the Queen in 1957 – and used by her again at the **Liverpool Garden Festival** in

The school 'push-pull' train leaves for Dymchurch every afternoon during term time.

The 'maxi' coaches built for the Ravenglass & Eskdale in 1990 – and used at the Gateshead Garden Festival – are the widest vehicles built for the 15-inch-gauge, seating three adults abreast. *Ravenglass & Eskdale Railway Co Ltd*

1984. A Pullman Observation Saloon coach, no less than 33 feet long, was built by Colin Bunn and his staff in 1977 and is still the longest passenger-carrying vehicle ever to run on the 15-inch-gauge; its central bar area for refreshment sales has resulted in its appearing under several guises of commercial sponsorship. The diesel-powered school train has given rise to an innovative 'driving trailer' conversion of a guard's coach, equipped with large end windows, a horn and a headlight, a brake control and a radio link to the locomotive, so that the train can run safely at full line speed in both directions.

Coaches of the Ravenglass & Eskdale Railway

Economy being the watchword during the latter years of Sir Aubrey Brocklebank's ownership, the deteriorating Heywood coaches were replaced by more wooden 16-seat opens from 1928 onwards, themselves created from second-hand ships' timbers. Three train sets could be operated and the entirely 'fresh-air' appearance of the trains certainly gave the line a unique character; perhaps it was reasonable to assume that passengers holidaying in the Lake District would be well-equipped with foul weather clothing! Ravenglass trains to this day include a proportion of traditional open vehicles in suitable weather, some having been rebuilt using old seasoned timber from the (demolished) Murthwaite stone-crushing plant. Unfortunately, one has to wonder how long the delights of riding up and down the valley in this fashion – with the hard-to-resist temptations to stand up or lean out for a better view! – will survive the over-zealous attention of the 21st-century Health and Safety industry.

Covered coaches reappeared at Ravenglass in the early 1960s in the shape of three

Right: The elegant
steel-bodied designs of
the Parkinsons, as used
at Great Yarmouth and
Southend, and later at
Sutton Coldfield.

Below: The 'Waggon-
Fabrik AG' builder's
plate (1937) on a coach
at the Waveney Valley
Railway, Bressingham.

time, some three-abreast seating, which exploits to the maximum the stability of the 15-inch-gauge, being no less than 3.4 times the track width. Five of the 'maxi' coaches were used at the **Gateshead Garden Festival**, and two have since been fitted with steam heating.

Steel or wooden bodies?

The Jaywick coaches had been preceded, by a few years, by the splendid enclosed and vacuum-braked coaches built at Sheringham by Harold and Nigel Parkinson. Their operation at **Southend** after 1930 used a five-coach articulated set, while **Great Yarmouth** had the twin-car Austin petrol railcar set and two extra bogie coaches with side doors, dummy 'corridor' connections, roof ventilators and electric light. In their original form they were handsome, one-third scale models of main-line coaches of the day, weighing 1 ton each, and perhaps deserved a better location than a 600-yard seaside line. Shortly after transfer to the **Sutton Miniature Railway**, the braking and lighting equipment was removed and the side doors soon followed suit. Three further examples were built in 1952-54 and, although the substantial proportions of all of them can still be admired at the **Cleethorpes Coast Light Railway**, it has to be said that the lack of doors has altered their appearance somewhat for the worse.

Open coaches were the order of the day on most of the German *parkeisenbahnen*, and the 19 examples that came from Köln to the **Waveney Valley Railway** at Bressingham in

luxurious eight-seater saloons built by Caffyns of Eastbourne, which had run on the 18-inch-gauge **Jaywick Railway** from 1936 and later at Tommy Mann's **New Brighton Miniature Railway**. They provided only a fraction of the accommodation needed, but pointed the way to a design of aluminium-bodied 20-seater saloons of very similar profile introduced from 1967; the fleet of 16 (10 being heated) includes semi-opens, guards' and wheelchair coaches, and the diesel railcar trailers that ran the 'Herculaneum Shuttle' at the **Liverpool Garden Festival**. The Jaywick coaches moved on yet again in 1976, to a life of quiet deterioration at the **Gloddfa Ganol Narrow Gauge Railway Centre** based in the former Oakley Quarry at Blaenau Ffestiniog. The Centre closed in 1998 with the resumption of large-scale slate extraction, and the Jaywick vehicles went briefly to the **Moors Valley Railway** in Hampshire, then to Austin Moss at the **Windmill Farm Railway**; only one of the bodies has survived.

From 1990 Ravenglass produced six 'maxi' coaches featuring sliding doors (giving access to more than one compartment) and, for the first

The Liverpool Garden Festival coaches have given remarkably good service since 1984. In this view at Cleethorpes, the former Sutton signal box can be seen, controlling the level crossing.

1972 were extremely substantial, the bodies including both teak and steel panelling, with elegantly curved skirting below frame level. They had been built by the Düsseldorf factory of Waggon-Fabrik AG, based at Uerdingen (Niederhein); for a number of years two sets were in use at Bressingham, but several examples have now passed to other venues.

Leaving aside for the moment the somewhat individualistic designs of John Wilkins for the Fairbourne Railway, the next substantial build of traditional British 15-inch-gauge coaches was for the **Liverpool Garden Festival Railway** in 1984. These were assembled at the Steamtown engineering workshops at Carnforth, with a similar outline to the modern Romney, Hythe & Dymchurch fleet, and reverted to mahogany bodies, 18 being semi-open and three fully enclosed with guards' compartments and wheelchair access. A full nine-coach train called for maximum effort from the locomotives on the steep gradients! After use at Liverpool (and at the unsuccessful **Britannia Park, Shipley**, venture), the vehicles were dispersed through the agency of Severn-Lamb Ltd, initially to the **Oakwood Adventure Park Railway** in Pembrokeshire and to a projected 18-inch-gauge line near Exmouth in Devon. The Ravenglass & Eskdale workshops overhauled ten vehicles for the 1990 **Gateshead Garden Festival**, the three guards' coaches afterwards being sold on to the Shuzenji Romney Railway in Japan. Four of the semi-opens are now at the **Windmill Farm Railway** and four others – from storage at the Sandy Bay, Exmoor, venture – can be seen at the **Cleethorpes Coast Light Railway**.

A typical articulated unit built by G&S Light Engineering Ltd for Dudley Zoo and Fairbourne; only the guard had weather protection!

Surplus coaches from the 'Réseau Guerlédan' venture have found their way to several locations. This example, at Evesham Vale, has an attractive Talyllyn Railway-style livery.

Modern carriage designs

The almost complete lack of usable carriages at the **Fairbourne Railway** in 1947 provided John Wilkins with not so much a problem as an opportunity to develop some innovative designs! First to arrive were a 'stopgap' set of six four-wheel coaches, followed in 1952 by the first set of three articulated open coaches (providing 72 seats) designed by Dr E. N. Corlett of Wilkins & Mitchell; a duplicate unit was built in 1960. Interestingly, these had a noticeably low centre of gravity, probably to give maximum stability in the strong winds that frequently swept the sand-and-shingle promontory leading out to Barmouth Ferry. By contrast, the 'Canteen'

vehicles of 1953 and 1969 were tall enough for a full-height person to stand under cover and serve, while they were sidetracked at the Ferry during the running day. Two bogie coaches (built by G&S Light Engineering in 1950) followed the usual migration route from Dudley Zoo to Fairbourne in 1960, and the pièce de résistance was a four-coach articulated set of covered coaches, again by Guest Engineering & Maintenance, in 1964. Especially when running with the petrol locomotives *Dingo* and *Sylvia*, these gave Fairbourne a thoroughly up-to-date, even futuristic appearance, and fully justified the dropping of the word 'Miniature' from the railway's title in 1958.

As already mentioned, these modern

Modern-style comfort: upholstered seats in a standard Bure Valley coach. *G. Sutton*

vehicles did not greatly appeal to John Ellerton in 1985, and their replacements were the 30 wooden-bodied coaches brought back from his venture in Brittany. These now look entirely at home, both at Fairbourne and at venues such as **Markeaton Park**, Derby, where the excess vehicles have come to rest. Fortunately there was a ready market for the Wilkins and Guest designs, two articulated sets going to the **Haigh Hall Country Park** and the third initially to the **Littlecote Railway** and since to **Evesham Vale**. Another can now be seen at the **Windmill Farm Railway**.

The **Bure Valley Railway** in Norfolk was well equipped with new, steel-bodied coaches from the outset, the prototype being built by John Edwards in 1988 and since converted to a generator vehicle for electric train heating. The majority of the fleet were built in 1989-90 by Electroplates of Great Yarmouth, comprising 19 standard coaches, a bogie brake coach and two four-wheel brake vans; a major refurbishment programme has been recently carried out. Six wheelchair-accessible Special Saloons with lower windows were built by Winson Engineering in 1998 and Fabcon in 2002. The uniform outline of the vehicles forming a Bure Valley train impressively conveys its 'main line in miniature' character, but there are also two ex-Fairbourne wooden-bodied carriages generally used for 'Thomas the Tank Engine' events.

The great increase in country and leisure park lines since the 1970s has naturally created a demand for simple, easily maintained passenger coaches to run – in the main – with internal-combustion power, and it is not surprising that locomotive-building firms have produced a broadly similar range of rolling stock, adaptable for gauges from 12¼ inches upwards. The basic unit tends to be a semi-open compartment coach with a light roof supported by welded steel framing, glazed ends, metal or plywood flooring, and slatted wooden seats. Customer enhancements can include better floor covering, fully enclosed sides with windows and doors, a wheelchair-accessible area, upholstered seating, electric lighting, and even a public address system!

Alan Keef Ltd entered the passenger-carrying field by way of work on the Butlins Holiday Camp lines and man-riding vehicles for industrial use. The company's notable recent achievements for 15-inch-gauge lines have included additional sets of coaches for the **Heatherslaw Light Railway** and **Perrygrove Railway**, and privately commissioned vehicles for the **Wotton Light Railway** in Buckinghamshire and the **Difflin Lake Railway** in County Donegal. The latter are modelled on carriages of the former 3-foot-gauge County Donegal Railway. The large-scale firm of Severn-Lamb Ltd offers a wide range of open and enclosed carriage types to accompany its standard locomotive designs, perhaps with a greater emphasis on supplying complete railway installations to new venues. 15-inch-gauge is the smallest currently advertised, 2-foot being more common; train seating capacities extend from 32 up to 320 passengers. Although the Exmoor Steam Railway is best known for its locomotive designs, 15-inch-gauge coaches have been constructed for both the **Perrygrove Railway** and the **Markeaton Park Light Railway**.

Sandy hauls a train on the private Wotton Light Railway, Buckinghamshire, in 1998. *P. Scott*

Goods wagons

Although perhaps of less interest to present-day enthusiasts, goods vehicles for agricultural and domestic traffic featured largely in the plans of Sir Arthur Heywood, the Duke of Westminster, Charles Bartholomew and Sir Robert Walker, while Sir Aubrey Brocklebank was quick to realise the carrying capacity of the 15-inch-gauge for his Beckfoot granite. Relatively less has been preserved, compared to locomotives and passenger coaches, but there are nevertheless some remarkable survivals.

It was hardly to be expected that Heywood would be content with the conventional railway trucks of his day in planning estate railways, where the train would replace sets of horses and carts. He duly produced his own multi-purpose design of 'top' wagon – essentially a flat-bed truck that could be used with bolsters for carrying timber, or built up with box-like sides of varying height for loads of minerals or agricultural produce. His earliest 15-inch-gauge

wagons measured 4 feet by 2 feet and carried 5cwt of coal; the later 'standard units' were 6 feet long and 3 feet wide, though there were experimental exceptions. There were also eight tipping wagons (two for Duffield Bank and six for Eaton Hall) and two bogie wagons for works use. Of special interest was the 'Dynamometer Carriage' with half-height sides, fitted with equipment for measuring the drawbar pulling power of the locomotives. A reconstruction of this vehicle often accompanies *Ursula* on her visits to special events at various railways.

The **Sand Hutton Light Railway** was essentially a garden line in its 15-inch-gauge days, with just one or two construction wagons, but Charles Bartholomew at **Blakesley Hall** used five tipping wagons to bring in coal supplies to the house, home farm and electricity station; the power equipment itself (an 8-ton generator and a 5-ton gas engine!) was brought in on a 15-inch-gauge 'trolley' built – like the bogie coaches – from spare rails. It is uncertain how much rolling stock, if any,

A rake of Heywood-type wagons on Rookwood siding at the Perrygrove Railway, the one to the right carrying a 'box' top.

The re-created 'Dynamometer Carriage', which usually accompanies *Ursula* on her visits, shows the Heywood type of arm-and-plate coupling.

existed at **Staughton Manor** and the **Higham Railway**, though Howey certainly had a set of goods trucks on his earlier 9½-inch-gauge line; his black dog, Peter, acted as guard and rode correctly in the last vehicle!

In the Narrow Gauge Railways Ltd years, the **Ravenglass & Eskdale** line was essentially a passenger operation; mineral traffic was re-introduced by Sir Aubrey Brocklebank from 1922. The stone quarried at Beckfoot was moved down to Murthwaite in 18 four-wheeled wagons built in wood and iron, with drop doors, by Francis Theakston Ltd of Crewe and Bristol, who also contrived an elevated 'tippler' at Ravenglass for up-ending and discharging the crushed railway ballast into standard-gauge trucks; road stone went down a chute to a lorry waiting on the road below. In 1928, after the Murthwaite crushing plant had been rebuilt to increase capacity, the Yorkshire Engine Company built six heavy-duty (6-ton) hopper wagons to handle its output, but it was quickly realised that a better option was to provide a standard-gauge track, 'gauntleted' outside the 15-inch rails, as far as the crushing plant to avoid transhipment of ballast for the LMS. After this came into use in 1929, the hoppers saw little use and were sold on to Captain Howey to move shingle ballast on the **Romney, Hythe & Dymchurch** line. As already related, two had their moments of glory as the constituents of the anti-aircraft armoured train during the Second World War. Apart from this conversion, the military engineers were content to use the underframes of passenger coaches for moving equipment – including the 'PLUTO' sections – during their control of Captain Howey's railway.

Train coupling and braking systems

Although this book has not set out to cover technical matters in great depth, the observant visitor to 15-inch-gauge railways is bound to notice the many different types of coupling and brake connections between locomotives and trains. While this displays the mechanical ingenuity of the owners and builders, it does place practical difficulties and limitations in the way of exchanges between different lines. It is not uncommon for a visiting locomotive to be used only as the 'pilot' engine in a double-headed formation, the 'train' engine of the home line being equipped with the correct brake operating system, the positions of the two machines naturally having to be reversed for the return trip down the line!

The intricacies of couplings were amusingly explored by Simon Townsend in 'In Search of the Perfect Coupling' in *The Heywood Society Journal* (Volume 40), beginning with Sir Arthur Heywood's design of a hinged tongue on one end of a vehicle engaging with a plate on the opposite end of its neighbour. The Heywood coupling was intended to be semi-automatic, permitting a degree of 'fly shunting', but close examination of photographs of demonstration trains (often left loaded, ready for use) suggests

Detail of a Heywood-pattern coupling, with modern safety chain. *G. Sutton*

that derailments were not entirely unknown.

Interestingly, the three longest 15-inch-gauge lines operating today use completely different coupling methods: the **Ravenglass & Eskdale** employs rigid steel bars and locating pins, the **Romney, Hythe & Dymchurch** hooks and chains, and the **Bure Valley** ball hitches derived from motor car and trailer linkages! Few, if any, lines using conventional buffers have gone to the extent of adopting main-line screw couplings rather than simple hooks and chains. Variants on the 'bar and pin' system are the most common, safety usually being assured by an R-shaped spring clip passed through the pin after coupling up, thus preventing the vehicles from accidentally parting company while in motion. A particularly simple device was adopted by Harry Barlow for the **Lakeside Miniature Railway** (Southport) and the **Far Tottering & Oystercreek Railway** (Battersea Park), where very frequent – and rapid – coupling and uncoupling was required; a hinged bar on the locomotive with a ball-shaped end dropped into a V-shaped slot on the ends of the articulated coach sets.

As we perhaps might expect, such home-grown practices did not greatly appeal to the builders of the German *liliputbahnen* in the 1930s, who preferred the interlocking or 'clasped hands' coupling then being adopted on the German State Railways, which even included automatic brake connections. These can be seen today on the **Waveney Valley Railway** at Bressingham; the similarity to the Scharfenberg coupling used on modern main-line trains is noticeable. Curiously, the nearest British equivalent – the 'chopper' couplings used on the Ffestiniog Railway – have been little favoured on the 15-inch-gauge, though they are in use on the **Kirklees Light Railway**.

The early 15-inch-gauge lines mostly relied on hand brakes on the coaches or brake vans, supplemented by a steam brake on the locomotive; the Heywood designs boasted a particularly complex piece of equipment. Vacuum braking systems were the logical development for passenger-carrying lines, as steam engines produce a natural vacuum in the smokebox for the working power. By 1911 Bassett-Lowke had introduced a type of 'simple'

vacuum brake in which air was exhausted from the system to apply the brakes; a rubber diaphragm in a hemispherical brake cylinder was lifted by the vacuum and pulled directly onto the brake levers. The system was first used at Rhyl at the August Bank Holiday of 1911, and also appeared at the Luna Park in Geneva the following year. The obvious disadvantage was that a serious leak, or the parting of the hoses between the carriages, prevented the brake from working at all! The **Romney, Hythe & Dymchurch** line has always used the fail-safe or 'automatic' vacuum system, the brakes being *released* by creation of a vacuum and fully applied should a leak occur. Working parts for all vacuum systems tend to be large and heavy, and of course petrol or diesel locomotives require an exhauster to operate them. The modern requirement, to meet the standards of Her Majesty's Inspectors of Railways, is to stop a train on level track from 20mph in 13 seconds.

Modern train braking systems mostly use compressed air supplied by a compressor on the engine, axle-driven mini-compressors on the coaches, or storage reservoirs topped up at stations. They fall generally into two types, identified by the use of a single hose or twin hoses. The single-pipe system, used at lines including the **Bure Valley, Ravenglass & Eskdale, Kirklees, Cleethorpes Coast** and **Markeaton Park**, relies on differential air pressures: 60psi fully releases the train brakes, a drop to 50psi produces a normal brake application, and a fall to 30psi or less causes an emergency stop. The twin-pipe system is based on modern articulated road vehicle practice, where compressed air admitted to the yellow hose provides normal braking but the release of air from the red hose (normally pressured above 40psi) triggers an emergency stop in the event of the train becoming divided or the engine detached.

As a footnote to the delights, or headaches, of gala events at 15-inch-gauge railways, one might think sympathetically of the organisers of the 2008 event at the **Cleethorpes Coast Light Railway**, where the 'home' and 'visiting' fleets comprised four types of coaches, three types of couplings – and two braking systems!

5. Track, stations and signalling

The permanent way

Above: 'Don't lose those spikes, they cost 35p each!' Assembling track panels at the Rhiw Valley with second-hand (ex-Romney) rail and pre-drilled new sleepers.

Right: Track renewal at the Rhiw Valley: new ballast has been spread on a plastic membrane, after the ground has been levelled by hand.

Although the 'infrastructure' of 15-inch-gauge railways is perhaps less distinctive than their locomotives and rolling stock, and has been generally paid less attention by enthusiasts, there are nevertheless many features of interest. As we might expect, the pioneering lines of Sir Arthur Heywood at Duffield Bank and Eaton Hall demanded high standards of equipment, and the same is true of the 'main lines in miniature', the

Romney, Hythe & Dymchurch and Bure Valley railways. On the other hand, pleasure and private lines have proved that 15-inch-gauge trains can operate successfully in much simpler circumstances, tracks being laid directly on the sand at the first Blackpool Miniature Railway and practically on the natural surface of the meadow at the Rhiw Valley Light Railway. And as we have already seen, the little Woodland Railway in Kent was happy to make do with any source of scrap rails and sleepers!

Heywood insisted that narrow-gauge track had not, up to the 1870s, received the attention it deserved, and characteristically carried out experiments to determine the best type – beginning with rails weighing 14lb per yard on sleepers only 5 inches wide and 2 inches deep, the rail joints being tried at first without fishplates. Slightly lighter (12lb per yard) and much heavier (22lb) rails were then used, on wooden sleepers secured in chairs by 'keys' on the *inside* of the rails, as was the fashion of the Midland Railway nearby; did he seek the advice of the local permanent way engineers, or merely observe, we might wonder? By the time of the Eaton Railway's construction, Heywood had devised a form of cast-iron sleeper with integral chairs to hold 16½lb rails, now with *outside* keys as used by the Great Western and most other railways. He had no hesitation in setting to work himself with 'beater, rammer and crowbar' while instructing the Duke of Westminster's labourers on the supreme importance of a firm, level trackbed. In later years Harry Wilde maintained the line in superb condition, using weedkiller so liberally that a labourer who thoughtlessly placed his sandwiches on the rail is said to have been hospitalised with arsenical poisoning!

Although Heywood used lengths of assembled track to move the Eaton Railway 'head of steel' forward, he never saw the advantages of using completely portable units such as points, crossings and curves of different radii. The idea of the narrow-gauge railway 'straight out of the box' for colonial use had been developed by Ransomes & Rapier of Ipswich in the 1870s, and widely promoted in that firm's catalogues and book, *Remunerative Railways for New Countries*. If a commercial manufacturer had combined the ideas of Ransomes & Rapier and Heywood, the story of the landed estate railway might have taken a very different course. The **Blakesley Hall Railway** used comparatively light (12lb) rail on steel sleepers, but with good-quality stone ballast, and had no difficulty in moving heavy equipment to the Hall. The early seaside lines also tended to use 12lb rail on either steel or wooden sleepers – the latter at wider centres – and in the case of Rhyl, a mixture of the two. At **Sand Hutton**, Sir Robert Walker went in for 16lb rail secured to main-line sleepers cut into three lengths, secured by clips and coach bolts. Interestingly, Captain Howey's first line (of 9½-inch gauge) at **Staughton Manor** used rail as light as 7½lb per yard; the sleepers were 2 feet in length, clearly to allow for future re-gauging, but it is uncertain whether the rails were ever replaced, though the model 'Forth Bridge' was prudently reinforced with steelwork. *John Anthony*, weighing nearly 3 tons on its six axles, would have tested the original rails to their limits!

At the **Ravenglass & Eskdale**, the newly converted 15-inch-gauge track encountered problems with the heavily worn wrought-iron rails of the original line, leading to some bad derailments, but under Sir Aubrey Brocklebank's control much was relaid with 25-30lb rail brought back from the Western Front military railways, with new sleepers and – of course – the granite ballast that was now the line's lifeblood. In building the miniature railway at **Dreamland Park, Margate**, in 1920, Greenly had used 20lb rail on main-line sleepers cut only in half, giving a decidedly 'over-scale' appearance. The rail bought for the **Romney, Hythe & Dymchurch** construction was (like Ravenglass) mixed grades of war surplus of varying lengths, so that most of the rail joints were staggered; the norm was later settled as 24lb per yard, British Standard flat-bottomed. Greenly, like Heywood, had a 'hands-on' – or rather 'feet-on' – approach to tracklaying, the Romney sleeper spacing of 22 inches being said to be his natural stride. The sleepers were quite substantial, being 3 feet long, 9 inches wide and 4½ inches deep, but as the shingle ballast settled under the weight of the trains passengers in the early four-wheeled coaches experienced a nauseous rolling effect!

One of the most substantial 15-inch-gauge permanent way constructions of the earlier period was enjoyed by the **Ettrick Bay Railway**, which operated only a lightweight Cagney locomotive but used the heavy flat-bottomed rails previously carrying the cars of the Rothesay Tramways Company. The **Dudley Zoo** and **Fairbourne** railways pioneered the use of concrete sleepers on the very narrow gauge, courtesy of the Guest family's building firm; the last shovelfuls of each 'mix' for door lintels and kerbstones were thriftily used for track sleepers, with fastening holes alternately inside and outside the foot of the rail. To prevent all mishaps, metal tie rods were also used to keep the lines strictly to gauge.

The last 50 years have seen a trend towards more and more substantial permanent way, as locomotives and coaches have tended to become larger and heavier. Fittingly, the **Ravenglass & Eskdale Railway** showed the way forward in the 1960s by the use of new 35lb per yard rail in 30-foot lengths – then manufactured for use in coal mines – laid on new sleepers of Jarrah, an Australian hardwood, which has since become something of a standard for narrow-gauge lines. In recent years rail tends to be imported from rolling mills in the Far East.

Track work remains labour-intensive, though mechanical aids have become commonplace and volunteers from preservation or support groups play an important part on many lines. Contractors such as Severn-Lamb Ltd and Alan Keef Ltd are also available to carry out works for fully commercial operations such as zoos and theme parks. Not the least remarkable achievement of the **Liverpool Garden Festival Railway** was the laying of its 2½ miles of curving, undulating track by Henry Boot Ltd & Sons in just 13 weeks, using two gangs of 40 men with little or no experience of 15-inch-gauge track construction.

Stations

The early miniature railway at Ardkinglas House had a terminal station with buildings and an engine shed with a servicing pit, but apparently all the structures were destroyed on 29 December 1879 as a minor consequence of the great storm that brought down the first Tay Bridge!

It will come as no surprise that the most elaborate constructions of the 'pioneering' years were to be seen at Duffield Bank and Eaton Hall, where cost was virtually of no consequence but the aesthetic effect of the buildings, to the owner, was of the highest importance. Sir Arthur Heywood's principal station was at the 'Tennis Ground', often used for family picnics, where an elegant rustic-style timber-framed building, with vertical

The former goods terminus of the Eaton Railway near Eaton Hall remains intact…

...as does the former locomotive shed within the present-day Grosvenor Garden Centre.

planking, was erected between 1875 and 1879 hard against the rock face of the old quarry. A somewhat similar, though less ornamental, style of construction survives today at Dove Leys, where a shed for railway equipment can be seen in the copse just south of the mansion, a mute witness to the frustrated ambitions of the Dove Bank Railway. The Eaton Railway went in for brick construction of walls up to the eaves with a timber superstructure; the coal store and carriage shed to the north of the Hall still remain, the latter being the depot for the Duke's present-day **Eaton Hall Railway**. The original all-brick engine shed at Belgrave also remains as an office within the Grosvenor Garden Centre, though the route of the associated trackwork has completely disappeared.

Blakesley station in Northamptonshire on the East & West Junction Railway began with just a wooden platform and shelter for Charles Bartholomew's **Blakesley Hall** line, but by 1906 the 15-inch-gauge line was provided with a rustic wooden 'summerhouse', from the comfort of which his guests could telephone the Hall for a train to be sent. The Edwardian fashion for rustic architecture was also to be seen, appropriately enough, in the stations and lineside gardens at G. V. Llewelyn's 1911 miniature railway at Southport and on the short-lived Luna Park Railway in Geneva. Miniature Railways of Great Britain had begun

in an extremely modest way with a narrow wooden station and ticket office ('Gipsyville') on the sands at **Blackpool**, but by 1911 Greenly had scope and resources enough to endow the **Rhyl Miniature Railway** with a clock tower on top of the wooden station – built by E. & E. L. Jones of Rhyl – and a signal gantry spanning the track to a water tower opposite.

The conversion of the **Ravenglass & Eskdale** line in 1916 inherited and re-used the remains of the 3-foot-gauge stations, except for the terminus at Boot, which was abandoned as too steeply graded to be reached by the scale-model locomotives. Both Ravenglass and Dalegarth have been extensively modernised in recent decades, but Irton Road retains its original stone building of 1873.

Fairbourne, having been a horse tramway, possessed precisely nothing in the way of station facilities when taken over by Narrow Gauge Railways Ltd, and the extreme narrowness of the site opposite the Cambrian Railways station, between road and stream, limited the possibilities to a run-round loop and engine shed. The village Post Office, shop and café of Mr and Mrs Wills on the opposite side of Beach Road were the passengers' only resort. At the opposite end of the line, winter storms and the ever-present threat of erosion militated against buildings of any kind, though a flag-pole was used to indicate that trains were running! The new four-tracked Fairbourne

The rebuilt Ravenglass station building nears completion early in 2012.

Although created in recent years, the platform at Evesham Vale station has a timeless rustic quality

station of 1959, on the south side of the stream, was indeed a major redevelopment.

Later seaside lines tended to invest more money in station buildings, as visible gateways to the attractions of the train ride itself, in much the same way that piers tended to have elegant, ornamental buildings at their shore entrances. At **Dreamland Park, Margate**, in 1919-20 Greenly erected concrete structures with steel overbridges, anticipating his more substantial use of concrete at the **Romney, Hythe & Dymchurch**; in their turn, the Parkinsons had two island platforms connected by footbridge at Pleasure Beach station on the **Yarmouth**

Miniature Railway and an overall roof of elliptical steelwork at the Central station at the Kürsaal, Southend.

It was, naturally, the **Romney, Hythe & Dymchurch** project that gave the freest rein to Greenly's architectural talent. The Hythe terminus originally had three platforms, covered for about a third of their length by a light, elegant overall roof, while New Romney had four platform tracks. The station building at New Romney combined the roles of general, booking and parcels offices; the frontage had an awning with an elegant fretwork fascia extending outwards to four columns on brick bases, and the whole was surmounted by a clock tower – a bigger and better version of the one at Rhyl. Dymchurch station was at first blessed with an overall roof (certain trains being intended to terminate there), but famously showed Greenly's economical or utilitarian side, with gentlemen's toilets built into the square concrete towers supporting the footbridge.

The rebuilt **Sutton Miniature Railway** of 1938 opened with an impressive timber station very much in the style of a covered fairground ride, probably erected by Pat Collins to set off the railway equipment brought from Great Yarmouth. As mentioned already, the station was rebuilt for the final time in 1957 with canopies in a more 'railway-like' style, but was destined to last barely five years.

Over at Southport, Harry Barlow seemed never to see the point of covered accommodation on the **Lakeside Miniature Railway** – on a rainy day any passengers were going to get wet in the open coaches anyway! – and the 1948 station at 'Peter Pan's Pool' opened with a small booking office of rendered construction, since replaced by a more modern brick building. At the other end of the line, Pleasureland, a simple wooden ticket hut survived precariously almost

Greenly as architect: the frontage of New Romney station retains his characteristic style.

No book on the 15-inch-gauge would be complete without the gentlemen's toilets supporting the Dymchurch footbridge!

Expense (almost) no object: the Aylsham headquarters of the Bure Valley, seen shortly after opening.

until the line's centenary, its latter years perhaps trying to emulate the 'Oystercreek' station in Battersea Park, which was furnished with a derelict fisherman's hut, courtesy of Rowland Emett.

The numerous theme park and zoo railways of the last 40 years often tend to have facilities in the same style as the main attraction, but elsewhere some fine buildings have been created resembling the classic late-Victorian or Edwardian country station. The **Perrygrove Railway** in the Forest of Dean, and the **Evesham Vale Light Railway**, are excellent examples of the genre, as is the delightful Lakeside station at the **Cleethorpes Coast Light Railway**, complete with a posting box, piles of period luggage, and – in the author's experience – an extremely affectionate ginger cat! The 'town' end of the line at Kingsway has a fine modern full-height booking office and shop, providing a spacious welcome to the passenger, the 'train shed' beyond being appropriately more in proportion to the size of the

rolling stock, while at North Sea Lane another wooden building withstands the force of the gales off the Humber Estuary.

Public space on a larger scale is enjoyed by the **Kirklees Light Railway** thanks to the generously proportioned original terminal building at Clayton West, though the platform elevation does rather tend to tower above the 15-inch-gauge trains.

The **Bure Valley Railway** does not use any original station buildings, those that survived having been sold as private residences, but the termini at Aylsham and Wroxham are noteworthy modern buildings, Aylsham in particular doubling as a Tourist Information Centre and providing substantial shop and catering facilities, which in themselves justify opening virtually all through the year, even when no trains are running.

The station cat at the Lakeside station at Cleethorpes presides over a fine display of vintage luggage.

Signalling and train operation

Although many 15-inch-gauge and other miniature railways have operated from first to last without any formal signalling, others have used quite elaborate systems, and the introduction of controller-to-driver radio communication has been a pioneering achievement that other, larger railways have since emulated. Of course, the enthusiast will easily recognise that some apparent signal installations are more decorative than utilitarian, with arms fixed at curious angles or even 'back to front'!

Sir Arthur Heywood recognised, correctly, that the small track gauge of the 15-inch-gauge railway does not reduce the possibility of accidents, and equipped the **Duffield Bank Railway** with two signal boxes, at Manor Copse and the Tennis Ground, linked by telephone, with a line also to his office. These were usually manned by the younger, female members of the family, and the signals had wooden arms mounted within slotted wooden posts, presenting a slightly archaic appearance even in the 1880s. Alternate trains, when the line was open to visitors, tended to run 'express' (taking 5 minutes) or 'stopping' (taking 7 minutes for a circuit of the line). By contrast, the Eaton Railway was never intended to have more than one engine in use at a time, and the owning family took little part in its actual operation. The driver, Harry Wilde, was given copious written rules on the procedures to be followed, but it was not envisaged that he might encounter a second train on any part of the line! Charles Bartholomew's love of technology led him to equip the **Blakesley Hall Railway** with the very modern – for 1903 – Sykes electric banner signals, as recently installed at Glasgow's St Enoch station, though in practice they functioned very much as point indicators.

The first Miniature Railways of Great Britain line, at **Blackpool**, had a starting signal at the end of the station platform, doubtless largely for appearance, though it may have served to give the 'right away' to the engine driver. Similar provision was later made at **Llewelyn's Miniature Railway** at Southport, where the line was just an out-and-back

shuttle, and at **Rhyl**, where the gantry also boasted a shunting signal (with a disc on the arm, as in main-line practice) for the engine shed siding. The White City exhibition line in London was signalled so that two trains could operate simultaneously – one waiting in a reversing siding until the other had left the platform – but in the end there was only business enough for a single train. The Brussels exhibition line could operate multiple trains at short intervals by an ingenious automatic system devised by a Belgian engineer, Mon. L. Hervé: as a train left a station, the locomotive's driving wheels pressed treadles set just inside the running rails, and these cleared the 'distant' and 'home' signals of the section behind for the following train. However, the Luna Park, Geneva, layout of 1912 reverted to manual signalling using traditional British semaphores, as operations required the train to travel over part of the circuit twice, diverging from the 'inner' to the 'outer' loop at facing points on the second part of the journey. In later years, an even more elaborate system was installed by the Parkinsons at their **Yarmouth Miniature Railway**, where safety was doubly ensured by mechanical interlocking within the 10-lever signal box on the footbridge, and by point locks on the track secured by the approaching trains closing electrical track circuits; the signals and points themselves were actuated by hydraulic power.

On the **Romney, Hythe & Dymchurch** line full signalling was installed from the start, with no fewer than four intermediate boxes between Hythe and New Romney. 'Block' (section clearance) working was by telephone, recorded centrally at the New Romney signal box; being operated under a Light Railway Order, it was not necessary to install the block bells and 'line occupied/line clear' instruments used on main-line railways. Similar signal provision was made on the Dungeness extension, though with less frequent train movements the equipment quickly fell out of use. A manual staff or token, supplemented by paper tickets for two or more train departures in the same direction, was introduced to the New Romney-Greatstone-Dungeness section when it was reduced to a single line in 1946.

At the **Ravenglass & Eskdale Railway**,

The Longleat Railway, the first of its kind at a wildlife park. Note the fine signals and twin pipe air brake system on the rear of the locomotive. *S. Bowditch*

A red-and-white disc point indicator at Irton Road, with electrical link to a white 'repeater' light further up the track.

traffic built up so rapidly after 1916 that a home-grown train control system was devised to replace the initial practice of sending out trains on 'time intervals', with *Katie* always in the rear as the most likely to run out of steam between stations! With mineral as well as passenger trains roaming the line, a pilotman rode on the engines on the busy Murthwaite to Eskdale Green section, and the trains carried red and white marker discs to indicate whether another service was, or was not, following behind. Even so, near-misses and at least one actual head-on collision did occur, the lightly built *Colossus* coming off second best to the solidity of *Muriel*. By the end of the 1920s a controller at Ravenglass had become responsible for all movements, using written orders and telephone communication to all stations, in some ways anticipating the sophisticated radio control system used today. In the 1960s there was a brief reversion to the old system of 10-minute time-interval working, with 'headway clocks' set by each train crew to indicate the time they had left designated points.

The system of single-line tokens, issued from and replaced into electrically linked frames, has never been widely used on 15-inch-gauge lines, though it is commonplace on standard-gauge (and many narrow-gauge) single lines. The **Fairbourne Railway** in the Wilkins era used simple tokens for its Fairbourne-Golf House Loop-Ferry sections, and – in theory at least – the engine in motion on busy days at the **Lakeside Miniature Railway** carried a token while the other two trains waited at the termini. However, the author recalls visiting Southport one Easter Saturday (the first day of operation) in the early 1960s and finding

much hilarity among the drivers, as by early afternoon the token had already bounced off one of the engines and disappeared without trace into the lineside bushes; for the rest of the year, operation was presumably just by common sense!

The automatic operation of points at passing places and locomotive run-round loops has long been a feature of miniature railways of all gauges: a compression spring or weighted lever sets the points to send an approaching train or engine onto the left-hand track. Wheel flanges on vehicles moving through the 'trailing' points momentarily open the switch blades, which then fall back into the closed position. The system works reliably and can be seen on lines as busy as the **Ravenglass & Eskdale** and the **Bure Valley**, where the point indicator arms have fixed and moving discs, the outer faces painted white and the inner faces red; if an approaching driver sees any part of a red disk, it is a warning that the blades have not fully reset and he (or she!) must stop and examine the points.

Modern train operation has come to rely very much on electronics. Colour-light signalling has replaced many semaphores on the **Romney, Hythe & Dymchurch** line, exactly as it did on British Railways in the last decades of main-line steam. At road level crossings, these are interlinked with flashing signals to warn road vehicles of an approaching train, and in very recent years these have had to be supplemented by automatic barriers in the locations where car drivers are prone to ignore lights alone. European light railway practice, of train control by VHF radio communication, came to Britain in 1977 when the **Ravenglass**

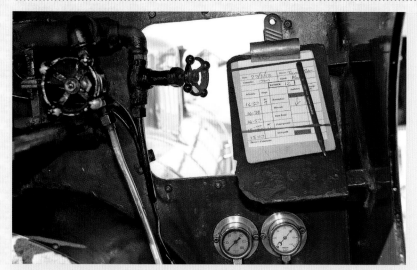

A train movement order (RANDER system) on the footplate of *Northern Rock*.

& Eskdale equipped its locomotive fleet with 'Redifon' two-way radios linking to a controller (whom the Americans would call a 'dispatcher') at Ravenglass. Each train movement has an identifying number, odd for down trains and even for up trains, and on leaving Ravenglass the driver has a written order setting out his round trip schedule. The controller makes red and green entries on a train graph to indicate occupied or vacant sections of the track, each driver reporting his arrival at a passing loop and requesting permission to proceed – which will usually confirm, or may occasionally vary, his written schedule. Based on the German *zügleitung*, the 'RANDER' ('R and E R') system does not involve any station staff and is highly flexible for varying line occupancy; it naturally requires a highly responsible person as Controller. The system can cope with up to six train units in use, four on the move and two at the termini, and has been so effective that similar principles have been used in the 'Radio Electronic Tokenless Block' developments for standard-gauge lines such as the Cambrian Coast in Wales and the West Highland in Scotland.

Elements of both the Romney and Ravenglass systems featured in the sadly short-lived **Liverpool Garden Festival** operation, track-circuiting and colour-light signalling controlling the spacing of the three trains while other track circuits warned level crossing keepers to manually lower their barriers for an approaching train. Telephone circuitry was provided to each signal, but in practice the VHF radios held by both drivers and train guards proved the most effective means of communication.

Simplicity is still the watchword on many pleasure park lines, where it is quite usual for only a single train to be in operation. The **Rhyl Miniature Railway** retains the time-honoured method of one train completing a circuit of the Marine Lake and halting at a 'home' signal position just outside the station, the engine then whistling to permit the second train to depart from the platform. Exceptionally, the Centenary Gala allowed three trains to be in use: one at the 'home' signal, one halfway round the circuit alongside the main-line railway, and the third ready to depart from Central station – a classic example of simple, safe miniature railway operation.

The driver's handset for RANDER radio control.

In the following section, brief details are provided for each of the 38 15-inch-gauge railways expected to be operating in Britain during 2013. A simple and standardised format has been adopted, and it is clearly not possible to do full justice here to the major lines, which have been described in more detail in the two 'History' chapters. Where publications covering the individual lines are known to the author, they have been noted as 'Further reading' at the end of the entries. The information given has been compiled, in large part, from publicly available sources and intending visitors are recommended to check opening arrangements, etc, in advance of a visit.

For the sake of comprehensiveness, the three lines known to exist in the Republic of Ireland have been included, as has the Fairbourne Railway (now 12¼-inch gauge), which still runs at its original location and played such an important part in the 15-inch-gauge story prior to 1985.

Many of the modern lines operating within adventure, safari and other theme parks require payment of the entry fee to the main attraction before access to the train is possible. In most cases travel on the train is then free; in others there is a small supplementary charge.

Billing Aquadrome: The 'Willow Lake' Miniature Railway
(Park entry fee applies)

Location
Crow Lane
Great Billing
Northampton NN3 9DA.
Tel: 01604 408181
Website: www.billingaquadrome.com

Route
The railway forms an irregular circuit of approximately 1,000 yards around Willow Lake, one of several lakes comprising the holiday and leisure park. The station is near the entrance to the Aquadrome.

Background
The first railway on the site was of 10¼-inch gauge, opened at Easter 1949 and using a Carland Engineering 'Royal Scot' 4-6-0 locomotive. In 1952 the line was doubled in length and widened to 2-foot gauge, latterly using a Simplex (Motor Rail) engine *Oliver* with a steam-outline body, built in 1953. This line was slightly longer than the present-day route, with a station on the north side of the lake.

The line was reconstructed to 15-inch-gauge in 2009-10, opening at Easter 2010.

Operating dates
Daily, from April to end of October, from 11.00am to 5.00pm (low season) or as late as 8.00pm (high season)

Locomotive
Severn-Lamb 'Rio Grande' 2-8-0 steam-outline diesel-hydraulic, numbered 362 (1978)

Carriages
Four, semi-open

Blackpool Zoo Miniature Railway
(Zoo entry fees apply)

Location
Blackpool Zoo
East Park Drive
Blackpool FY3 8PP
Tel: 01253 830830
Website: www.blackpoolzoo.org.uk

Route
A single line of 700 yards runs through a woodland setting within the Zoo, from North to South stations; the route was considerably altered in 2011.

Background
Constructed by Severn-Lamb Ltd under contract in 1972, this is a characteristic example of the firm's all-inclusive, 'out of the box' provision.

Operating dates
Open daily from March to October, from 10.00am

Locomotive
'Rio Grande' 2-8-0 steam-outline diesel-hydraulic (no name or number) (1972)

Carriages
Six bogie open; normally four used at one time

Blenheim Park Railway
(Park entry fees apply)

Location
Blenheim Palace
Woodstock
Oxfordshire OX20 1PX
Tel: 01993 811091
Website: www.blenheimpalace.com

Route
The present line links the Palace to the Pleasure Gardens and other attractions, with a length of 1,000 yards in the shape of a figure 7, passing through a small wood. Both terminal stations have run-round loops and there is a three-road engine and carriage shed.

Background
The railway was built by Pleasurerail Ltd in 1975, originally as an out-and-back run of 700 yards within the Pleasure Gardens. The initial motive power was Twining and Guest's (steam) 4-6-2 *Prince Charles*, formerly at Dudley Zoo and Fairbourne, purchased by W. McAlpine (Chairman of Pleasurerail Ltd) and renamed *Sir Winston Churchill*. Other locomotives used from time to time were David Curwen's *Muffin* and Trevor Guest's *Tracy-Jo*.

Operating dates
The railway operates daily from April to October at a half-hourly frequency. Travel requires purchase of a Park and Gardens ticket; prices are higher if admission to the Palace is included.

Locomotives
Anna 4-6w diesel-mechanical (G&S Light Engineering, 1960)
Sir Winston Churchill 0-6-2 steam-outline diesel-hydraulic (Alan Keef Ltd, 1992)

Carriages
Four 16-seat bogie semi-open, with canopy roofs

'It's behind you!' Enthusiasts at the Bure Valley Gala in 2009. *G. Sutton*

Bure Valley Railway

Location
Bure Valley Railway Co Ltd
Aylsham Station
Norwich Road
Aylsham
Norfolk NR11 6BW
Tel: 01263 733858
Website: www.bvrw.co.uk

Route
The railway uses the trackbed of the former East Norfolk standard-gauge railway between Aylsham (South) and Wroxham, a distance of 8.9 miles, with a headquarters and depot at Aylsham. There are intermediate stations (served as request stops) at Brampton, Buxton and Coltishall. Aylsham and Wroxham stations both have extensive car parking, and connections with the 'Bittern Line' Norwich to Sheringham trains are available at Hoveton & Wroxham station.

Background
Standard-gauge train services on the route ceased in 1952 (passenger) and 1955 (freight). In order to promote tourism within the Broads National Park, the trackbed was purchased by Broadland District Council in 1987 for use as a footpath and cycleway as well as for the operation of 15-inch-gauge passenger trains. The pedestrian and cycle routes completed in 1991 make numerous links to other paths in the area, including the River Bure. The railway was constructed by the Bure Valley Railway Co at a cost of £2.5 million and opened on 10 July 1990, but its parent company (RKF Holdings) ceased to trade in 1991; after some changes of control the railway has been principally owned by Westernasset Ltd since 1995. The company is vigorously supported by the Friends of the Bure Valley Railway.

Engineering works
The innovative, fully fenced foot and cycle route parallels the entire length of the railway (and continues westward to Lenwade, under Norfolk County Council ownership). The only

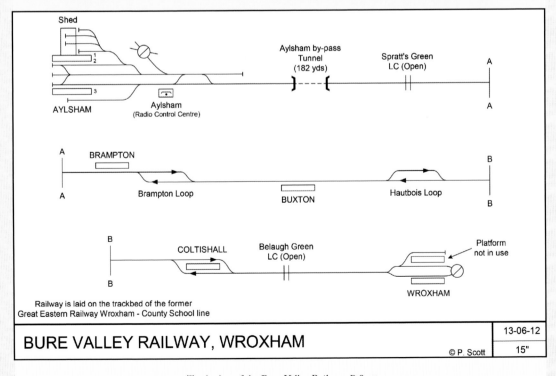

Track plan of the Bure Valley Railway. *P. Scott*

Giant of the 15-inch-gauge: *Lydia* towers above the Bure Valley Railway standard carriages while visiting for a Gala weekend on 10 October 2009. *G. Sutton*

operational railway tunnel in Norfolk takes the line under the A140 Aylsham by-pass road, and the River Bure at Buxton Lammas is crossed by a 32-metre girder bridge (one of 17 bridges along the line). Both terminal station buildings are substantial and well-equipped; remains of some original station buildings, not in railway ownership, can be seen at other locations. Passing loops are provided at Brampton, Hautbois (pronounced 'Hobbis') and Coltishall.

Operating dates
Normally February half-term; weekends in March; daily April-October (various timetable frequencies); weekends in November; special trains in December and at New Year.

Events
The Bure Valley is noted for its special enthusiast events such as an 'Everything Goes' gala at Spring Bank Holiday and a Steam Gala with visiting locomotives in late September. One- and two-day Driver Experience courses are available for advance booking.

Locomotives
Steam
No 1 *Wroxham Broad* 2-6-4T (G&S Light Engineering, (1964); originally internal-combustion, converted to live steam by Winson Engineering
No 6 *Blickling Hall* 2-6-2 (Winson Engineering, 1994)
No 7 *Spitfire* 2-6-2 Winson Engineering, 1994)
No 8 *Thunder* 2-6-2T by BVR (Winson kit, 1997)
No 9 *Mark Timothy* 2-6-4T (Winson Engineering and Alan Keef, 1999)

Nos 6, 7, 8 and 9 are mechanically similar, based on a half-scale version of the 'ZB' Class locomotives built for service in India and Pakistan.

Diesel
No 3 *2nd Air Division USAAF* 4w-4w diesel-hydraulic (BVR, 1989); equipped for passenger train operation
No 4 *Rusty* 4w diesel-hydraulic (Hunslet Engine Co, 1954)
No 5 Steam-outline 4w diesel-mechanical 'tram' engine (Lister Blackstone, 1960)
-    2-2w-4 battery-electric (Greenwood & Batley, 1966); currently dismantled, to be rebuilt

Carriages
20 standard bogies; five wheelchair-accessible Special Saloons; two four-wheel brake vans; electric train heating generator (all steel-bodied, built 1989-2002)
Two wooden-bodied bogie coaches, ex-Réseau Guerlédan and Fairbourne railways, used for special events

Wagons
Six for permanent way work, including 'flail' vehicle for cutting and spraying lineside vegetation.

Further reading
Vaughan, Adrian *A History of the Bure Valley Railway* (BVR Co, Aylsham, 2000)

Cleethorpes Coast Light Railway

Location
Cleethorpes Coast Light Railway
Lakeside Station
Kings Road
Cleethorpes
North East Lincolnshire DN35 0AG
Tel: 01472 604657
Website: www.cleethorpescoastlightrailway.co.uk

Route
The line runs from a terminus at Kingsway alongside a boating lake, then turns inland to Lakeside, formerly a terminus but since 2007 adapted as a through station. It then continues to North Sea Lane (on the Meridian Line) with distant views across the Humber estuary to Spurn Point. A busy road crossing at Lakeside is protected by lights operated from the former Sutton Miniature Railway signal box. The total length is 2 miles.

Background
The first miniature railway on the site was of 10¼-inch gauge, constructed by Botterills of Nottingham and opened in 1948, comprising a half-mile run alongside the boating lake. The concession was taken over by Arthur Clethro in 1954, using battery-electric power, but operation was handed back to Cleethorpes Borough Council in 1959 and the track was doubled. In 1971 the line was rebuilt to a virtually unique gauge of 14½ inches and extended to the Zoo near Lakeside, using Severn-Lamb 'Rio Grande'-type locomotives and one with a *Flying Scotsman* outline, all fuelled on propane gas. After closure

Many pubs claim to be the 'smallest', but the Signal Box Inn at Cleethorpes makes the strongest claim!

of the Zoo in 1978 the line's fortunes declined and it was reduced to single track in 1982, the far terminus being appropriately named 'Witts End'! The track was relaid to the conventional 15-inch-gauge in 1990-91, since when there has been extensive development by Chris and Debra Shaw, including the acquisition of the Sutton Collection in 2002, the extension to North Sea Lane in 2007, and a new station at Kingsway, including a short route extension. Visitor facilities include a shop at Kingsway, a tea room, and the 'Signal Box Inn' at Lakeside – said to be the smallest on the planet! Special events include occasional Steam Galas with visiting locomotives, and 1940s-style weekends.

Part of the Sutton Collection is normally on display in the Griffin Hall at Lakeside, together with a historical miniature railway exhibition.

There is an active Supporters' Association, which successfully raised matching funding for the Heritage Lottery Memorial Fund grant for the Sutton Collection.

A possible further extension to South Sea Lane, Humberstone, would give a total distance of 3 miles.

Operating dates
Normally weekends in March, April and May; daily end May to early September; weekends in October; specials in December

Locomotives
Steam
No 111 *Yvette* 4-4-0 (E. Craven/T. Tate, 1970), based on LNER Class 'D49'
No 24 *Sandy River* 2-6-2 (Fairbourne Railway, 1990), based on American prototype
Effie 0-4-0T (Great Northern Steam, 1990); rebuilt 2006; replica of Heywood design
Mountaineer 0-4-0 (W. van der Heiden, 1970); formerly at Bush Mill Railway, Tasmania
No 6284 2-8-0 (Turner/Croome & Loxley, 2009), based on LNER Class 'O4'

Sutton Collection
No 1 *Sutton Belle* 4-4-2 (Cannon Ironfounders, 1933)
No 2 *Sutton Flyer* 4-4-2 (Cannon Ironfounders and Griffin Foundry, 1950)
No 3 *Mighty Atom* 4-4-2 (Bassett-Lowke, 1908); also named *Prince of Wales*

Left: Taking a well-earned rest, *Sutton Flyer* is displayed in the Griffin Hall at Lakeside station, Cleethorpes. *D. Holroyde*

Below: The Sutton Miniature Railway 'GWR Railcar' No 4. *P. Green*

There is a long-term project to restore *Crompton*, an 18-inch-gauge 4-4-2 built by David Curwen (1951), and convert it for 15-inch-gauge operation.

Internal combustion

Toby 4w steam-outline diesel-mechanical
    (Lister, 1944)
The Cub   4-4w diesel-hydraulic
    (Minirail, 1954)
No 5 *Battison* 2-6-4T steam-outline diesel-
    electric (S. Battison, 1958)
DA1 4w diesel-mechanical
    (Bush Mill Railway, 1986)
(KD1) four-car diesel-electric railcar 'Rapido'
    (Rail Systems, 1983)

Sutton Collection

No 4 *Dudley* 4-4w petrol-hydraulic (G&S
    Light Engineering, 1946) to GWR
    'Streamlined Railcar' outline

Carriages

Approximately 15 covered or semi-open bogie vehicles from the Longleat, Liverpool Garden Festival and Bush Mill Railways

Sutton Collection

Six covered steel-bodied bogie coaches (Nos 1-3 being originally from Great Yarmouth); four open *cars de luxe* with slatted seats.

Left: Coaches at rest at Lakeside Station, Cleethorpes, including (left) an example from the Longleat Railway and (right) a 'corridor' connection from Great Yarmouth.

The American-
style 2-6-2 No 24
Sandy River from
Cleethorpes, in fine
form at a Kirklees
Light Railway gala on
12 September 2009.
P. Green

(Combe St Martin) Wildlife and Dinosaur Adventure Park Railway

(Park entry fees apply)

Location
Leigh
Combe Martin
Ilfracombe
Devon EX34 0NG
Tel: 01271 882 486
Website: www.wildlifedinosaurpark.co.uk

Route
The line is 500 yards long, end-to-end, with a station, tunnel and a torrent of 7,500 gallons of water that rushes alongside the train (now named the 'Earthquake Canyon Train Ride') on each trip.

Background
The Park extends to 26 acres featuring many live animal attractions, dinosaur models and animations. The railway – opened in 1989 and extended two years later – draws its inspiration from an American theme park.

Operating dates
Easter to end October or early November, 10.00am to 5.00pm

Locomotive
Severn-Lamb Mk 2 2-8-0 steam-outline
    petrol-hydraulic (1987)

Carriages
Two bogie carriages, with canopies

Clevedon Miniature Railway

Location
Salthouse Fields,
Clevedon
North Somerset BS21 7XP

Background
The railway was originally built to a gauge of 9½ inches in 1952, and ran in this form for exactly 60 years. Initially an out-and-back run with a live steam 4-4-2 locomotive, it was converted to a circuit in 1962, and operated by diesel power. A later 'Rio Grande' 2-8-0 petrol-electric locomotive was the smallest of its kind built by Severn-Lamb.

The line, circling a field near the seafront, gives a run of 900 yards, and at the end of 2012 the new leaseholder, Harvey Amusements, announced that it is to be re-gauged to 15 inches for operation by a battery-electric (steam-outline) 4-6-0 with two carriages. The 9½-inch-gauge stock has been retained by the previous operator.

Craigtoun Park Railway

Location
Craigtoun Park,
St Andrews
Fife KY16 8NX
Tel: (not available)
Website: www.craigtounparkrailway.co.uk

Route
The line consists of a quarter-mile circuit around a lake at the Park, passing the listed Dutch Village and crossing two bridges.

Background
A short 7¼-inch-gauge railway was first opened in 1960 and regauged to 15 inches by Severn-Lamb Ltd in 1976; the present layout was adopted in 1996. It is owned by Fife Council but since 2011 has been operated on a yearly concession basis (in 2012, by MRW Railways Ltd), with a second locomotive (previously used in Ireland) brought in.

Operating dates
(2011) July and August, daily, 10.30am to 5.30pm. Operation in 2012 and future years is expected to be from mid-June until September.

Locomotive
2-8-0 steam-outline diesel-hydraulic with Perkins engine (Severn-Lamb, 1973)

Carriages
Two open and two semi-open

Difflin Lake Railway
(Garden entry fees apply)

Location
Oakfield Park
Raphoe
County Donegal
Republic of Ireland   Tel: 07491 73068
Website: www.oakfieldpark.com

Route
The railway is an integral feature of the restored gardens. A complex layout around the lakes and gardens, it was originally 3.3km and has been recently extended to 4km, comprising three interconnected loops allowing various lengths of run.

Background
Oakfield Park is the private residence of retired businessman Sir Gerry Robinson; the house is *not* open to the public at any time but the gardens are generally open from Wednesday to Sunday during the summer months. The architects of the railway were A. & E. Wright of Belfast, with technical consultants Martin's Models Garden Railways of Kington, Herefordshire. The choice of 15-inch-gauge (rather than 12¼ inches) was influenced by the availability of a partly built 'Exmoor' Class locomotive.

Operating dates
The railway operates on Saturdays and Sundays only, from May to end August, and is normally worked by the diesel locomotive, except for 'Steam Sunday' – the last Sunday of each month. Railway tickets, supplementary to garden entry, are obtained from the station building, which is also licensed for the sale of refreshments.

Locomotives
No 1 *The Duchess of Difflin* 0-4-2T (Exmoor Steam Railway, 2003)
No 2 *The Earl of Oakfield* 4w diesel-hydraulic (Alan Keef Ltd, 2002); Perkins diesel engine with hydrostatic transmission

Carriages
Two covered, externally resembling and liveried as (3-foot-gauge) County Donegal Joint Railway – one bogie 3rd Class, one bogie Brake 1st with provision to carry wheelchairs. Two four-wheel open, general design similar to Bassett-Lowke coaches of early 20th century. Air braking is in use.

Wagons
Two four-wheel open; one bogie flat car (air-braked)

Right: A typical Severn-Lamb 'Rio Grande' locomotive, in use at the Craigtoun Park Railway at St Andrews. *P. Bryant*

Left: The Duchess of Difflin hauls two 'County Donegal'-type coaches on the Difflin Lake Railway in 2007. *P. Scott*

Eaton (Hall) Railway
(Garden entry fees apply)

Location
Eaton Hall
Eccleston
Chester CH4 9ET
Tel: 01244 684400 (Estate Office)
Website: www.eatonestate.co.uk

Route
The restored railway starts from the original Coal Store and Carriage Shed and follows the original (1896) route for a short distance through the gate into the park, where it divides at a triangular junction and forms a loop, 1½ miles in length, round the cricket ground and the woodland beyond.

Background
The original Eaton Railway closed and was completely dismantled in 1947, most of the surviving equipment going to the Romney, Hythe & Dymchurch Railway. The three remaining coaches were presented back to the Eaton Estate for preservation in 1980, but the Duke did not progress the idea of rebuilding the railway until 1996, when one of the four replicas of the 0-4-0 *Katie* was purchased and a short length of track laid. The route through the Park received planning permission in 1998 and was complete by 2000, the first public open day taking place in 2004.

Operating dates
The railway usually runs on the four Sundays when the gardens are opened to the public for charity. Tickets for morning trains are sold from 10.30am and for afternoon trains from 1.30pm, but usually sell out quickly.
      Occasional 'Steam at Eaton' days for

Always a good idea... An Open Day at Eaton Hall.

Left: Katie (a replica) emerges into the Park at Eaton Hall, where the rebuilt railway follows the original course.

Below: Ursula (renamed as *Shelagh*) and *Katie* double-head at the 'Steam at Eaton' event on 25 July 2009. P. Green

enthusiasts have taken place, bringing visiting locomotives such as *Ursula* from Perrygrove, *Effie* from Cleethorpes and *Synolda* from the Ravenglass & Eskdale Railway.

Locomotive
Katie 0-4-0T replica of original Heywood design, begun by FMB Engineering, completed by P. Stileman (1995); repaired by Alan Keef Ltd (2001)

Carriages
Open bogie carriage and four-wheel brake van (2000); the 'Duchess's Coach' (covered, 2004); bogie brake van (rebuilt to original height). The majority of the rebuilding work was carried out by the Eaton Hall estate staff; the remaining sections of original bodywork unable to be restored were donated to the Heywood Collection at the Perrygrove Railway.

Evesham Vale Light Railway

Location
Evesham Vale Country Park
Twyford
Evesham WR11 4TP
Tel: 01386 422282
Website: www.evlr.co.uk

Route
Beginning at Twyford station adjoining the car park, the line swings to the right into the Country Park and has a current length of just over a mile including a tunnel on the balloon loop. Evesham Vale station, also on the loop, is a convenient venue for walks and picnics. There is the possibility of future extension of the railway.

Background
The railway was built by Jim and Helen Shackell in 2002 as a venue for the operation of their collection of magnificently restored locomotives and rolling stock. The station buildings are some

of the most impressive on recent 15-inch-gauge railways, Twyford in particular with its overall roof fitting perfectly into its setting. Apart from the busy shopping village, the Country Park itself is currently rather undeveloped, but the site owners are believed to have plans for significant enhancements. In January 2012 the railway was sold to Adrian and Susan Corke – experienced preservationists – who plan to develop it further with the assistance of a small group of volunteers. The historic locomotive *Count Louis* was based here until the end of the 2012 season.

Operating dates
Weekends throughout the year, and daily during school holidays, from 10.30am to 5.00pm (4.00pm in winter months). Steam Gala weekend in early July.

Locomotives
The regular operating fleet comprises:
Dougal 0-6-2T+T (Severn-Lamb, 1970)
St Egwin 0-4-0T+T (Exmoor Steam Railway, 2003)

Diesel locomotives in use include
Cromwell 4w diesel-hydraulic (Ruston & Hornsby, 1960); originally diesel-mechanical; rebuilt 1984
Sludge 4w (Lister, 1955)
Bessie self-propelled tipping unit (2002) (currently away on loan)

Although modern, the Evesham Vale station building has a timeless rustic charm.

The restored *Count Louis* at work overlooking the Vale of Evesham on 29 August 2011.

Carriages
Four bogie, ex-Réseau Guerlédan and Fairbourne, some liveried similar to Talyllyn Railway (1978)
Three-car articulated semi-open set, ex-Fairbourne (Alfred Hope & Co, 1952)
One German-type open coach

Fairbourne Railway
(Recently Fairbourne & Barmouth Railway and Fairbourne Steam Railway – 12¼-inch-gauge since 1985)

Location
Fairbourne Railway Co
Beach Road
Fairbourne
Gwynedd LL38 2EX
Tel: 01341 250362
Website: www.fairbournerailway.com

Route
The line extends for just under 2 miles from the station in Beach Road, Fairbourne (adjoining the Cambrian Coast line level crossing and station), to Barmouth Ferry, partially roadside to Golf Halt. There are three road crossings between Fairbourne and Beach Halt, and a tunnel between Estuary Halt and Barmouth Ferry. The balloon loop on the seaward side of the sand dunes at the Ferry, out of use for five years, was cleared early in 2012 for occasional trains.

Fairbourne's splendid half-scale *Sherpa* is as much 'at home' on the Welsh coast as the full-sized 'B' class engines are in the Himalayan foothills.

Background

What other railway has operated on no fewer than four different gauges, two of them at the same time? Although the Fairbourne to Barmouth Ferry line, in its current form, is laid to 12¼-inch gauge, it would be unfair and ungenerous to exclude it from this book since it has played a major role in the history of the 15-inch-gauge. The route and purpose of the line are unaltered, and its essential character and ambience have been revived under its more recent owners.

The general story has been covered in the two 'History' sections of this book. In 1995 the line was bought from the Ellerton family by Prof and Mrs Tony Atkinson and Dr and Mrs John Melton, who invested heavily in improvements – taking no income – and covered annual revenue shortfalls. In a most generous act, they transferred ownership to a charitable company (North Wales Coast Light Railway Ltd) in 2009 and thus wrote off £500,000 of invested funds. Operation is now in the hands of the Fairbourne Railway Preservation Society, which, following the death of Prof Atkinson, launched an appeal for funds in October 2011.

Operating dates

Limited service in February, March, September and October; daily April to early September; Gala event in early June. The connecting ferry to Barmouth harbour operates from Easter onwards

Cafés are operated at Fairbourne station when trains are running and at Barmouth Ferry in high season.

Locomotives

Steam

The four locomotives are half-scale replicas of 2-foot-gauge prototypes:

No E759 *Yeo* (originally *Jubilee*) 2-6-2 T Lynton & Barnstaple Railway type (David Curwen, 1978)

No 2 *Beddgelert* (originally *David Curwen*) 0-6-4 ST, North Wales Narrow Gauge Railways type (David Curwen, 1979)

No 4 *Sherpa* (originally *France*) 0-4-0 ST, Darjeeling Himalayan Railway 'B' Class (Milner Engineering, 1978)

No 5 *Russell* 2-6-4T, Welsh Highland Railway type (Milner Engineering, 1979)

Internal-combustion

Gwril [III] 4w diesel-hydraulic, originally 2-foot-gauge, with Kubota engine (Hunslet, 1994; overhauled by Alan Keef, 1997)

No 5 *Tony* (recently *Lilian Walter*) 4w-4w diesel-mechanical, originally 15-inch-gauge *Sylvia* (G&S Light Engineering, 1961); rebuilt 1985; re-engined 2000 and currently receiving new body)

Carriages

Approximately 20 covered bogie coaches, several with balconies, to North Wales Narrow Gauge Railways outline, ex Réseau Guerlédan (further examples dispersed)

Three bogie by Bagnalls, Stafford, ex-Butlins, Skegness (2009) – to be rebuilt

Further reading

anon *Fairbourne Railway, one of the Welsh Narrow Gauge lines* (Photo Precision, c1970)

Boyd, J. I. C. *Narrow Gauge Railways in Mid Wales*, pp175-191 (Oakwood Press, 1965)

Buck, S. *Siân and Katie – The Twining Sisters* (Siân Project Group, 1995)

Butcher, Alan C. (ed) *Railways Restored 2005* (Ian Allan Publishing Co, 2005)

Milner, W. J. *Rails through the Sand* (Rail Romances, Chester, 1996)

Souvenir Guide Book (Fairbourne Railway, 2005)

Wilkins, J. *Fairbourne Railway – A Short History of Its Development and Progress* (Fairbourne Railway Co, c1964)

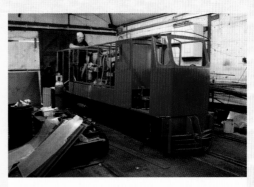

The only locomotive from the Wilkins era still running at Fairbourne is the former *Sylvia*, re-gauged to 12¼ inches as *Lilian Walter*, and now being fitted with new bodywork as *Tony*.

Gulliver's Railroad at Gulliver's Land
(Theme park entry fees apply; adults must be accompanied by a child)

Location
Gulliver's Land
Livingstone Drive
Newlands
Milton Keynes MK15 0DT
Tel: 01925 444888
Website: www.gulliversfun.co.uk/miltonkeynes

Route
A circular line of 600 yards runs round the outskirts of the Park; trains call at four stations.

Background
This children's theme park, just within the City of Milton Keynes, opened in 1999 and has seven sections aimed mainly at children under ten. A campsite nearby opened in 2010.

Operating dates
School holidays; most weekends from April; limited weekdays in May and June; daily July-August; weekends September and October; certain dates in December. Site entry fee includes the train.

Locomotive
0-6-0 (steam outline) with 6w diesel-electric powered tender, built on site (1999)

Carriages
Two bogie, semi-open

Gulliver's Railroad at Gulliver's World (Theme park entry fees apply; adults must be accompanied by a child)

Location
Gulliver's World
Old Hall
Warrington
WA5 9YZ
Tel: 01925 444888
Website: www.gulliversfun.co.uk/warrington

Route
A circular line of 500 yards.

Background
This children's family theme park lies in a forest setting just west of Warrington and includes a man-made lake. It was opened in 1989 and contains more than 50 rides and attractions.

Operating dates
School holidays; most weekends from April;

limited weekdays in May and June; daily July-August; weekends September and October; certain dates in December. Site entry fee includes train.

Locomotive
0-6-0 (steam outline) with 6w diesel-electric powered tender (Meridian Motioneering, 1989)

Carriages
Two bogie, semi-open

Alan Keef's 0-6-2T steam-outline diesel *Helen* finally displaced live steam on the Haigh Country Park Railway. *P. Scott*

Haigh Country Park Railway

Note: this railway was closed during 2012, but was expected to resume operation after overhaul in 2013, probably by an external contractor under licence.

Location
Haigh Country Park
Haigh
Wigan
WN2 1PE
Tel: 01942 832895
Website: www.wlct.org/haigh/haigh-country-park.htm

Route
A circular scenic ride of 1 mile around woodlands and past the walled gardens and the Swan Pond. There are two stations on the circuit (Haigh Hall North and South), the latter having a passing loop and a three-road engine shed.

Background
Haigh Hall, built 1827-40, is the former home of the Earls of Crawford and Balcarras, and is surrounded by 250 acres of park and woodland. It lies about 3 miles NNE of Wigan town centre and was purchased by Wigan Borough Council in 1947, and subsequently developed for public recreation. A number of attempts to establish a railway were made by Gilbert Swift, Director of Leisure Services, from 1982 onwards, success being achieved with the purchase of the locomotive *Rachel*, three open and four enclosed coaches and some wagons – including the former canteen vehicle – from the Fairbourne Railway. Rail mostly came from the Yorkshire Water Authority at Distington, with cut-down standard-gauge sleepers. For about ten years from 1986 the line operated live steam with E. W. Twining's 2-4-2 *Katie* (also from Fairbourne), which ran here as *Haigh Hall* and later moved to Cleethorpes, then to Windmill Farm for restoration.

Nearby, the Wigan Model Engineering Society operate a dual 3½/5-inch-gauge locomotive track.

Operating dates
Weekends from Easter to end October and daily during school holidays (weather permitting), from 12.00 to 4.00pm (Easter to September) and to 3.30pm (October)

Locomotives
Helen 0-6-2T steam-outline diesel-hydraulic

(Alan Keef, 1992)
Rachel 0-6-0 diesel-mechanical (originally petrol-mechanical) (G&S Light Engineering, 1961); renamed *W. Brogan MBE* for some years after 1986

Carriages
Four, semi-open (Alan Keef Ltd)

Heatherslaw Light Railway

Location
Ford Forge
Heatherslaw
Cornhill-on-Tweed
TD12 4QA
Tel: 01890 820244 / 820317
Website: www.heatherslawlightrailway.co.uk

Route
From the Old Forge near Heatherslaw Mill, the line follows the right bank of the River Till to Castle Bank below Etal Castle, both interesting sites for visitors. The line is now 2 miles long, an earlier 'short cut' across the Haugh away from the river having been taken out, and a passing loop installed. Trains climb a short length of 1 in 35 gradient on the approach to Etal station.

Background
The railway was a 'dream come true' for the late Neville Smith, planned in the late 1980s on a site leased from the Ford and Etal Estate of Lord Joicey, and opened in 1989. The track was laid by local labour, using 20lb per yard rail. Despite the provision of flood relief channels, the line has been damaged by the river in 1992, 2008 and 2009, the most serious flash flood being in August-September 2008, which also badly affected Heatherslaw Mill and the associated buildings. A short deviation of route has since been installed, and concrete sleepers were experimented with (unsuccessfully) to give better resistance to inundation. Heatherslaw station has an overall roof, and also houses a model railway display. Operation of the railway is now assisted by the Heatherslaw Railway Society, and between 25,000 and 30,000 visitors are carried annually.

Above: Rural delight: *The Lady Augusta*, with her magnificent tall chimney, waits at Etal on the Heatherslaw Light Railway.

Below: The Lady Augusta at work on the Heatherslaw Light Railway on 19 April 2009. *D. Verity*

Operating dates

Daily service April to October, 11.00am to 3.00pm (or 4.00pm in July and August); basic timetable hourly but half-hourly if required in July and August in some years (not 2012). Running time, 18 minutes.

Locomotives
Steam

The Lady Augusta 0-4-2 (Brian Taylor, as sub-contractor to R&ER, 1989); under overhaul off-site in 2012

Bunty 2-6-0T+T (designed by Neville Smith with bar frames, completed by Alan Keef, 2010)

Both are equipped to burn wood fuel (i.e. 'carbon neutral') and have air brakes.

Internal-combustion

Clive 4-4w diesel-hydraulic (Neville Smith, 2000); since re-engined; may be further rebuilt in future

A simple 'fresh air' solution to the carriage of wheelchairs at Etal!

Carriages

Twelve bogie (eight in normal use), total carrying capacity 100 passengers with steam locomotive; normal maximum of four with diesel locomotive

Kirklees Light Railway

Location

Clayton West Station
Park Mill Way
Clayton West
HD8 9XJ
Tel: 01484 865727
Website: www.kirkleeslightrailway.com

Route

The line uses 3½ miles of the trackbed of the former Clayton West standard-gauge branch to Shelley Woodhouse, mainly on embankment but including a 511-yard-long tunnel. There are views of the Emley Moor radio and TV mast and of an ancient woodland, Blacker Wood.

Background

The railway was developed by the late Brian Taylor and his wife Doreen to provide a range of attractions for visiting families, while the variety and technical aspects of the steam locomotive designs are of great interest to enthusiasts. The line enjoys a large site at Clayton West where facilities include a café, indoor play area and shop, an outdoor railway-themed play area, a 7¼-inch-gauge line encircling a duck pond, and a raised model engineers' track.

Operating dates

Weekends throughout the year, normally every 40 minutes from 11.00am to 3.40pm; daily during school holidays, either as above or every 70 minutes from 10.30am

Locomotives
Steam

Fox 2-6-2T Hunslet Engine Co outline (B. Taylor, 1990)

Badger 0-6-4T, freelance design (B. Taylor, 1991)

Hawk 0-4-4-0T Kitson-Meyer articulated (B. Taylor, 1998)

Owl 0-4-4-0T Avonside-Heisler articulated with shaft, chain and geared drive (B. Taylor, 2000)

Internal-combustion

Jay 4-w diesel for works use (B. Taylor, 1992; rebuilt 2002)

No 7 2-2w steam-outline petrol-hydraulic, tram body (B. Taylor, 1991)

Above: The enlarged, former standard-gauge terminus at Clayton West dominates a fine display of 4-4-2 locomotives at a gala event. *Kirklees Light Railway/S. Ross*

Right: Many lines have tunnels – but the Kirklees Light Railway has one of standard-gauge proportions, 511 yards long! The Avonside-Heisler geared locomotive *Owl* emerges with a train in 2011. *Kirklees Light Railway/S. Ross*

Carriages

Fourteen bogie, mostly built on-site, including two brake, two semi-open, and two 1st Class (built 2007-08). All covered vehicles are steam-heated.

Wagons

Two bogie rail flats; one 4w rail flat; one ballast open; one tool van

Further reading

Earnshaw, Alan *One Man's Line to Clayton West* (Trans-Pennine Publications, 1993)

Above: Hawk, based on a Kitson-Meyer design, is seen at Kirklees in 2007. The exhaust steam pipe from the rear cylinders can clearly be seen in the coal bunker.

Right: It is hard to believe that Martens's *Black Prince* from New Romney and the diminutive Cagney No 44 from Rhyl both run on 15-inch-gauge track, as seen at the Kirklees Light Railway on 10 September 2011. *D. Verity*

Knowsley Safari Park Railway

(Park entry fees apply)

Location
Knowsley Safari Park
Prescot
Knowsley
L34 4AN
Tel: 0151 430 9009
Website: www.knowsleysafariexperience.co.uk

Route
The 'dumb-bell'-shaped line is 800 yards in length, with the second loop running through woodland and round Mizzy Lake, giving views of the elephant paddock.

Background
The 'Lakeside Railway' was built in 1991 as one aspect of the amusement area associated with the pioneering safari park created by the Earl of Derby in 1971, one of the first where animals were allowed to roam in relative freedom while visitors were confined to touring the park by car.

Operating dates
Daily (except Christmas Day) from 10.00am A fare additional to the park entry fee is payable.

Locomotive
2-6-0 steam outline diesel-hydraulic (no name or number) (Severn Lamb, 1991)

Carriages
Bogie; two semi-open, three open

Lakeside Miniature Railway

Location
Marine Lake
Esplanade
Southport
Merseyside PR8 1RX
Tel: 01772 745511
Website: www.lakesideminiaturerailway.co.uk

Route
The line is 800 yards in length, from Pleasureland at the south-west corner of the Marine Lake to Marine Parade, passing under Southport Pier.

Background
As one of the pioneering seaside lines of 1911, Llewelyn's (now Lakeside) Miniature Railway has had an influence out of all proportion to its length, notably in being the home base of Harry N. Barlow's fleet of streamlined diesel-electric 'Pacifics' from 1948 and in setting up the 'Far Tottering & Oystercreek Railway' at the Festival of Britain in 1951. Regular steam operation ended with Barlow's 1969 sale of the line, and the surrounding area has suffered by the removal of several holiday and leisure attractions such as the 1928-built outdoor Sea

Top: The Lakeside Miniature Railway depot at Southport recalls busy times in the past, when three locomotives would have been used daily.

Above: Pleasureland station, Southport, at the height of its elegance in 1997, with Curwen's *Princess Anne* on a short train. *P. Scott*

Bathing Lake and the Pleasureland fairground rides, which included a veteran wooden roller-coaster.

However, under the ownership of the late John Spencer (to 2006), and since of Don Clark, the railway has continued to defy economics and occasional vandalism and to operate each season – sometimes earlier and later than the advertised dates, when weather conditions are favourable for visitors. As the first such line he knew as a child, and one of the inspirations for this book, the author wishes this grand centenarian every future success.

Operating dates
Easter to end of October, 11.00am to 5.00pm

Locomotives
Duke of Edinburgh [II] 4-6-2 diesel-electric (H. Barlow, 1950)
Golden Jubilee 1911-1961 4-6-0 diesel-hydraulic (H. Barlow, 1963)
Princess Anne 6-6w diesel-hydraulic, 'Western' Class outline (designed by David Curwen, built by Severn-Lamb, 1971)
No 3 *Jenny* 2-6-2T steam-outline diesel-hydraulic (A. Moss, 2006)

Carriages
The full fleet comprised 24 open bogie vehicles, mostly as articulated pairs, some having been built for operation in Battersea Park in 1951. Several units are out of use awaiting restoration, one train set having been refurbished for the 2011 Centenary.

Top: The new station building at Princes Parade, seen from Southport Pier; the 'Trains to Pleasureland' sign recalls an earlier era.

Above: The railway celebrated its centenary in 2011. *Golden Jubilee*, built for the 50th anniversary, was Barlow's last design.

Lappa Valley Steam Railway

Location
Benny Halt
St Newlyn East
Newquay
TR8 5LX
Tel: 01872 510317
Website: www.lappavalley.co.uk

Route
The railway is a successful conversion of the 1-mile Benny Halt to East Wheal Rose section of the standard-gauge line originally built by Joseph Treffry in 1849 for mineral extraction, which later passed to the Great Western Railway and British Railways. Access, car parking and ticket office, are at Benny Halt.

Background
The Lappa Valley is an important wildlife conservation and industrial heritage site, the preserved East Wheal Rose mine engine house (closed for structural repair in early 2012) being a notable feature, recalling the 1846 flooding disaster that claimed 39 lives underground. The 15-inch-gauge railway was constructed by Eric Booth and opened in 1974 to give better

Zebedee heads a Lappa Valley train, conveying visitors to the attractions of the East Wheal Rose site in 2006. *G. Sutton*

public access to the site, and is now owned by the Lappa Valley Railway Co. Visitor facilities at the landscaped East Wheal Rose site include a boating lake, a locomotive-themed maze, play areas and woodland walks; there is also a nine-hole golf course nearby.

Two further miniature railway trips are available, the 10¼-inch-gauge Newlyn Branch Line continuing along a further mile of trackbed to Newlyn Halt (using two diesel locomotives), and the 7¼-inch-gauge Woodland Railway giving a 350-yard circular ride (using petrol units based on the 1970s High Speed Train and Advanced Passenger Train).

Operating dates
Daily, 1 April to 2 September; daily except Saturdays rest of September; Sundays to Thursdays in October; daily in autumn half-term school holiday Train fare includes use of almost all amenities at East Wheal Rose.

Locomotives (15-inch-gauge)
No 1 *Zebedee* 0-6-4T (designed by David Curwen, built by Severn-Lamb, 1974)
No 2 *Muffin* 0-6-0 (designed David Curwen, built by Berwyn Engineering, 1967)
(No 3) *Gladiator* 4-4w diesel-hydraulic (Minirail, 1960)
No 4 *Arthur* 4w diesel-mechanical (Lister, 1942)

Carriages (15-inch-gauge)
Ten (originally four) bogie, mostly semi-open but one fully enclosed and upholstered as 'First Class'; all locally built

Responsibility for the main-road Metha Bridge was a major problem in the conversion of the standard-gauge route to the 'heritage' Lappa Valley Railway. *Lappa Valley Railway*

Lightwater Valley Miniature Railway
(Park entry fees apply)

Location
Lightwater Valley Theme Park
North Stainley
Ripon
HG4 3HT
Tel: 0870 458 0040
Website: www.lightwatervalley.co.uk

Route
The circular, three-quarter-mile line includes one bridge and a 20-yard tunnel, from Lightwater Station stopping at 'Fort William' and 'Whistle Stop'.

Background
The theme park, evolving from a small farm attraction, was opened by Robert Staveley in 1969 and rapidly expanded. It passed into corporate ownership in 1997 and now includes more than 40 rides, including Europe's longest roller-coaster, 'The Ultimate', besides natural attractions such as a lake.

The railway was opened in 1979 and has remained a useful asset to move visitors around the Park, although some of its early interest has been lost with the dispersal of its fleet of historic locomotives. In its early years these included Henry Greenly's original *Little Giant* of 1905, his petrol locomotive *Blacolvesley* of 1909, the only 15-inch-gauge 'Royal Scot' built by Carland Engineering, and *Yvette*, built in 1946 (her prototype being the LNER 'D49' Class 4-4-0) – truly a remarkable collection at the line's outset.

Operating dates
Weekends from Easter; Wednesdays to Sundays in June; daily in July and August; weekends in September and October. Train is included within the Park entry fee.

Locomotive
No 278   'Rio Grande' 2-8-0 steam-outline
           diesel-hydraulic (Severn-Lamb, 1984)

Carriages
Six bogie, semi-open, one adapted for passengers in wheelchairs

Longleat Railway – 'Jungle Express'
(Park entry fees apply)

Location
Longleat House
Warminster
Wilts BA12 7N
Tel: 01985 844400 (Estate Office)
Website: www.longleat.co.uk

Route
The line was originally a 600-yard 'push-pull' operation to a point near the spillway, halfway along Longleat Lake. Later it was extended with steep gradients to Hazelwood Hill near the Safari Park entrance. A major reconstruction under the auspices of John Hayton took place in 1977, the line becoming a balloon loop using the old lakeside section on the return. The outward route was modified further in 1987-88, and in 1998 a tunnel was formed in part of a cutting at the extreme end of the loop. The

current length is 1 mile; a further realignment in 2008 introduced steeper gradients and tighter curves where the line now bisects the 'Jungle Kingdom' with a foot crossing.

Background
The railway is operated by Longleat Enterprises as part of the Safari and Adventure Parks associated with Longleat House, ancestral home of the 7th Marquess of Bath, whose son Viscount Weymouth is now chief executive. The house was opened to the public in 1949; the railway (constructed by Minirail – Matthew and Les Andersen) opened in 1965, and the pioneering Safari Park in 1966. Recently (2011-12) the railway has been rebranded the 'Jungle Express', bringing it closely in line with the theme park, and new colour schemes have been applied to the station and rolling stock, coupled with sound effects.

The main station, Longleat Central, has three platforms and a three-road engine shed. Points and indicator lights are controlled from

Longleat Junction Signal Box; the semaphore arms do not operate.

Operating dates
Weekends in March; daily April to end of October, from 10.00am. Travel on the 'Jungle Express' is restricted to holders of the All in One Day ticket; it is not available to holders of the Safari Only, or House and Gardens Only, tickets.

Locomotives
No 4 *Lenka* 4-4w diesel-hydraulic railcar with Deutz engine (built Longleat, 1984)
No 5 *Ceawlin* 2-8-2T GWR 'Pannier tank'-outline diesel-hydraulic with Petter engine (rebuilt Longleat 1989 from parts of former Severn-Lamb 'Rio Grande' No 2)
No 6 *Rudolph* 2-6-2T (Exmoor Steam Railway, 2004); formerly *John Hayton*)
No 7 *Flynn* 6w diesel-mechanical (Alan Keef, 2007)

Former motive power included an earlier No 1 railcar *Lenka*, sold to Oakwood Park in 1987; 0-6-0 *Muffin* designed by David Curwen, sold to Lappa Valley in 1974; and 0-6-2T No 3 *Dougal*, sold to Evesham Vale in 2004

Carriages
Eleven bogie, 16-seat and 20-seat, two (Nos 14 & 16) having access for disabled passengers. Four 16-seater bogie coaches (built by Severn-Lamb) were sold to the Cleethorpes Coast Light Railway in 1991, and one early bogie open coach has also survived, currently at the Sherwood Forest Railway.

Top: The Longleat Railway's No 7 *Flynn*, an Alan Keef design, stands on the turntable with the depot in the background. *S. Bowditch*

Above: John Hayton simmers in the spacious layout of the Longleat Railway on 23 September 2006. *G. Sutton*

Wagons
One bogie open; one bogie multi-purpose; one four-wheel open

Markeaton Park Light Railway

Location
Markeaton Park
Derby
Tel: 01623 552292
Website: this is currently (2012) closed

Route
The line runs from the Ashbourne Road/Queensway entrance to the Park (adjacent to the large roundabout) to Mundy Halt at the opposite (north-west) corner, a distance of 1,440 yards.

Background
The line opened in 1989. There is plentiful car parking at the Queensway terminus, and a large children's playground adjoins Mundy Halt. The 'Exmoor' Class steam engine *Markeaton Lady* operated here until 2010.

Operating dates
Weekends throughout the year and daily in school holidays; normally every 20 minutes from 11.00am to dusk (dependant on weather)

Locomotive
D5905 *City of Derby* 4w-4w diesel-mechanical (J. Brown 1995; rebuilt J. Bull)

Carriages
Three enclosed bogie, by Exmoor Steam Railway (1996); three end-balcony enclosed bogie, ex-Réseau Guerlédan and Fairbourne, acquired from Windmill Farm (2007)

The English *parkeisenbahn*: the Markeaton Park Light Railway on the outskirts of Derby.

Marwell Wildlife Railway
(Site entry fee applies)

Location
Marwell Wildlife
Colden Common
Winchester
SO21 1JH
Tel: 01962 777407
Website: www.marwell.org.uk

Route
A run of 900 yards, in 'dumb-bell' format, links stations named Treetops Junction and Park End Halt.

The Marwell Wildlife Railway, a comparatively little-photographed line, has a Severn-Lamb locomotive with a traditional British 'narrow-gauge' outline, as seen on 15 April 2012. *P. Scott*

Background
The line, operated by Marwell Preservation Trust, was first opened in 1987 and gives close-up views of the animals. Marwell Wildlife (formerly 'Zoo') is a conservation charity. The railway is supplemented by a 'road train' conveying visitors around the site.

Operating dates
Daily, except Christmas Day and Boxing Day, from 10.30am. A fare is charged for train travel in addition to the site entry fee.

Locomotive
Princess Anne 2-6-0 steam-outline diesel-hydraulic (Severn-Lamb, 1987); the first of its class built with English narrow-gauge outline bodywork

Carriages
Four bogie, semi-open

Oakwood Park Miniature Railway

(Park entry fees apply)

Location
Oakwood Theme Park
Canaston Bridge
Narberth
Dyfed SA67 8DE
Tel: 01843 891373
Website: www.oakwoodthemepark.co.uk

Route
The line is 1,100 yards long, basically circular, linking the entrance to the main area of the Park; the return journey is shorter.

Background
Oakwood Theme Park began as a very small family attraction, and has operated for 25 years. It now includes five large 'thrill' rides and a long wooden roller-coaster. In April 2008 operation of the Park was taken over by a Spanish company.

Operating dates
Most days (except some Tuesdays and Wednesdays) in April and May; daily June-August; weekends in September and October. Travel on the train is included in the Park entrance fee.

Locomotives
Lindy-Lou 0-8-0 steam-outline diesel-hydraulic (Severn-Lamb, 1972)
- 0-8-0 steam-outline diesel-hydraulic (Severn-Lamb, 1976)
Lenka 4-4w diesel-hydraulic railcar, ex-Longleat (Severn-Lamb, 1973)
Lorna 4-4w diesel-hydraulic railcar (Goold Bros, 1989)

Carriages
Eight bogie, partially enclosed, built for Liverpool International Garden Festival (1984); three also used at Gateshead, 1996. Three bogie open, by Severn-Lamb.

Paradise Railway

(Park entry fees apply)

Location
Paradise Park
Hayle
Cornwall TR27 4HY
Tel: 01736 753365
Website: www.paradisepark.org.uk

Route
Although only 250 yards in length, the circular line includes three level crossings, a bridge and a tunnel.

Background
Opened in 1976, the line is within the Bird Garden and encircles the house. At one time it was operated by the W. van der Heiden-built 0-4-0 steam locomotive *Chough*, named after the preservation project based here for that member of the crow family.

Operating dates
Daily, 1 April-31 October, from 10.30am to 5.30pm (operation dependant on weather). A fare is charged for train travel in addition to the site entry fee.

Locomotive
No 3 *Jungle Express* 4w diesel-mechanical (Lister, 1938)

Carriages
Two bogie, open

Paulton's Park Railway – 'Rio Grande'
(Park entry fees apply)

Location
Paulton's Park
Ower
Romsey
Hants SO51 6AL
Tel: 023 8081 4442
Website: https://paultonspark.co.uk

Route
A circular line of 700 yards, passing animal enclosures and the lake.

Background
Paulton's Family Theme Park, on the former Paulton's Estate, offers 60 rides and attractions and also houses 80 species of birds and animals. A recent addition is the 'Peppa Pig World' based on the children's TV fantasy characters. The railway, opened in 1987, is now designated 'Rio Grande'.

Operating dates
February school half-term; Fridays to Mondays until late March; then daily to 1 October; Thursday to Tuesday in early October and daily

A typical 'theme park' scene on the Paulton's Park Railway on 16 June 2012. *P. Scott*

in October half-term; opens at 10.00am (high season) or 10.30am (low season)

Locomotive
- 2-8-0 steam-outline diesel-hydraulic (Severn-Lamb, 1986)

Carriages
Five bogie, semi-open

Perrygrove Railway

Location
Perrygrove Farm
Perrygrove Road
Coleford
Glos GL16 8QB
Tel: 01594 834991
Website: perrygrove.co.uk

Route
The line extends from Perrygrove station in sweeping reverse loops for a distance of 1,320 yards, climbing past Rookwood station and Heywood Halt to the present terminus at Oakiron station, the former site of the Oak Iron Pit. Sharp curves and two sections of 1 in 30 gradient are encountered, demonstrating the full potential of the 'minimum gauge' railway. There is the possibility of a quarter-mile

Firing up: *Ursula* at the Perrygrove Railway on 30 September 2008. *G. Sutton*

extension, beyond Oakiron, to a final terminus at Crow's Nest. The workshops at Perrygrove are reached by a short tramway section from the station. There are numerous footpaths around the route, one steep example linking Perrygrove, Heywood and Oakiron directly so that the same train can be viewed at all three locations on its journey. A passing loop near Rookwood is used at busy times.

Background
The building of this unique railway by Michael and Frances Crofts in 1995-96 has already been mentioned in the 'History' sections. In addition to being a worthy tribute to the vision of Sir Arthur Heywood, and consequently a 'Mecca' for steam enthusiasts, Perrygrove has developed as a family leisure destination with picnic and extensive outdoor play facilities, an Indoor Village with secret passages, and a Treasure Hunt adventure.

The Heywood Collection, which is preserved at Perrygrove station, can be viewed by visitors and operates on special Vintage Train days each year (full particulars are given under 'Museums' below). Notably, from 2005 the railway has also been home to the Beyer-Garratt articulated locomotive (based on the 'K1' prototype) built in Hobart in 1990 and formerly used on the (now closed) Bush Mill Railway.

Operating dates
Every weekend from February until end of October, and daily during school holidays. The timetable normally provides nine or ten return trips, and passengers may ride several times.

Locomotives
Steam
Spirit of Adventure 0-6-0T (Exmoor Steam Railway, 1993)
Lydia 2-6-2T (Alan Keef, 2008)
No 3 0-4-4-0T Beyer-Garratt articulated (Bush Mill Railway, 1990)

Diesel
No 2 *Workhorse* 4w diesel-mechanical (Motor Rail, 1963); originally 2ft 6in gauge
Jubilee 4w diesel-hydraulic (Hunslet, 1994); originally 2-foot gauge
- 4w diesel-mechanical (Lister, 1954; originally 2-foot gauge)

Top: Sun and shadow surround *Ursula* on the Perrygrove Railway on 26 May 2012. *G. Sutton*

Centre: The magnificent 15-inch-gauge Beyer-Garrett model built by the Bush Mill Railway in Tasmania, running at the Perrygrove Railway on 30 September 2008. *M. Sutton*

Bottom: Detail of the front bogie and tank of the Garrett No 3 at Perrygrove in 2008.

Carriages

Excluding the Heywood Collection (see under 'Museums' below), the vehicles in regular use comprise three enclosed bogie carriages by Exmoor Steam Railway and three by Alan Keef Ltd. Four open coaches of the German *parkeisenbahn* type, by Waggon-Fabrik AG, have recently been acquired from the Windmill Farm Railway.

Lydia, with the new carriage set, descends towards Perrygrove station on 26 May 2011. *G. Sutton*

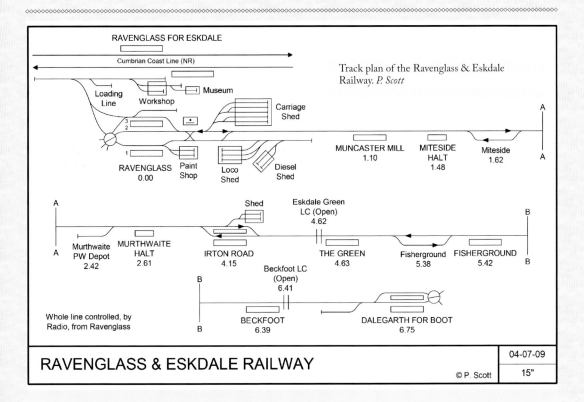

Track plan of the Ravenglass & Eskdale Railway. *P. Scott*

	04-07-09
RAVENGLASS & ESKDALE RAILWAY	
© P. Scott	15"

Ravenglass & Eskdale Railway

Location

Ravenglass & Eskdale Railway
Ravenglass
Cumbria CA18 1SW
Tel: 01229 717171
Website: www.ravenglass-railway.co.uk

Route

The line runs from Ravenglass (adjoining the standard-gauge station) through Miterdale to Muncaster Mill (1 mile), Miteside (1¾ miles), Murthwaite (2¾ miles) and Irton Road (4¼ miles); then through Eskdale to The Green (formerly Eskdale Green, 4¾ miles), Fisherground Halt (5½ miles), Beckfoot (6½ miles) and Dalegarth (7 miles).

Background

The Ravenglass & Eskdale has featured at length in the 'History' chapters of this book, and has an extensive literature of its own. Although not in the most accessible of locations, the railway has gone from strength to strength since preservation, drawing on the (virtually year-round) Lake District tourist industry. It opens some of the finest scenery in England to passengers, the varied landscape in different seasons ensuring than no two journeys can ever seem identical, while for enthusiasts the locomotive fleet and the operating challenges of the route are a constant delight. In recent years, extensive refreshment, shop and other visitor facilities have been developed at both Ravenglass and Dalegarth, while in contrast Irton Road retains much of its 1879 ambience. There is a small Museum at Ravenglass (see under 'Museums' below).

Operating dates

Weekends and school holidays in February (also November and December); daily from mid-March to end-October, with between 5 and 14 departures daily in each direction, according to season. Note: two round trips only in special Christmas period timetable.

Locomotives (see also under 'Museums' below)

Steam

No 3 *River Irt* 0-8-2 (Heywood, 1894; rebuilt Ravenglass 1927)

No 6 *River Esk* 2-8-2 (Davey, Paxman, 1923)

No 9 *River Mite* 2-8-2 (Clarksons, 1966)

No 10 *Northern Rock* 2-6-2 (Ravenglass, 1976)

No 11 *Bonnie Dundee* 0-4-2 (Kerr, Stuart, 1901; originally 2-foot gauge)

Top; River Irt on a down Ravenglass & Eskdale train at Fisherground in December 2008. *P. Ashworth*

Centre: River Irt at Fisherground Halt with a 'Santa Special' on 21 December 2009. *E. Andersen*

Bottom: River Irt descends towards Miteside loop, with Muncaster Fell in the background, on 14 June 2011. *E. Andersen*

Katie 0-4-0T (A. Heywood,
    1896) – under restoration
The Flower of the Forest 2w-2
    tank, vertical boiler
    (Ravenglass, 1985)

Internal-combustion
ICL4 *Perkins* 4w-4 diesel-
    mechanical (Muir-Hill,
    1929)
ICL7 *Shelagh of Eskdale* 4-6-4
    diesel-hydraulic (Severn-
    Lamb, 1969)
ICL8 *Lady Wakefield* 4w-4w
    diesel-hydraulic (Ravenglass,
    1980)
ICL9 *Cyril* 4w diesel-
    mechanical (Lister, 1932)
ICL11 *Douglas Ferreira*
    4w-4w diesel-hydraulic
    (TMA Engineering, 2005)
Quarryman 4w petrol-
    mechanical (Muir-Hill,
    1926)
- 4w battery-electric
    (Greenwood & Batley, 1957)
No 21 *Les* 4w diesel-mechanical
    (Lister Blackstone, 1960)

Carriages
Fifty bogie, including 12 heated saloons
(two equipped for wheelchairs); six
'maxi' saloons seating three persons
abreast; 10 semi-opens; 13 opens; and
one staff mess coach.

Wagons
Nine four-wheel flat wagons (seven
having 'top' boxes for ballast); a four-
wheel rail-bender, bogie manrider, bogie
flat, and emergency van

Further reading
Greenly, H. *The Ravenglass & Eskdale
    Railway* (R&ER Co, 1923)
Butler, P. E. B. and Lyne, J. D. *The
    Ravenglass & Eskdale Railway*
    (Oakwood Press, 'Locomotion
    Papers No 44', 1969)
Davies, W. J. K. *The Ravenglass &
    Eskdale Railway* (David &
    Charles, 2nd ed, 1981)

Top: Green Goddess (visiting from New Romney) and *River Mite*
are viewed from across the River Mite at Barrow Marsh, with
Scafell in the background, on 2 May 2011. *E. Andersen*

Centre: River Mite is seen amid the rhododendrons in Horsefalls
Wood between Murthwaite and Irton Road on 2 June 2011.
E. Andersen

Bottom: Northern Chief (visiting from New Romney) crosses
Barrow Marsh on the approach to Ravenglass on 29 April 2011. *E.
Andersen*

Gradon, W. McG. *'Ratty': History
    of the Ravenglass & Eskdale Railway*
    (Plateway Press, new ed, 1997)
Jenkins, S. and Jenner, D. *The Ratty
    Album, Vol 1* (2002)
Jenner, D. and Smith, A. *The Ratty
    Album, Vol 2* (c2003)
Andersen, E. and Jenner, D. *The Ratty
    Album, Vol 3* (2011)
Jenner, D., Smith A., and Van Zeller, P.
    *Ravenglass & Eskdale Railway –
    Journey through Historic Postcards*
    (1991)
Van Zeller, P. and Higginson, M.
    *Ravenglass & Eskdale Railway
    Stockbook* (2006)
Visitor's Guide (Ravenglass & Eskdale
    Railway Co, 2009)

Above right: Northern Rock runs through
plantations at the eastern end of Muncaster Fell
on 30 April 2011. *E. Andersen*

Right: A striking view of *Northern Rock* passing
the bluebells at Eskdale Green on 2 May 2011.
E. Andersen

Below: Douglas Ferreira approaches Eskdale
Green station down Hollin Head Bank on 2 May
2011. *E. Andersen*

The end of the line at Dalegarth, looking towards the head of Eskdale.

Rhiw Valley Light Railway

Location
Lower House Farm
Manafon
Berriew
Powys SY21 8BJ
Tel: n/a
Website: www.rvlr.co.uk

Route
The present line is approximately 1 mile in length, forming a kidney-shaped circuit from a triangular junction immediately outside the station area, running around meadows and alongside the beautiful River Rhiw. Trains may travel around the line in either direction.

Background
The line was constructed by the late Mr J. Woodroffe for the pleasure of family and friends, building on the experience of an earlier 7¼-inch-gauge garden railway. Construction began in 1971 and the gauge of 15 inches was inspired by the sight of the locomotive *Dougal* (now at Evesham Vale) under construction by Severn-Lamb. The railway was operational by 1973 using home-built coaches, and for many years there were regular public openings. Following the death of the builder in 2003, these were restricted to coincide with the Welshpool & Llanfair Light Railway annual steam gala in early September.

In 2011 the present owner, Mr M. Woodroffe, announced ambitious expansion plans including a change of route (part of the circle may be replaced by a longer run, alongside the river, to the western boundary of the farm), additional coaches, and the design and building of a third steam locomotive. A Friends organisation has been formed to support the project, and it is planned to offer, in due course, more public openings and 'Driver Experience' opportunities.

Operating dates
The railway is privately owned so there is only public access on certain dates. In 2013 it is hoped to open on four weekends. Check dates and times of future openings in the railway press, or on the Rhiw Valley's website.

Above: The Rhiw Valley Light Railway has the perfect setting near Manafon in Powys, seen here during a public open day in 2011.

Right: A 15-inch-gauge dog! Rupert Jones at the Rhiw Valley Railway.

Locomotives
Steam
Powys 0-6-2T (designed by David Curwen, built by Severn-Lamb, 1973)

Jack 0-4-0 (J. Woodroffe/TMA Engineering, 2003)

Rhiw 2-6-2T based on Manning Wardle 2-foot-gauge prototype for Lynton & Barnstaple Railway – design in progress

Petrol
Monty 4-w petrol-mechanical, based on BMC 'Mini' components with extra reduction gearbox (J. Woodroffe/H. Brunning, 1989)

Carriages
Two bogie enclosed; one 4-wheel enclosed; one 4-wheel brake van – all wooden-bodied.

Wagons
Three 4-wheel, flat

Rhyl Miniature Railway

Location
Marine Lake
Wellington Road
Rhyl
LL18 1LN
Tel: 01352 759109
Website:
www.rhylminiaturerailway.co.uk

Route
The line is 1,700 yards long, basically circular around Marine Lake, but with numerous curves and minor earthworks.

Background
As one of the pioneering 'Miniature Railways of Great Britain' seaside ventures, the history of the line has been largely covered in the main text. The original character has been faithfully retained, passengers still being carried in the Greenly *cars de luxe* dating from 1913, usually pulled by locomotives built locally by Albert Barnes. The new Central station building (2007) is a superb asset, providing a museum (see also under 'Museums' below), workshop and storage facilities.

The railway is confident of a secure future, evidenced by work having commenced on a re-creation of a Bassett-Lowke 'Class 10' locomotive, the type that opened the railway in 1911.

Operating dates
Weekends and Bank Holidays in April and May; Thursdays to Sundays in June and July; daily in late July and August; weekends in September. Normally 11.00am-4.00pm. Gala Event in early June.

Locomotives
Steam
No 44 4-4-0 (Cagney Brothers, c1910)
No 101 *Joan* 4-4-2 (A. Barnes, 1920)
No 102 *Railway Queen* 4-4-2 (A. Barnes, c1921); restoration to working order is planned

No 105 *Michael* 4-4-2 (A. Barnes, c1927)

Diesel and electric
Clara 0-4-2 steam-outline diesel-hydraulic (G&S Light Engineering, 1961); ex-Dudley Zoo; restored 2012
Electric saloon railcar 2w-2-4 (Minirail, 1957/8); converted as battery-powered vehicle by A. Hayne, 1983)

Top: A close-up of Lancaster & Chester Railway No 44 (Narrow Gauge Division) at Rhyl Miniature Railway.

Above: A driver's eye view of the 'Welsh' side of the Central station at Rhyl.

Right: Several enthusiasts, and a wooden man in a boat, wait for the next train at Rhyl!

Below right: Generations of volunteers relax together at Rhyl Central station.

Carriages

Eight bogie open *cars de luxe* (1913); one adapted for wheelchairs.
Two Cagney bogie open (c1910; from Lima, Peru, 2002)

Further reading

Bell. J. and B. *A Guide to Rhyl Miniature Railway – Canllaw I Reilffordd Fach y Rhyl* (RMR, c2008)

Romney, Hythe & Dymchurch Railway

Location

The Station
New Romney
TN28 8PL
Tel: 01797 362353
Website: www.rhdr.co.uk

Route

Double track from Hythe to Burmarsh Road (3¾ miles), Dymchurch (5 miles), St Mary's Bay (6¼ miles), Romney Warren Halt (7½ miles) and New Romney (8 miles); single track to Romney Sands (11½ miles) and a balloon loop at Dungeness (13 miles).

Background

The Romney, Hythe & Dymchurch Railway has played a central role in the story of the 15-inch-gauge lines and has, naturally, featured largely in the two 'History' chapters. Since 1972 the line has been continuously improved and has, through gala events and locomotive exchanges, adopted an outgoing stance greatly to the benefit of the wider miniature railway community, while gaining valuable publicity for itself.

Although its surroundings lack the scenic splendour of some other lines, there are still relatively unspoiled locations where the original character can be enjoyed – the open countryside between Dymchurch and Botolph's Bridge, and the unique shingle expanse of Dungeness, whose remoteness is emphasised rather than

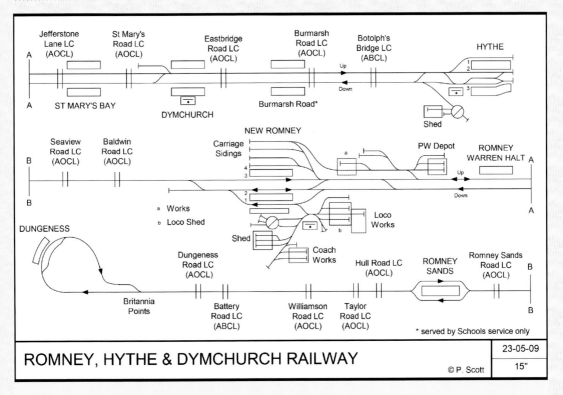

ROMNEY, HYTHE & DYMCHURCH RAILWAY

© P. Scott

23-05-09

15"

diminished by the brooding presence of the Nuclear Power Station. Howey's and Greenly's creation of their 'main line in miniature' is perhaps best appreciated in the peak season, or at a gala event, when New Romney sees frequent train arrivals and departures, locomotive changes, etc, unmistakeably recalling (for the older generation!) the atmosphere of a busy station in the 1950s. Romney Warren Halt, opened in 2009 to serve the Marsh Visitor Centre, Country Park and Local Nature Reserve, was the first new station for more than 60 years (excluding military stopping places during the Second World War).

It is truly remarkable that the large fleet of steam locomotives has remained intact and (except for planned overhaul stoppages) in working order. The railway does not operate a museum as such, the 1947 acquisitions from Eaton Hall having since returned for preservation there and at Perrygrove, but three fine examples of coachbuilding are treated as heritage vehicles and reserved from everyday use.

Operating dates

Weekends and school holidays, January to March and October to December; daily from late March to end of September with between four and 11 return journeys depending on season; numerous special events throughout the year.

Top: Track plan of the Romney, Hythe & Dymchurch Railway. *P. Scott*

Above: The majesty of *Dr Syn*, recently overhauled, waiting to take over a Dungeness-bound train.

Above: The countryside near Hythe retains its character, as *Dr Syn* speeds towards Dymchurch with an attractive blue-liveried rake of carriages.

Right: The ultimate in 'main-line' diesel power: No 12 *John Southland* at New Romney.

Locomotives
Steam
No 1 *Green Goddess* 4-6-2
  (Davey, Paxman, 1925)
No 2 *Northern Chief*
  4-6-2 (Davey, Paxman, 1926)
No 3 *Southern Maid*
  4-6-2 (Davey, Paxman, 1927)
No 4 *The Bug* 0-4-0 (Krauss,
  1926)
No 5 *Hercules* 4-8-2 (Davey,
  Paxman, 1926)
No 6 *Samson* 4-8-2 (Davey, Paxman, 1926)
No 7 *Typhoon* 4-6-2 (Davey, Paxman, 1926)
No 8 *Hurricane* (*Bluebottle* 1939-46) 4-6-2
  (Davey, Paxman, 1926)
No 9 *Winston Churchill* (*Dr Syn* until 1946)
  4-6-2 (Jackson, Rigby and Yorkshire
  Engine Co, 1929-31)
No 10 *Dr Syn* (*Black Prince* until 1946)
  4-6-2 (Jackson, Rigby and Yorkshire
  Engine Co, 1929-31)
No 11 *Black Prince* (originally *Fleissig Lieschen*)
  4-6-2 (Krupp, 1937)

Internal-combustion
No 12 *John Southland* 4w-4w diesel-hydraulic
  (TMA Engineering, 1983)
No 14 *Captain Howey* 4w-4w diesel-hydraulic
  (TMA Engineering, 1989)
4   4w diesel-mechanical (Motor Rail, 1938)
(PW2) *Scooter* 2w-2 petrol-mechanical
  (RHDR, 1949)

(PW3) *Redgauntlet* 4w petrol-mechanical (M.
  Jacot/A. Keef, 1977)

Carriages
The rolling stock has been almost entirely re-bodied or replaced between 1973 and 2004, the 30 new units being constructed by E. Charlier & Sons of Hythe and by the RHDR itself. There are a total of 59 bogie coaches, 54 of which are in regular service. These comprise eight 20-seat saloons in varnished teak, three 20-seat saloons in painted teak, and 20 20-seat saloons in painted aluminium; two luggage vans in teak (one painted, one varnished); two painted aluminium luggage vans; one driving trailer (for the school train); seven 16-seat saloons in painted aluminium; two 20-seat semi-opens in varnished teak; one 20-seat semi-open in painted teak; seven 20-seat semi-opens in painted aluminium; and one 16-seat disabled access coach in painted aluminium.

The carriage of wheelchairs poses a problem for 15-inch-gauge vehicles – an elegant enclosed version is seen at Dungeness.

Different liveries for the painted vehicles have been introduced in recent years, requiring these to run in relatively fixed train sets.

The five 'non-standard' vehicles comprise the Royal Saloon, used by HM the Queen in 1957 (and again at the Liverpool Garden Festival in 1984); a 12-seat saloon; a restored 'Clayton Pullman' of 1927; the 32-foot-long Bar Car *Gladys* designed by John Snell in 1977; and a platelayers' mess coach.

Further reading
Anon *The Line that Jack Built – the Romney Hythe & Dymchurch Railway in Pictures* (Ian Allan, c1969)

Davies, W. J. K. *Romney Hythe & Dymchurch Railway* (David & Charles, 1st ed, 1975 and 2nd ed, 1988)

Mitchell, V. and Smith, K. *Narrow Gauge Branch Lines: Romneyrail, a Journey through Time on the RHDR* (Middleton Press, 1999) – a photographic journey along the line

Ransome-Wallis, P. *Romney Hythe & Dymchurch Railway – the World's Smallest Public Railway* (Ian Allan, 3rd ed, 1961 and 5th ed, 1968)

Romney Hythe & Dymchurch Railway – Railway World Special (*Railway World*, Ian Allan, 1985)

Snell, J. B. *One Man's Railway – J. E. P. Howey and the RHDR* (David & Charles, 1983)

Numerous editions of Official Guide Books and Timetables have appeared at various dates, notably the Golden Jubilee Edition 1927-1977 (RHDR, 1977)

Saltburn Miniature Railway

Location
Cat Nab Station
Valley Gardens
Saltburn Bank
Saltburn
Tel: 07813 153975
Website: www.saltburn-miniature-railway.org.uk

Route
Starting from Cat Nab station, near the beach, the line turns inland and runs for half a mile through Valley Gardens to Forest Walk station, having been extended and substantially rerouted by the present operators in 2000-03. The depot is situated approximately at the halfway point.

Background
This classic seaside line was built by Herbert Dunn of Bishop Auckland in 1947 and was the home of Henry Greenly's pioneering internal-combustion locomotive (*Blacolvesley*) from 1948 to 1960, running here as *Elizabeth*. In 1953 the railway was sold to Cyril Pickering of Saltburn Motor Services and the route was extended across Skelton Beck to the present Forest Halt. Subsequently the line came into local authority

'Barlow Pacific' *Prince Charles* at Saltburn in 1998. *P. Scott*

hands, but was closed in 1975 due to falling visitor numbers, and the track suffered landslip damage in 1979. Re-opening by the Saltburn Miniature Railway Association took place in 1987, since when the railway has flourished with the acquisition of new coaches and further (diesel) locomotives to supplement H. Barlow's classic *Prince Charles* of 1953.

Forest Halt is close to tea rooms, a picnic area, woodland centre and gardens. Other features of interest in Saltburn include the Cliff Lift and Pier, though the elegant Halfpenny Bridge (which once spanned the Valley Gardens) was demolished in 1974.

Operating dates
Saturdays, Sundays and public holidays, Easter to end September; daily (except Mondays)

during main school summer holidays, 1.00pm to 5.00pm, weather permitting

Locomotives
Prince Charles 4-6-2 steam-outline diesel-electric (H. Barlow, 1953)
George Outhwaite 0-4-0 diesel-hydraulic (SMRA, 1994)
Saltburn 150 4-6-2 steam-outline diesel-hydraulic (Artisair, 1972; rebuilt SMRA, 2012)

Carriages
Three bogie, semi-open; one bogie, open

Wagons
General work truck; air-compressor wagon; tanker truck

Sherwood Forest Railway

Location
Gorsethorpe Lane
Edwinstone
Mansfield
NG21 9HL
Tel: 01623 515339
Website: www.sherwoodforestrailway.com

Route
The line runs for 800 yards, originally within the Sherwood Forest Farm Park (which closed in 2010), and includes two level crossings, a tunnel constructed from former colliery rope

containers, and two stations named Loxley and Welldale. There is scope for future expansion.

Background
The railway was built by the Colley family between 1999 and 2007, and extended in stages to its present length. The route utilises some of the earthworks from an early-19th-century irrigation scheme built by the Duke of Portland. Despite closure of the Farm Park, nearby facilities include an adventure play area, an under-5s' play area, and picnic sites.

Operating dates
Weekends and school holidays, 11.00am to 5.00pm; Tuesdays (outside school holidays) 12.00 to 4.00pm

Locomotives
Steam
No 1 *Smokey Joe* 0-4-0ST 'Bagnall' outline (K. Hardy, 1991)
No 2 *Pet* 0-4-0ST 'Kerr Stuart' outline (K. Hardy, 1998)

Petrol and electric
No 5 *Pioneer* 2-2w petrol-mechanical (K. Rosewell, 1947)
BE3 *Anne* 4-w battery-electric (K. Hardy, 1993)
No 4 *Lottie* 4-w petrol-hydraulic (D. Colley, 2006)

Carriages
Four bogie, semi-open (one by Exmoor Steam Railway, three ex-Longleat Railway); bogies re-

Many lines now open at weekends all year round: *Smokey Joe* hauls two recently built Sherwood Forest Railway 'Winter Saloons', which can run as an articulated unit of either two or three coaches. *D. Colley*

used under three-car enclosed articulated set, including guard's compartment (2012)

Wagons
Two four-wheel

Thorpe Light Railway

Location
Near the Tees Suspension Bridge between Whorlton and Wycliffe, near Barnard Castle, County Durham.
For information please call 07833 194286 or email ajcoulls@yahoo.co.uk

Route
Half a mile long, the line has a balloon loop at each end, with a station in the middle. Trains leave the station, plunge into a cutting and through a wooded avenue, then enter a tunnel. Exiting the tunnel, the line skirts a lake and returns on a through line past the station. Another cutting follows, curving past the stone-built former loco shed and returning past a paddock to the station. Two old North Eastern Railway signals provide atmosphere, and facilities are still being developed.

Background
The railway was built by Raymond Dunn in 1972 as the Whorlton Lido Railway and ran for many seasons delighting visitors to this

picturesque spot until closure in 2005. Now under private ownership, it has been renamed the Thorpe Light Railway and is being rebuilt and run by an active Friends group.

Operating dates
The railway operates on occasional open days from June 2013. Please contact Anthony Coulls of the Friends as above for details.

Locomotive
Wendy -4w-4w diesel-mechanical built by Dunn Coleby Simkins in 1972.

A locomotive will be lent for initial operations on the railway while Wendy is under repair.

Carriages
Four 16-seat bogie 'toastrack' opens, built by Dunn; coaches will be lent for initial operations

Tramore Miniature Railway

Location
Amusement Park
Sea Front
Tramore
Co Waterford
Republic of Ireland
Tel: 00353 51 81403

Route
The 400-yard circular line around a boating lake includes a short tunnel.

Background
The line opened in 1973 as part of a 50-acre amusement park, and is operated by Tramore Failté Ltd.

Operating dates
Daily June to early September, from 12.00 noon; weekends only in rest of September

Locomotive
2-8-0 steam-outline petrol-hydraulic (Severn-Lamb, 1973)

Carriages
Two, open and semi-open

Twinlakes Miniature Railway – the 'Iron Moose Express'
(Park entry fee applies)

Location
Twinlakes Park
Melton Spinney Road
Melton Mowbray
LE14 4SB
Tel: 01664 567777
Website: www.twinlakespark.co.uk

Route
A balloon loop of 1km from Canada Quay station to 'Imoogi Dragon' station, providing transport between two areas of the Park.

Background
Twinlakes Park, covering 70 acres, is a family attraction aimed mainly at younger children; adult groups without children are not admitted. The railway opened in 2008 using track, locomotives and rolling stock previously at the 'American Adventure Theme Park' at Shipley, Derbyshire.

Operating dates
Daily except 24-27 December, from 10.00am

Locomotives
No 1423　2-6-0 steam-outline diesel-hydraulic (Severn-Lamb, 1986)
-　　2-6-0 steam-outline diesel-hydraulic (Severn-Lamb, 1988)

Carriages
Five, covered

Two Severn-Lamb 'American Mogul' locomotives are in use at the recently built Twinlakes Miniature Railway near Melton Mowbray, as seen on 16 August 2010. *P. Green*

Waveney Valley Railway
(Museum entry fee applies)

Location
Bressingham Steam Museum and Gardens
Low Road
Bressingham
Diss
Norfolk IP22 2AA
Tel: 01379 686900
Website: www.bressingham.co.uk

Route
One of three narrow-gauge railways at Bressingham, the Waveney Valley line is 1.55 miles long and circular in form, crossing the River Waveney twice, intersecting the 2-foot-gauge Nursery Line, and later running parallel to the standard-gauge demonstration line. There is no lineside access except at the departure and alighting points.

Background
The site at Bressingham was purchased by Alan Bloom in 1947, and the railway museum and steam collection were established gradually from 1965 onwards, now including numerous traction engines and the famous 'Steam Gallopers'. The opportunity to purchase the two Krupp-built locomotives in 1972 provided the stimulus for the Waveney Valley Railway for which, until recent years, they provided the sole motive power. The line opened to visitors in 1974.

Operating dates
Museum open daily from 10.30am to 5.00pm; Mondays and Tuesdays outside main school holidays are normally non-steam days. At least

Forging through the woodland: a view from the footplate of *Rosenkavalier*.

one narrow-gauge line is in use Wednesdays to Sundays; outside weekends, a phone enquiry will confirm whether the Waveney Valley line is in operation. The museum entry fee on steam days includes unlimited train rides.

Locomotives
Steam
No 1662 *Rosenkavalier* 4-6-2 (Krupp, 1937)
No 1663 *Männertreu* 4-6-2 (Krupp, 1937)
St Christopher 2-6-2T (Exmoor Steam Railway, 2001)

Diesel
D63534w-4w diesel-mechanical (J. Brown, 1998)

Carriages
Originally 19 German *parkeisenbahn* bogie opens (by Waggon-Fabrik AG, 1937); some now fitted with roofs and two converted to wagons; four-wheel guard's van with brake air compressor. Approximately ten units in service, some sold.

Wagons
Multi-gauge ballast hopper; bogie flat wagon; bogie cabin truck

Further reading
Bloom, A. *Steam Engines at Bressingham* (Faber & Faber, 1970, and later eds; ISBN 0 571 10867 9)

Poetry in motion: Roland Martens's magnificent *Rosenkavalier* at the Waveney Valley Railway.

West Midland Safari Express
(Park entry fee applies)

Location
West Midland Safari and Leisure Park
Spring Grove
Bewdley
DY12 1LF
Tel: 01299 402114
Website: www.wmsp.co.uk

Route
The railway is 700 yards in length, linking the main car park to the amusement area. It runs along the back of the walkways, with level crossings over access roads, and passes the back of the hippopotamus enclosure.

Background
The Park was established in 1973 within the grounds of Spring Grove House. It is centred on a 4-mile 'safari' drive in visitors' own cars, during which 600 animals of 30 different species may

be viewed. The Park holds many endangered species and is especially famous for its pride of white lions. The railway was installed in 1979.

Operating dates
Daily from 11 February to 2 November, from 11.00am (2012). In addition to the site entry fee, wristbands (for unlimited rides) or ride tickets must be purchased.

Locomotive
2-8-0 steam-outline diesel-hydraulic (Severn-Lamb, 1979)

Carriages
Four bogie semi-open, with clerestory roofs

The railway at the West Midland Safari and Leisure Park serves a practical need, linking the main car park to the amusement area.

Westport House Express
(Park entry fee applies)

Location
Westport House and Country Park
Westport
Knock
Co Mayo
Republic of Ireland
Tel: 00359 98 27766
Website: www.westporthouse.ie

Route
A balloon loop of 700 yards from Westport

Central station, the lines diverging and joining at 'Monkey Junction', giving extensive views of Westport House and its lake, Croagh Patrick and Clew Bay.

Background
The house is the seat of the Marquess of Sligo, built in the 18th century (largely to a design by James Wyatt) and is now recognised as one of the finest country houses in Ireland in its parkland setting, with lake, terraces and magnificent coastal scenery. The Country Park, claimed to be 'Ireland's Adventure Capital', contains an amusements section within which the railway, opened in 1990, reflects the theme

of pirates in its alternative name, the 'Treasure Island Express'.

Operating dates
Two weeks at Easter, daily; Sundays and Bank Holidays in May; daily in June, July and August, 11.30am to 5.30pm

Locomotive
WH 2-6-0 steam-outline diesel-hydraulic (Severn-Lamb, 1989)

Carriages
Three bogie semi-open with clerestory roofs

Windmill Farm Railway
(Animal Farm entry fees apply)

Location
Windmill Animal Farm
Red Cat Lane
Burscough
Ormskirk
L40 1UQ
Tel: 01704 892282
Website: www.windmillanimalfarm.co.uk

Route
The line is 1.1 miles long from Windmill Farm station to Lake View station, with numerous curves following the layout of fields. The depot – also housing the '15-inch-gauge Heritage Collection' – is at Windmill Farm (see under 'Museums' below).

Background
The Windmill Farm Railway is the brainchild of Austin Moss, whose ambition to create a working museum began with the acquisition of one locomotive in 1988. Equipment, especially locomotives, moves between 'museum' and 'active' status as restoration takes place or overhaul becomes necessary.

In addition to the family attractions of the host Animal Farm itself, there are a picnic site and play area available at Lake View.

Operating dates
Weekends and school holidays between February and Easter and from October to December; daily from Easter to mid-September. A small fare,

additional to the site entry, is charged for travel on the train.

Locomotives
Steam (not all in active service)
No 4 *Blue Pacific* 4-6-2, vertical boiler (N. Guinness, c1935)
Siân 2-4-2 (designed by E. Twining, built by G&S Light Engineering, 1956); ex-Fairbourne
Katie 2-4-2 (designed by E. Twining, built G&S Light Engineering, 1963); ex-Fairbourne
Red Dragon 4-4-2 (Moss/Walker, 1991); incorporates parts of a Bassett-Lowke original

Internal-combustion/electric (not all in active service)
Whippet Quick 4w-4 diesel-mechanical (Lister, 1935); ex-Fairbourne
Gwril 4-w diesel-mechanical (Lister, 1943); ex-Fairbourne
No 4468 *Duke of Edinburgh* (I) 4-6-2 steam-outline diesel-electric (H. Barlow, 1948)
Princess Anne 4-6-2 steam-outline diesel-electric (H. Barlow, 1956)

The reconstructed *Red Dragon* at Windmill Farm with her owner, Austin Moss.

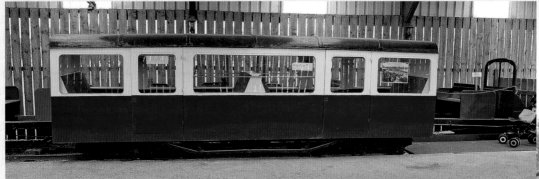

The luxurious two-compartment coach, originally from the Jaywick Railway, restored at Windmill Farm.

No 2510 *Prince Charles* 4-6-2 steam-outline diesel-electric (H. Barlow, 1951)

Blacksmoke 2-4-2 steam-outline petrol-mechanical (E. Smith, c1956)

- 4wh-4wh diesel-hydraulic (G&S Light Engineering, 1957); ex-Dudley Zoo

Königswinter 2-8-2 steam-outline diesel-hydraulic (Severn-Lamb, 1972); built as 2-8-0 and converted to 'tank' outline while at Cleethorpes

No 2870 *City of London* 4-6-0 steam-outline diesel-mechanical (Jubilee, 1987)

No 5305 4-6-0 steam-outline battery-electric (A. Moss, 1999)

14 2w-2 petrol-mechanical (G. Walker, 1985)

- 4w diesel-electric (C. Gluyas/D. Madden, 2012)

Carriages
Two-car articulated set, ex-Dudley Zoo, with covered guard's compartment; four bogie enclosed (two with glazed ends), ex-Liverpool Garden Festival; three open bogie (by Waggon-Fabrik), ex-Waveney Valley; one bogie enclosed ex-Réseau Guerlédan; one bogie saloon (by Caffyns), ex-Jaywick (also two underframes for restoration); three Severn-Lamb semi-open bogie (stored off-site for restoration). Carriages in use are liable to change, as vehicles are restored or exchanged.

Additionally, a number of vehicles have been built for other railways or private customers.

Rural scene: *Red Dragon* arrives at the picturesque Lake View station on 21 May 2011

7. Museums

Many, perhaps most, of the 15-inch-gauge railways operating today hold, and often still operate, some equipment of historic interest, the exceptions being the modern lines set up recently for the purely practical purpose of transport within theme parks and similar visitor attractions.

However, there are a number of museum sites that have set out deliberately to preserve locomotives and rolling stock, the most important being the Heywood Collection at the Perrygrove Railway and the Heritage Collection at the Windmill Farm Railway. The Sutton Collection at the Cleethorpes Coast Light Railway unusually shares in the regular operation of the line.

Although not directly connected with railways, Bassett-Lowke's first home in Northampton is now the 78 Derngate Charles Rennie Mackintosh House and Galleries, remodelled in the architect's iconic Modernist style and including a Dining Room restaurant. The house reflects Bassett-Lowke's philosophy, to have no possessions in his home older than himself!

The Albert Barnes Room (Rhyl Miniature Railway)

Background
The Albert Barnes Room, named after the famous local miniature railway and fairground equipment engineer, is located adjacent to the platform of the fine new Central station building opened in 2007. Admission is free.

There are comprehensive displays on the history of miniature railways, a working signal frame, and a showcase of Bassett-Lowke model locomotives and railway vehicles.

Locomotive
106 *Billy* 4-4-2 (Albert Barnes, Rhyl, c1930)

The last of the six 'Albion' Class engines to be built, *Billy* has always worked at Rhyl and was purchased by the Town Council in 1978. Restoration to exhibition condition was carried out by Gratton Engineering in 1985-86.

Other historic equipment
All the working locomotives and carriages at Rhyl are of significance, but particular mention should be made of the imported Cagney 4-4-0 locomotive (No 44) and four-wheel Cagney carriages, which can normally be seen within the Central station.

Footplate detail of 'Albion' Class *Billy*, exhibited in the Albert Barnes room at Rhyl.

Conwy Valley Railway Museum

Location
Conwy Valley Railway Museum
The Old Station
Betws-y-Coed
Conwy
LL24 0AL
Tel: 01690 710568

Route
There is a half-mile single-track 15-inch-gauge line from end to end of the site. There is also a 7¼-inch-gauge dumb-bell-shaped line.

Background
The Museum was established in the early 1970s in the former goods yard of Betws-y-Coed station, on the opposite side of the track from the standard-gauge passenger station. A number of standard-gauge vehicles are preserved, including a refreshment facility. The principal operating feature is the extensive (950-yard) 7¼-inch-gauge line installed about 1974 by Allan Pratt. In 1989 a 15-inch-gauge electric tramway was added (with overhead current collection by trolley pole), and the Museum collection itself includes a magnificent quarter-scale model of British Railways No 70000 *Britannia*. Other interesting narrow-gauge vehicles include an 18-inch-gauge covered van from the Woolwich Arsenal Railway and an 18-inch-gauge flangeless tub from a plateway at Wyke near Halifax, which operated until 1981.

Operating dates
Open daily, from 10.30am. There are separate charges for the 7¼-inch-gauge train, the 15-inch-gauge tramcar, and the Museum.

Locomotive
No 70000 *Britannia* 15-inch-gauge 4-6-2 built to true quarter-scale (begun by Longfleet Engineering, Poole, c1965, and completed by TMA Engineering, Birmingham, 1988); on static display

Tramcar
Single-deck, one side enclosed and one semi-open (chassis by Brett Rogers and TMA Engineering, Birmingham)

The Heywood Collection (Perrygrove Railway, Gloucestershire)

Background
This is almost certainly the most extensive collection of historic miniature railway equipment in existence, and is under the patronage of Sir Peter Heywood Bt. The Trustees are James Waterfield and Michael Crofts (the creator of the Perrygrove Railway). A special building is provided adjacent to Perrygrove station to house the exhibits.

The objects of the Collection are firstly to preserve surviving artefacts from Sir Arthur Heywood's work, and secondly to provide a public educational resource concerning minimum gauge railways. The

Frames for a future replica of *Ella* support steel sleepers and a variety of artefacts at the Heywood Collection at Perrygrove.

Ursula hauls wagons from the Heywood Collection on a private charter at the Perrygrove Railway.

Trustees work within a detailed conservation policy (set out in full on the Collection's website), under which artefacts are carefully assessed for condition before a decision is made as to their treatment. Objects with the potential for occasional 'light use' are repaired to the necessary extent, without causing damage to surviving original material; where this cannot be done, objects are conserved for Museum preservation as educational resources.

In the case of certain locomotives, carriages and wagons, 're-creations' have been built according to the best current understanding of how the original appeared and worked, to enable the visiting public to fully experience and appreciate Heywood's achievements. Most of the Collection can be enjoyed, on a static basis, whenever the Perrygrove Railway is open to the public, and on certain 'Vintage Trains Days' the historic vehicles operate up and down the line in all their splendour. However, it should be noted that certain items – especially the re-created locomotive *Ursula* with the Eaton Hall brake-van – are occasionally loaned away to run at special events on other lines.

Original vehicles
Eaton Hall bogie saloon coach, 1904 (restored 2004-07)

Duffield Bank and Dove Leys 'Top' wagon, 1886 (at Dove Leys until 1948)
Rail-bending wagon from Duffield Bank (restored at Windmill Farm Railway)
Eaton Hall platelayers wagon, 1895
Eaton Hall 'Top' wagon, c1895
Eaton Hall sawmill trolley-type wagon, c1916

There is also a surviving fragment from the Eaton Hall open coach.

Re-created locomotives and vehicles
These represent the ongoing work of Mr James Waterfield of Boston, Trustee.

Ursula 0-6-0T locomotive, as built for Eaton Hall
Ella 0-6-0T locomotive, as built for Duffield Bank (frames only to date; work in progress)
Duffield Bank bogie Dining Carriage (built from original drawings)
Eaton Hall bogie brake van
Duffield Bank 'Dynamometer Carriage' – open vehicle with instruments to record locomotive power output

The Miniature Railway Museum Trust (Lakeside station, Cleethorpes Coast Light Railway)

Background

The Trust was launched in September 2008 to preserve and interpret artefacts and other materials relating to British miniature railways of all types and gauges. Its long-term goal is to establish a permanent and wide-ranging museum, probably in Cleethorpes; the Trust's early activities have been closely associated with, and supported by, the Cleethorpes Coast Light Railway.

An original Bassett-Lowke four-wheel coach, used at Porthcawl until the 1980s, displayed at the 'Rails to the Sands' exhibition at Cleethorpes.

The first activity was a display on the history of the Sutton Miniature Railway mounted in the Griffin Hall at Lakeside station; the project was led by Simon Townsend, drawing on his experience in setting up the Albert Barnes Room at Rhyl. In 2010 and 2011 a major exhibition on seaside railways – 'Rails to the Sands' – was mounted in a 1,000-square-foot exhibition space nearby, including Greenly's 15-inch-gauge *Blacolvesley* and an original Bassett-Lowke four-wheeled coach formerly used at Porthcawl.

As readers will already be aware, the Cleethorpes Coast Light Railway preserves and operates the locomotives and coaches forming the Sutton Collection.

Ravenglass Station Museum (Ravenglass & Eskdale Railway)

Background

Despite the small size of the building, the Museum is extremely well laid out with every inch of space used to advantage. The displays cover the history of the Eskdale area, the iron mines and quarries, the original 3-foot-gauge railway and its conversion to 15-inch-gauge by Narrow Gauge Railways Ltd. There is a showcase of Bassett-Lowke small-scale models and a replica of part of a Heywood coach; the two main exhibits normally stand behind glass windows facing the car park.

Locomotive

Synolda Class 30 4-4-2 (Bassett-Lowke, 1912); sometimes absent on working visits to special events elsewhere

Rolling stock

Four-wheel coach No 10, with 'Bassett-Lowke, London and Northampton' cast plates in

Blacolvesley at Ravenglass, displayed for a visit of the Heywood Society on 10 October 2009. *D. Holroyde*

the doorways. Outside the Museum are the frame and wheels of a 3-foot-gauge quarry truck.

Other historic equipment in use

Although not on public display, Ravenglass was for many years the normal home of the privately-owned 4-4-4T (petrol-driven) *Blacolvesley*, designed by Henry Greenly. Restoration of the Heywood 0-4-0T *Katie* on the original frames is making progress in the workshops, while other historic artefacts can be seen in everyday use on the railway. The diesel locomotive *Shelagh of Eskdale* incorporates some running gear of the Heywood *Ella*, the chassis of *Muriel* continues to run under *River Irt*, and the veteran Muir-Hill passenger tractor – surely

Part of the excellent museum display at Ravenglass, including a fragment of a Duffield Bank closed carriage.

the railway equivalent of the 'Irishman's knife', as it originally made use of the discarded front bogie from *Sans Pareil* – is still around, despite changes of both bodywork and engine unit, as ICL4 *Perkins*!

Strumpshaw Steam Museum

Location
Strumpshaw Steam Museum
Strumpshaw
Norwich
NR13 4HR
Tel: 01603 714535

Background
The Museum is part of the 1,000-acre working Strumpshaw estate and was begun by Wesley Key and continued by his son James and grandson William Key, the present owner. The collection of steam engines (road and stationary) was originally kept at North Walsham and moved to Strumpshaw in 1954; it is the largest private collection in Britain and also includes fairground organs and a Christie cinema organ.

A narrow-gauge railway with a steam-outline diesel locomotive and one carriage tours part of the grounds, but the particular relevance to the 15-inch-gauge is the display of an early Cagney locomotive, which – if not Charles Bartholomew's own engine – was certainly a visitor to the railway at Blakesley Hall in 1904 or 1905. In 1936 it was used at Ettrick Bay in Bute – and might just possibly have featured in a short-lived re-opening of the Sutton Miniature Railway in the interim. It then passed into private preservation, with several owners before being purchased at auction in 1968 by Mr Laurence C. Brooks of Brooks Railroad Models Ltd and restored to working order. With tender lettering for 'Brooks Railroad', it has visited special events at New Romney, Cleethorpes and elsewhere.

Opening dates
Sundays and certain weekdays in April, May and June; daily from late June to early October, 10.30am to 3.30pm

Locomotive
15-inch-gauge 4-4-0 (Cagney/Herschell-
  Spillman, late 1890s)

Further reading
Heywood Society Journal, No 47
*Cagney Special
Issue* (Autumn 2011)
Tebb, Dr Bob *The Blakesley Miniature
Railway and the Bartholomew
Family* (Silver Link Publishing,
2009)

This much-travelled early Cagney
locomotive, which ran at least briefly at
Blakesley Hall, is now at Strumpshaw Steam
Museum. *D. Armstrong*

15-inch-gauge Heritage Centre (Windmill Farm Railway, Burscough)

Background

The Centre was established by Mr Austin Moss in
1997 as a place to restore and operate his collection
of historic 15-inch-gauge equipment, which had begun
with a single locomotive in 1988. All are in the private
ownership of Mr Moss, of his friends and volunteers,
or (in one case) the 'Siân Project Group'. In the nature
of preservation work, locomotives and coaches move
between 'museum' and 'working' status and back again
over the years.

In this workshop scene at the Windmill
Farm 15-inch-gauge Heritage Centre, E. W.
Twining's *Katie* undergoes heavy overhaul.

Visitors to the Windmill Farm Railway can view a
selection of restored locomotives through large display
windows in the entrance area. Items under restoration
in the workshop, and rolling stock in storage, are not
available to be seen except by special permission of Mr
Moss.

Locomotives

The Centre has brought together the two E. W.
Twining-designed 2-4-2T locomotives *Katie* (1954)
and *Siân* (1963) and the Lister petrol tractors *Whippet
Quick* (1935) and *Gwril* (1943) from the Fairbourne
Railway, the reconstructed Bassett-Lowke Class 10
'Little Giant' *Red Dragon,* and three of the streamlined
diesel 4-6-2s designed by Harry N. Barlow: *Duke of
Edinburgh* (1948), *Princess Anne* (1956), and *Prince
Charles* (1951).

Other interesting locomotives include the un-

Exhibits at the Windmill Farm 15-inch-gauge Heritage Centre, seen
through the spectacle plate of the rebuilt Severn-Lamb locomotive
Königswinter on 21 May 2011. *J. Murgatroyd*

named 1957 bogie diesel built by T. Guest for Dudley Zoo in 1957, the Barlow-inspired 4-6-0 *City of London*, the 2-8-2(T) diesel-hydraulic *Königswinter* (rebuilt from a Severn-Lamb 'Rio Grande' type), and the unique vertical-boilered (live-steam) 4-6-2 *Blue Pacific* built by N. L. Guinness in 1935.

Rolling stock

The collection includes examples from the Fairbourne, Romney Hythe & Dymchurch, Liverpool Garden Festival, and Dudley Zoo railways. Of special interest are the three Jaywick Railway coaches (originally 18-inch gauge), one fully restored and the other two as chassis awaiting rebuilding.

8. Tail lamp

Ready to depart: Humberstone North Sea Lane, on the Cleethorpes Coast Light Railway.

Our journey through 140 years of 15-inch-gauge railways – more than a century of passenger-carrying – is nearly over, and the author hopes that the reader has not been wearied by the tour around 38 working lines and several museums! They are to be found in so many beautiful parts of Britain, with endless opportunities for filming and photography. Friendliness is an almost universal characteristic of miniature railway staff; a polite request to take a particular photograph, or to look round an engine shed at a sensible time of day, is rarely refused, and the author owes an immense debt of gratitude to the staff and volunteers who have assisted his work and patiently answered his questions.

In the electronic age, most of the railways described maintain websites giving the most up-to-date information about opening dates, fares or admission charges, locomotives and rolling stock currently in use, and special gala events for enthusiasts. To gain further insight, it is necessary only to search the excellent 'Miniature Railway World' website, with its database of working lines, and as one's interest deepens there is no more fascinating source for news, discussion and research than the on-line 'Miniature Railway World Forum', which is free to join. Visits to working lines are now possible for the greater part of the year, at least at weekends thanks to the expanding tourist industry and milder winter conditions in the last few decades. For the rest of the closed season, we have the summer's harvest of books and DVDs to enjoy, and time to plan next year's holiday: our children or grandchildren are sure to love it! Possibly, one year, we might even receive a special birthday present – a never-to-be-forgotten engine-driving experience on a line such as the Bure Valley or the Romney, Hythe & Dymchurch, taking the controls of a living, breathing machine under the tuition of an expert driver.

And so this journey draws to a close, as a new season begins with summer temperatures in late March of 2012! Northern Rock, the epitome of modern locomotive design, has pounded her way up Miterdale and now runs easily down from Irton Road towards The Green, sun gleaming on yellow-green paint and polished brass as she rounds the bend at Long Yocking, and the spring colours of Eskdale open out in all their glory on our right. Ahead, the Lakeland fells shimmer purple in the morning haze, and in a few minutes the train will pause under the trees at Fisherground Halt, then race through Gilbert's Cutting and alongside the valley road to Stanley House at Beckfoot. As we swing to the right at Dalegarth Cottages, the clatter of carriage wheels will echo back from dry-stone walls, slowing as we cross the stream and Northern Rock comes to a stand just short of the turntable. Will it be tea and cake at the station café, or a cool Robinsons beer and Cumberland sausage at the Boot Inn? Such decisions! A little later, as we stroll back down the lane, a distinctive whistle tells us that the venerable River Irt is bringing up our return train; if we have indulged in that second pint we may well imagine the gaunt figure of Captain Howey leaning on the wall by the buffer stop, forever dreaming of the tunnels under the fells on his Ambleside extension that was never to be... Enjoy the ride, wherever you may travel. Who knows, the author may be sitting in the next carriage!

Further Reading

General works

Bryant, P. and Holroyde, D. *Miniature Railways of Great Britain and Ireland* (Platform 5 Publishing Ltd, 2012; ISBN 978-1902336930)

Butterell, R. *Miniature Railways* (Ian Allan, 1966)

Butterell, R., Holroyde, D., and Townsend, S. *ABC of Miniature Railways* (Ian Allan, 2000; ISBN 0-7110-2593-2)

Clayton, H. *The Duffield Bank and Eaton Railways, with particular reference to Sir Arthur Heywood* (Oakwood Press, 1968)

Clayton, H., Butterell, R., and Jacot, M. *Miniature Railways, Vol 1: 15 Inch Gauge* (Oakwood Press, 1971)

Croft, D. J. *A Survey of Seaside Miniature Railways* (Oakwood Press, 1992)

Heywood, Sir A. *Minimum Gauge Railways* (privately published 1881, reprinted 1894, 1898 and 1976)

Household, H. *Narrow Gauge Railways – England and the Fifteen Inch* (Ian Allan, 1989; reprinted by Promotional Reprint Co, 1995; ISBN 1-85648-478-9)

Howson, F. H. *Narrow Gauge Railways of Britain* (Ian Allan, 1948)

Kitchenside, G. *A Source Book of Miniature and Narrow Gauge Railways* (Ward Lock, 1981; ISBN 0-7063-6070-2)

Knight, N. R. *British Miniature Railways* (Rail Romances, 1999; ISBN 1-900622-02-5)

Lambert, A. *Miniature Railways Past and Present* (David & Charles, 1982; ISBN 0-7153-8108-1)

Mosley, D. and Van Zeller, P. *Fifteen Inch Gauge Railways* (David & Charles, 1986; ISBN 0-7153-8694-8)

Neale, A. *Narrow Gauge and Miniature Railways* [from old picture postcards] (Plateway Press, 1986; ISBN 0-9511108-0-2)

Scott, P. *Minor Railways* (Branch Line Society, 2000; ISBN 1-902368-11-8)

Strauss, Dr W. *Liliputbahnen* [a survey of passenger-carrying miniature railways] (original German edition, Kichler, 1938; English translation ed Butterell, R. 1988; ISBN 0-9514796-0-1)

Biographical

Bassett-Lowke, J. and Milner, J. *Bassett-Lowke – A Memoir of his Life and Achievements* (Rail Romances, 1999; ISBN 1-900622-01-7)

Fuller, R. *The Bassett-Lowke Story* (New Cavendish Books, 1984)

Keef, A. M. *A Tale of Many Railways – an Autobiography and History of Alan Keef Ltd* (Lightmoor Press, 2008; ISBN 978-1-8998893-0-3)

Smithers, M. *Sir Arthur Heywood and the Fifteen Inch Gauge Railway* (Plateway Press, 1995; ISBN 1-871980-22-4)

Steel, E. A. and E. H. *The Miniature World of Henry Greenly* (MAP, 1973; ISBN 0-85242-306-3)

Locomotives

Anon *Cagney's Locomotive Works* (reprint, Plateway Press, 1998)

Buck, S. *Katie's Other Sisters: the 15-inch-gauge Locomotives of E. W. Twining and Trevor Guest* (Siân Project Group, 2007; ISBN 0-9549-3301-X)

Butterell, R. and Milner, J. *The Little Giant Story* (Rail Romances, 2003)
Steam on Britain's Miniature Railways – 7¼-inch to 15-inch (Bradford Barton, 1976)

Holroyde, D. and Little, L. *The Locomotives of Severn-Lamb Ltd* (Narrow Gauge Railway Society, 2010; ISBN 978-0-9554326-2-0)

Little, L. and Holroyde, D. *The Miniature Locomotives of David Curwen* (Narrow Gauge Railway Society, 2008; ISBN 978-0-9554326-1-3)

Tonks, E. *Light and Miniature Railway Locomotives of Great Britain* (Birmingham Locomotive Club, 1950)

Woodcock, G. *Miniature Steam Locomotives* (David & Charles, 1964)

Journals

The historical importance of miniature railway artefacts (of all gauges) is well described in the article by A. J. Coulls, 'The Ephemeral Archaeology of the Miniature Railway', in the electronic journal *Industrial Archaeology Review* (Vol XXV No 1, 2003)

The Heywood Society has published its Journal since 1977 (issue 70 having appeared in Spring 2012) and, although the Society has a limited membership criterion, copies are available for purchase by non-members.

Since 2006 the fully illustrated magazine *Miniature Railway* (three issues per year) has been available through many preserved railway outlets and by paper or on-line subscription.

The Narrow Gauge Railway Society publishes a journal, *The Narrow Gauge*, and a newsletter, *Narrow Gauge News*, containing articles of relevance to 15-inch-gauge and other

miniature railways, as well as monographs such as those of David Holroyde and Lawson Little.

Web sites

Among the many Internet sites dealing with miniature railways, in one form or another, special mention must be made of 'Miniature Railway World' with its comprehensive database of operating railways. Associated with this is the discussion forum 'Miniature Railway World Forums', which is free to join and offers a platform for the exchange of information on a huge variety of related topics. The author is deeply indebted to numerous contributors for their generous input of information assisting in the compilation of this present book.

Sources on specific historic (closed) lines

Blakesley Hall
Kingston, P. B. *Blakesley Hall and its Miniature Railway: the Story of the Railway which ran through the Estate for 37 Years* (1903-1939) (Centenary ed, paperback, pub Dr Bob Tebb, 2003)

Tebb, Dr Bob *The Blakesley Miniature Railway and the Bartholomew Family* (Silver Link Publishing Ltd, 2009)

Jaywick
Little, L. 'A Single to the Seashore: The Jaywick Miniature Railway' (NGRS, *The Narrow Gauge*, No 186, 2004; ISSN 0-1452-5587) – contains information relevant to the Fairbourne and Ravenglass & Eskdale 15-inch-gauge railways

Sand Hutton
Hartley, K. E. 'The Sand Hutton Light Railway' (NGRS, *The Narrow Gauge*, Nos 95/96, 1982; ISBN 0-9507619-X)

Sutton Coldfield
Tidmarsh, J. G. *Sutton Coldfield Fifteen Inch Gauge Railway* (Plateway Press, 1990 and 2009)

Index

Running through Eskdale in March 2012.